Poetics

Aristotle

Poetics I

with

The *Tractatus Coislinianus*

A Hypothetical Reconstruction of
Poetics II

The Fragments of the *On Poets*

translated with notes by
Richard Janko

Hackett Publishing Company
Indianapolis / Cambridge

Aristotle: 384–322 B.C.

Designed by Dan Kirklin

Cover design by Listenberger Design Associates

Printed in the United States of America

10 09 08 07 06 05 04   6 7 8 9 10

For further information, please address

Hackett Publishing Company, Inc.
P.O. Box 44937
Indianapolis, Indiana 46244-0937

Library of Congress Cataloging in Publication Data

Aristotle.
  Poetics.
  (Hackett classics)
  Bibliography: p.
  Includes index.
  Contains, in addition to the translation of the
extant portion of Aristotle's Poetics (here called
Poetics I), a translation of the anonymous Tractatus
Coislinianus, which Janko sees as an outline of the
lost Poetics II, together with Janko's hypothetical
reconstruction of Poetics II, and the extant fragments
of Aristotle's Peri poiētōn, also in translation.
  1. Poetry—Early works to 1800.   2. Aesthetics—
Early works to 1800.   3. Comedy.   I. Janko, Richard,
1955–   .   II. Janko, Richard, 1955–   .
Hypothetical reconstruction of Poetics II.   1987.
III. Aristotle. Peri poiētōn. English. 1987.
IV. Tractatus Coislinianus. English. 1987.
V. Title.
PN1040.A513   1987   808.2   87-14845
ISBN 0-87220-034-5
ISBN 0-87220-033-7 (pbk.)

The paper used in this publication meets the minimum requirements of American National Standard for Information Sciences—Permanence of Paper for Printed Library Materials, ANSI Z39.48-1984.
∞

Contents

Preface and Acknowledgements

"Aristotle was the first accurate critic and truest judge—nay, the greatest philosopher the world ever had." So wrote Ben Jonson, whose assessment is still defensible today. Although no excuse is needed for studying the *Poetics*, it may be as well to justify the appearance of yet another translation of it. This one differs considerably, for better or worse, from its predecessors. I intend it primarily for students of literature, philosophy and literary theory, at both the undergraduate and postgraduate level, who know no Greek; it is meant to supply them with a readable yet accurate translation, accompanied by notes and a glossary to which they can refer as required (hence these sections contain more repetition than I would otherwise have allowed). But I also have in mind the needs of their hard-pressed instructors, who presently lack an adequate commentary on the *Poetics* which assumes no knowledge of Greek; and it is above all for them that I include the fragmentary material deriving from the lost *Poetics* II and *On Poets*, since this is not readily available and goes far to fill the two major gaps in our knowledge of Aristotle's theory, his views of comedy and of catharsis. Much of this material is new and exciting, but it is also very difficult, despite my best efforts to render it as accessible as possible; so not every class should be asked to spend time on these sections.

This book will also be of interest to specialists in Greek literature and Aristotelian philosophy. Although its format precluded me from discussing previous scholarship or doing much more than indicating alternative interpretations, my debt to earlier scholars will be apparent at every turn: I should mention especially the work of Vahlen, Butcher, Bywater, Rostagni, Else, Lucas and lastly Dupont-Roc and Lallot. The translation entailed considerable work on the Greek text, since I came to the conclusion that current editions still give insufficient weight to MS B and the Arabic; for knowledge of the latter I am dependent on the annotated Latin version of Tkatsch. The result is that both the text and the interpretation are new in places. As for the fragmentary material, I have altered my controversial views on the *Tractatus Coislinianus* hardly at all, although the curious will discover some minor revisions; subsequent research on the *On Poets* has strengthened my belief that these views are on the right lines. I have now connected with that dialogue two neglected Herculaneum papyri which needed substantial re-editing, as study in Naples confirmed; the translations of them included here are based on transcriptions I made during that visit, from which I will produce a new edition of them as soon as possible. Meanwhile the expert will find these texts in F. Sbordone, *Ricerche sui papiri Ercolanesi* I (Naples, 1969), 287–372, and M.L. Nardelli, *Cronache Ercolanesi* 8 (1978) 96–103. [I have now republished the former text in *Cronache Ercolanesi* 21 (1991) 5–64; see also A. O. Rorty, *Essays in Aristotle's "Poetics"*, Princeton 1992, 341–58.]

On the basis of this and other material, I have come to understand Aristotelian catharsis in a way that will seem new even to some specialists. In fact it is less new than may appear, because in recent years several scholars have been moving towards an interpretation more like that of Lessing than that of Bernays. That they have reached it by different routes, and without knowing the texts from Herculaneum, encourages my sense that we are finally on the right track. Among these scholars I should mention H. House, L. Golden, M. Nussbaum, J.M. Redfield and especially C. Lord. A very similar view of catharsis is now propounded by S. Halliwell, whose volume reached me only after this book was written. I find his attitude particularly encouraging, since he eschews the fragmentary material on which my views are partly based.

This book has gained much from discussion and correspondence with friends and colleagues in two continents and two islands. Above all, I thank Myles Burnyeat of Cambridge, who suggested that I write it for this series, Jonathan Barnes of Oxford, and J.M. Bremer of Amsterdam; without their reaction to my earlier work, I might well have reverted to other projects. The publisher's reader was Cynthia Freeland; to her sure judgement and critical acuity I owe many valuable suggestions, most of which were adopted without hesitation. The same must be said of my colleague Dirk Obbink, who read the entire manuscript, produced many pages of incisive comments, and never ceased to seem surprised at my acceptance of his corrections; his combined expertise in Aristotelian philosophy and the Herculaneum papyri proved particularly helpful. My wife Michele read the whole book in draft; her unfailing sense of style, eye for difficulties, and profound understanding of literary theory in all its ramifications made her contribution invaluable. She and Dirk were patient participants in seemingly interminable discussions of catharsis.

I wish to thank my colleagues in the Classics Department for providing so friendly an atmosphere in which to work; Columbia College, for a Lawrence Chamberlain Fellowship (awarded to those who have survived teaching the Core Curriculum), which gave me the time essential for completing this book; and IBM for its gift to Columbia University, Project Aurora, which supplied the microcomputer that speeded its editing. I am grateful to Mr. Colin Haycraft of G. Duckworth and Co. Ltd, and to the University of California Press, for permission to present material adapted from the more scholarly context of *Aristotle on Comedy*. I thank the National Endowment for the Humanities for a grant to travel to Naples, and my wife for graciously accompanying me thither. I also thank Umberto Eco for his indulgence to an unexpected companion on a certain journey back in time; coincidence can be stranger than fiction, but it is rarely as amusing. The staff of the Classics Faculty Library at Cambridge University assisted me greatly with their kindness, as did Ms. Jackie Maksymowicz with her expert typing of the first draft. Last but not least, the staff of the Hackett Publishing Company have shown me great forbearance during various delays. I much regret that William Hackett did not live to see this book through to publication himself.

Aristotelian poetics is one of those fields where new discoveries and new research may at any time bring more surprises and improve our understanding of detail; and no translation is ever satisfactory. Since the catharsis of this version's errors is far from accomplished, any suggestions for correction and clarification will be welcomed by the author.

Manhattan, January 1987 R. Janko

Introduction

1
The Importance of the *Poetics*

Aristotle was the first person ever to write a treatise devoted to literary theory. Before his time others had practised literary criticism in various simple forms, mostly to do with the use (and abuse) of literature as a vehicle for social, moral, religious and political ideas; and Plato, his teacher, was the first to raise many of the questions which he himself sought to answer. But to Aristotle belongs the credit for recognising that literature has its own set of principles, which can be discovered by careful analysis; from this recognition came the *Poetics*.

This brief treatise does not deserve attention only for its pioneering qualities or its incisive comments about ancient epic and drama; it has also had a profound effect on the way we read and analyse literature today. Once the *Poetics* was rediscovered and published in about A.D. 1500, its concepts, methods of analysis and conclusions acquired fundamental importance among Renaissance and seventeenth-century dramatists and literary critics in Italy, France and England. Interest in the *Poetics* has redoubled recently, because it has been acknowledged as a crucial text in the continuing and vigorous debates about the nature and purpose of literature, and about language itself. Nor is this interest likely to decline in the future. Some aspects of Aristotle's theory (notably catharsis) are only now becoming clear in the light of new evidence. Moreover, his analysis has already proved flexible enough to be applied to literary forms that did not exist in his time, like the detective novel; it would still be relevant even to a culture based exclusively on media like cinema or television. There is nothing outdated in Aristotle's construction of a complex yet challenging theory, except perhaps for the breadth of its foundations. These include his own careful analysis of human action, speech and thought, and many aspects of his wider philosophy. Because of this exceptional breadth, as well as his remarkably acute reasoning, Aristotle has much to offer that is still timely about literature and its relation to life, topics which are no less vital now than they were twenty-three centuries ago when he wrote.

2
Plato's Challenge to Poetry

To understand the importance of poetry to the Greeks, we need to remember that it long occupied the place held by all our modern mass-media put together—books, cinema, theatre and television. As a basic part of Greek education, poems, especially Homer's epics, were copied out, read aloud, memorised and recited. This method taught the practical skills of reading and writing, but was also meant to instill social, religious and moral values. Poetry was no less important in adult life. Performances of poetry and song at public festivals and dinner-parties supplied most of the available entertainment. At Athens there was only one place where the citizens could be addressed as a group on any question not of immediate political concern: the theatre. Many poets perceived part of their task as reasserting or revising the moral, social and religious standards of their time. It is not surprising that, as values changed, what the poets said was sometimes challenged. Thus the early thinker Xenophanes attacked Homer for his portrayal of the gods.

During the fifth century B.C., technical and philosophical prose, and polished public lectures and speeches, began to grow in significance, but poetry maintained its prestige and its claim to be the educator of Greece. The spectacularly successful tragic and comic dramatists of Athens could speak powerfully via their characters to all the citizens. It was a jury of those same citizens who condemned to death Plato's revered teacher, the philosopher Socrates (469–399 B.C.). Whether or not Aristophanes' caricature of Socrates in his comedy the *Clouds* had prejudiced the jury against him, in the aftermath of his execution Plato (ca 427–347 B.C.) argued vigorously that philosophy, rather than poetry, should be the source of values. Putting his arguments into Socrates' mouth in a series of prose dialogues, Plato attacked poetry on four main grounds, to be explained more fully below. They are, in brief:

(i)   Poets compose under inspiration, not by using reason.
(ii) Poetry teaches the wrong things.
(iii) Poetry is a *mimēsis* (imitation), at two removes from reality.
(iv) Poetry encourages the emotions of those who perform or listen to it.

Of these charges, the first two refute claims that poetry is a skill (*technē*) which can be learned, and from which we learn. Although such claims were common, nobody could say exactly what poetry taught, or how poets knew about it. Forced by Socrates to specify the contribution of particular poets, his interlocutors reply, for example, that Homer teaches war, or Hesiod farming. Socrates then objects that one could learn these arts better from a general or a farmer. He adds that, if poets do say things that are valid, they do so without knowing what they are saying, since they compose by an inspiration which comes from outside themselves. Both these arguments, used in Plato's early work, the *Apology* (22 B–C), were probably advanced by Socrates himself. In another early work of Plato's, the *Ion*, Socrates adds the charge that epic and tragic poetry encourage the audience to indulge their emotions, notably pity and fear, to the detriment of their powers of reason.

Plato expanded and elaborated this critique of poetry in his *Republic*, which clearly formed the starting-point for Aristotle's reply. In *Republic* II–III (377A–398B) Plato charges that much of the poetry currently used in education is unsuitable for educating the Guardians of his ideal state. Poetry sets a bad moral example, since it misrepresents the nature of divinity, notably in the crude and violent tales of the Olympian gods, and there are similar faults in its depiction of the heroes of old, who are shown as unable to control their emotions. It also presents problems of form. Since the poet or performer puts himself in the place of the character who is speaking, much of it involves *mimēsis* (imitation or impersonation); as ancient poetry was always read aloud, this applies to the reader too. Plato objects that the Guardians should not depart from their own characters by impersonating others, especially people who are morally inferior, because this experience will influence their characters in the wrong way.

In *Republic* X (595A–608B), Plato makes a much more fundamental attack on the nature of poetry itself, based on a vital tenet of his philosophy, the so-called Theory of Forms. He held that perceptible reality, i.e. the particulars of the universe we perceive with our senses, is not the object of true knowledge but only of opinion; for these particulars derive, by a relation of *mimēsis* (imitation), from transcendental "Forms" which we can apprehend only with our intellects, and not with our senses. We recognise e.g. a bed, a chair, justice or goodness, because a Form of each exists, from which particular beds or just acts derive (we can recognise the Forms embodied in the particulars because our souls knew the Forms before we were born).

From this theory, Plato concluded that art relates to our world of appearances in the same way that our world of appearances relates to the world of the Forms, i.e. by *mimēsis*. An artist depicts a bed, or a poet dramatises a just act, with his eye on particular beds or just acts in our world of appearances; but these particulars are already at one remove from the true reality of the Forms. Art is thus an imitation of an imitation; it is at two removes from reality.

Although art is thus mere illusion, it is a dangerous one, because we can mistake its products for reality. Worse still, we find poetry attractive because it appeals to what Plato considered the lower part of the soul, the part concerned with the emotions. Comedy makes us laugh, tragedy makes us weep, and poetry in general makes us give in to grief, pity, laughter, lust, anger, and so forth. But in his view we should control our emotions rather than indulge them.

For these reasons, Plato concludes in the *Republic* that the only poems to be allowed in the ideal state are hymns to the gods and poems in praise of good men; tragedy, epic and comedy are banned. But, as a lover of poetry himself, he issues a challenge to the poets, and to people who love poetry but are not poets themselves, to prove that it can be a source of benefit as well as of pleasure. This is the challenge to which Aristotle, Plato's greatest student, responds in the *Poetics*.

3
Aristotle and His Reply

Aristotle could afford to adopt a more relaxed attitude towards poetry than his teacher's had been, because times had changed and his own philosophy differed radically from Plato's.

Born in 384 B.C. at Stagira in northern Greece, Aristotle was the son of the court physician to the King of Macedon, a state whose power was to grow as that of Athens declined. Sent to Athens at age seventeen to complete his education, he soon joined Plato's Academy, and stayed there, first as student and then as professor, for two decades till 348, just before Plato died. Passed over as Plato's successor, he moved first to Assos near Troy (now in N.W. Turkey), where two of Plato's disciples had set up a college with the local ruler's encouragement, and then to the nearby island of Lesbos. In 342 he was invited back to Macedon by King Philip III, to supervise the secondary education of his son and heir Alexander (the Great). Philip's military victory at Chaeronea in 338 was a decisive defeat for the Athenian politicians opposed to the Macedonian domination of Greece; and in 335 Aristotle returned to Athens to set up a college of his own, the Lyceum. Here scholars could teach and research in every branch of knowledge, covering what we now call the humanities, sciences and social sciences (Plato's Academy had a narrower focus). During these years Alexander the Great conquered the vast Persian empire; his early death in 323 set off an anti-Macedonian revolt in most of Greece, and Aristotle was obliged to leave Athens. He died on the nearby island of Euboea the year after, aged sixty-two.

Aristotle combined an intensely analytical approach with an eye for practical details. His writings cover every area of learning except mathematics. The basis for his interest in studying—and indeed in defining for the first time—such diverse fields as logic, physics, meteorology, biology, metaphysics, politics, ethics, rhetoric and poetics, was his rejection of Plato's theory of Forms. Replacing it with his own theory of what "being" is, he reasserted the value of studying the particulars of the perceived world. His method was to analyse and classify the phenomena we perceive with our senses, and draw general conclusions in the process, which can then be applied back to the phenomena. The philosophy which results is less radical and Utopian than Plato's, and more willing to take account of, and to reshape, the opinions of ordinary people. Moreover Plato had to struggle bitterly to get the enterprise of philosophy taken seriously; it was still competing with poetry and rhetoric as a path to wisdom. But when Aristotle formulated his ideas, the kind of teaching and research practised in Plato's Academy clearly had a more secure future.

For these reasons, Aristotle's attitude to poetry was less hostile than his teacher's. Like everything else, poetry has its place in life, and is a worthy object of study by the philosopher. Philosophy should classify the different kinds of poetry, explain how they work and what their purpose is, and subject them to critical appraisal rather than outright condemnation. Aristotle's tone is detached and objective, unlike Plato who suggests that we should reject poetry like "a lover who renounces a passion that is doing him no good" (*Republic* X 608E).

Aristotle made public his refusal to accept Plato's views on poetry in his dialogue *On Poets*, the surviving fragments of which are newly collected and translated in this volume (for his disagreement with Plato see frags. 1–2). The *On Poets* was a polished work intended for a wide audience. Aristotle most probably published it while Plato was still alive; some of Plato's late works may even respond to the ideas it contained. But Aristotle never published the *Poetics*, which is probably the script for his lectures on poetry. There is no solid evidence that he drafted it much later than he wrote the *On Poets*, although he may well have tinkered with it until almost the end of his life. Most scholars suppose that he waited to deliver these lectures until his last years, when under his direction his students had compiled the *Didascaliae*, a chronological list of Athenian plays; but this seems very unlikely.

Among his own students Aristotle had no need to signal that his theory is fundamentally a refutation of Plato's, but so it is. However, far from rejecting his teacher's views as a whole, he retained much in them that he found valuable; his reformulation and reversal of Plato's positions is complex and subtle.

4

Aristotle's Concept of Representation

Aristotle responds to Plato's charges against poetry by arguing that poetry can be of philosophical value without being philosophy, and of educational value without being education. The four main grounds of Plato's attack were: (i) poetry is composed under inspiration; (ii) it teaches the wrong things; (iii) it is a *mimēsis* (imitation), at two removes from reality, and (iv) it encourages the emotions. To reply to Plato effectively Aristotle must answer all four points, which he does as follows:

(a) Poetry is a skill or art (*technē*) which can be learned, with rules comprehensible by reason. The mere fact that the *Poetics* sets out the principles of poetic composition answers Plato's first argument.

(b) Poetry is a *mimēsis* (representation) of reality, but a useful one from which we can learn: this will be explained below, and is the response to Plato's second and third points.

arouse emotion & does, but catharsis

(c) Poetry does work by arousing the emotions of the audience, but this can be beneficial. This answer to Plato's last argument involves the concept of catharsis, which will be discussed in the next section.

The Greeks drew no clear distinction between imitation, copying, impersonation and representation—all these concepts were included in the word *mimēsis*. Plato and Aristotle agreed that this was the right word to describe the relation between verbal and visual art (e.g. poetry and painting) on the one hand, and the perceived world on the other, but they used it with significantly different emphases. Plato tends to stress the idea that visual art *copies* nature and Homer *impersonates* his characters; neither aspect of *mimēsis* is very complimentary to art. Aristotle redefines *mimēsis* to stress that poetry *represents* action and life, just as language *represents* ideas (see *Rhetoric* III 1.1404a21, and compare *On Interpretation* 1.16a2ff.). Plato often suggests that art deceives us about reality; Aristotle argues that we can learn about reality from it, even at the most basic level, because of how representation works.

Plato
↳ copy
Aristotle
↳ represents
deceive
v.
teach

According to Aristotle, recognising that something is a representation is an intellectual process—we identify what is represented because it has some features of the actual object (*Poetics* 48b10ff.). Thus we recognise a sketch of a cow because it has four legs, horns and so on. To the complaint that such a sketch involves a loss of detail, Aristotle would reply that this loss is accompanied by an increased clarity of the basic form. This explains his high valuation of plot, the structure of the action which poetry represents; for him, a clearly structured art-work is preferable to one cluttered with formless detail.

At the beginning of the *Poetics*, Aristotle rejects the popular equation of poetry with anything written in verse (47b13–23). From the theory of representation just outlined he draws a still more significant conclusion. He argues that poetry is "more philosophical" than history, because history represents real actions and events ("particulars"), i.e. what actual historical characters said or did, whereas poetry tends to represent generalised ones ("universals"), i.e. what a certain kind of person would say or do in a certain kind of situation. A historian has to keep to the facts, where sequences of cause and effect are often unclear; but a poet can and should make sure that the action he represents (the "plot") is clear in terms of cause and effect (see *Poetics* 51a35–b11). Here Aristotle comes close to redefining poetry as a representation of universals, whether it is in verse or in prose. It follows that his theory is concerned not merely with anything that happens to be in verse, but rather with the whole range of what we call fiction.

5
Aristotle on the Purpose of Literature

As we have it, the *Poetics* provides no explicit reply to Plato's argument that tragedy, comedy and epic stir up our emotions, which we should instead seek to control. Since this aspect of his attack on poetry is so important, scholars have rightly assumed that Aristotle tried to answer it.

Aristotle accepted that these kinds of poetry have powerful emotional effects on the audience, since he often says so in the *Poetics*. In fact he defines the function of tragedy as the "catharsis" of emotions, i.e. their "purgation" or "purification" (49b27); the presence of catharsis in his definition of tragedy proves its importance to his theory, but he gives no further explanation. In a passage on the use of music and poetry in education (*Politics* VIII 7.1341b37–40), he speaks briefly of catharsis, and promises a full account of it in the *Poetics*; since no such account appears in that part of the text we still have, he is most probably referring to its second book (on comedy), now lost. The *On Poets* seems also to have discussed this question. If we are to understand his poetic theory completely, this gap needs to be filled.

Scholars have tried to reconstruct Aristotle's view of catharsis in two ways, either by comparing what he says in *Politics* VIII with his account of the emotional effects of tragedy in the *Poetics*, or by searching for later writers who knew his theory directly or indirectly; both approaches are valuable. The relevant passages from the *Politics* and from these later writers are newly collected, translated and equipped with notes in this volume; some of them have not appeared in English before. Since the later writers who talk about catharsis seem to have known the theory from the more widely read *On Poets* rather than from *Poetics* II, the evidence about it is presented together with *On Poets* frag. *4.

The interpretation of catharsis which has prevailed until very recently is that advanced by Jacob Bernays, the uncle by marriage of Sigmund Freud, in a famous essay published in 1857. At *Politics* VIII 7.1342a4–16 Aristotle explains tragic catharsis by comparing it with the healing of people suffering from hysterical outbreaks of emotion (*enthousiasmos*); these people are cured by 'cathartic songs', which *arouse* their emotions and thereby relieve them. Bernays concluded that the catharsis we obtain from tragedy is a similar process of psychological

healing; we all have build-ups of undesirable emotions of pity and terror, which can be aroused and then released by watching tragedy.

  Bernays' medical interpretation allows the theory of catharsis to answer Plato's point that poetry stimulates undesirable emotions, but it is
otherwise unsatisfactory. His view makes catharsis an accidental by-
product of tragedy, rather than something essential to its nature, as
Aristotle implies by including it in his definition of tragedy (*Poetics*
49b27). According to Bernays' theory the best audience for a tragedy,
in terms of its emotional effect, would surely be an audience of people
who are emotionally disturbed and unbalanced. This seems peculiar;
in the *Poetics* Aristotle implies several times that ordinary audiences are
inferior to the man of judgement, who is no doubt a philosopher, and
therefore less subject to emotional disturbance. The *Poetics* assumes
normal audiences in normal emotional states, and nowhere suggests
that we go to the theatre for the same reason that we visit the doctor.
Moreover, Bernays assumes that the emotions are inherently undesirable, just as Plato thought; but we shall see below that Aristotle did not
regard them as necessarily undesirable in themselves.

  Since Bernays' interpretation presents these difficulties, others have
looked again at either Aristotle's own remarks or later sources for an
alternative; and several scholars have arrived by different routes at
roughly the same hypothesis. The following interpretation of what Aristotle meant by catharsis is based on a combination of approaches,
including some evidence neglected or undiscovered until the last few
years.

  The *Poetics* indicates that poetry's arousal of the emotions is connected with the core of Aristotle's poetic theory, i.e. his concept of
representation. This is especially evident when he says that the tragic
poet must aim to bring about the pleasure that comes from pity and
terror *by means of representation* (53b12). Pity and terror are painful emotions in themselves, but much depends on why we feel them. Aristotle
is distinguishing between experiencing pity and terror in real life,
which is not pleasant, and experiencing them because of the tragic representation, which leads to the pleasure proper to tragedy. Similarly at
48b10–12 he says that we derive pleasure from seeing representations
even of things that are painful to look at in actuality. According to the
argument of the *Poetics*, if the action represented (the plot) is correctly
structured, it will arouse in the audience the correct emotional response; in the case of tragedy this is pity and terror. If the action is
badly structured, it will arouse the wrong emotional response, which
Aristotle calls "shock" or "revulsion" (52b36), literally "dirtiness"—the
opposite, surely, of *catharsis*, which means "cleansing" or "purification". These passages show that the theory of catharsis is not an acci-

53b12

dental appendage to the rest of Aristotle's literary theory, but an essential part of it.

To progress further, we need to consider Aristotle's general view of the emotions. Plato tended to regard them as merely irrational, but Aristotle considered them an important factor in taking correct decisions and forming good character. In his *Ethics* he argues that we should feel the correct emotion towards the right object, at the right time, to the proper degree and so forth. There are things about which it is right to feel e.g. anger, pity or terror; such correct emotional reactions as proper compassion, justified anger and the right degree of courage can and should affect decision or moral choice (see, for example, *Ethics* III 7.1115b11–20). It is important to feel the emotions rightly. For example, if we feel too much fear, we are cowardly, but if we feel too little we are foolhardy; only if we feel fear to the correct extent, no more no less, are we courageous. Such correct reactions attain the mean between the extremes; in Aristotle's view, this is where virtue lies, e.g. courage is the virtue lying at the mid-point between the extremes, namely cowardice and foolhardiness, which are both errors relative to it.

For Aristotle, one of the main factors in the building of good character is to develop a settled disposition to feel emotion correctly, since this will lead to good decisions. Just as, in Aristotle's moral theory, we become good by habitually doing good, so too by feeling emotion appropriately (towards the right object, at the right time etc.), we become habituated to having the right emotional responses, those emotional responses which attain the mean between the extremes; these help us to take the correct decisions, so that we come nearer to the mean, where virtue lies, and become virtuous in character.

Now poetry offers an obvious way in which we can learn these responses without the hazardous process of undergoing in actuality the experiences represented in poetry. By responding emotionally to the representation, we can learn to develop the correct emotional responses. Aristotle says precisely this about music, *in which he includes poetry*, at *Politics* VIII 5.1340a14–25, translated in this volume as Testimonium A(i) on catharsis.

Thus poetry undoubtedly has an educative and moral function, that is, it helps to form character. This may seem to have little to do with catharsis, but the later writers indicate that it did. Thus Proclus, explicitly referring to Aristotle, says that tragedy and comedy "make it possible to satisfy the emotions in due measure, and, by satisfying them, to keep them tractable for *education*" (Testimonium C(ii): my italics). The remarkable new text about catharsis from Herculaneum states "poetry is useful with regard to virtue, *purifying*, as we said, the [related] part [of the soul]" (*On Poets* frag. *4.7: my italics). This text even indicates that catharsis applies no less to errors in the intellectual virtue of practical intelligence, than to errors of character and emotion, like excessive fear: poetry contributes to virtue as a whole, which in Aristotle's moral theory depends on both intellect and character. Catharsis and the mean in terms of the emotions are also linked by Iamblichus and the *Tractatus Coislinianus*.

Unfortunately Aristotle himself never states this clearly in his surviving works; but it accords with his theories of character and education, and also with the general sense of his discussion of catharsis in the *Politics*. There he says that music (and poetry) confer three benefits, the education of children, catharsis and entertainment (VIII 1341b32–1342a16, translated as Testimonium A(ii) below). Like the songs used for healing abnormal emotional states, which produce a catharsis in hysterical people, tragedy produces "a sort of" catharsis of pity and terror; but this affects everybody, insofar as we are all prone to excess in the emotions to some degree. From this statement it surely follows that tragedy reduces these emotions so that they are no longer excessive and divergent from the mean, but in due proportion and in accord with it (which is what the *Tractatus Coislinianus* says it does). Both kinds of catharsis are homoeopathic; both work on the emotions by arousing the emotions, just as we treat a fever by piling on blankets.

If the interpretation advanced above is right, tragedy confers the other two benefits as well. It is obviously a form of entertainment, a concept which Aristotle associates not merely with relaxation but also with acquiring intelligence (*Politics* VIII 5.1339a25). However, like the poetry used in education (which surely includes Homer), tragedy also habituates us to feel the correct emotional as well as intellectual responses to the people and actions it represents; this is important for the development of good character and virtue. Thus catharsis falls in between—and combines—education and entertainment.

If this ethical aspect of catharsis is accepted, Aristotle's theory becomes a complete answer to Plato, and a far more subtle and sophisticated one. The above interpretation seems superior to Bernays', because it accords better with Aristotle's view of the emotions and their relation to character; it shows how catharsis is an integral part of poetry, as a representation of actions which arouse the emotions; and it explains how catharsis can benefit everyone, not just people who are emotionally unstable.

Taking tragedy as an example, the cathartic process works as follows. By representing pitiable, terrifying and other painful events, tragedy arouses pity, terror and other painful emotions in the audience, for each according to his own emotional capacity, and so stimulates these emotions as to relieve them by giving them moderate and harmless exercise, thereby bringing the audience nearer to the mean in their emotional responses, and so nearer to virtue in their characters; and with this relief comes pleasure. Comedy works on the pleasant emotions in the same way.

It must be stressed that this reconstruction of Aristotle's theory of catharsis is, and seems likely to remain, highly controversial. His incidental remarks in the *Politics*, and the scattered statements of later writers, are a poor substitute for a full account of his own.

6

The Structure of the Poetics

We do not know who arranged the *Poetics* in two 'books', i.e. separate rolls of papyrus. *Poetics* I ends at a major break in terms of content, the conclusion of the account of tragedy and epic; the lost Book II was concerned with comedy. The difficulty of the *Poetics* has led to considerable disagreement about its structure. The explanatory headings, and the paragraphs into which this translation is divided, are my own interpretations, since ancient manuscripts gave the reader no such help. Renaissance editors divided the work into twenty-six chapters, but these divisions are not very helpful for understanding its structure. The summary below may be more useful; it is based on the main headings supplied in this translation. For convenience I give in brackets ( ) the old chapter-numbers where each section starts.

1. *Poetry in general* (i)
1.1 Poetry is a kind of representation
1.2 Its kinds classified by (a) the media of representation
1.3 Its kinds classified by (b) the objects represented (ii)
1.4 Its kinds classified by (c) the manner of representation (iii)
2. *The origins and development of tragedy, comedy and epic* (iv)
3. *The nature of tragedy* (vi)
3.1 The definition of tragedy, and its six qualitative parts
3.2 The nature of plot (vii)
3.3 The kinds of plot (ix.51b33)
3.4 The three parts of plot (xi)

It may be valuable to compare this outline with the topics covered in the *Tractatus Coislinianus*, which I argue to be a summary of the lost second Book of the *Poetics*. The contents of the latter are as follows:

A list of the major sections of each work will show how they resemble each other (this is discussed further in the notes on the *Tractatus*):

Poetics	*Tractatus*
Poetry and its kinds	Poetry and its kinds
The origins of poetry	The end of poetry, catharsis
Definition of tragedy	Definition of comedy
The nature of plot	The nature of laughter
Quantitative parts	Qualitative parts
Qualitative parts	Quantitative parts
Comparison with epic	Comparison of kinds of comedy

7

The Present Translation

As I remarked above, the *Poetics* is probably Aristotle's script for his own lectures, intended for oral expansion and clarification. The structure of his argument is not very clearly marked, his use of terms is not always consistent, and the work is far from polished. These reasons would suffice to make the *Poetics* difficult; but its history as a text has made matters worse. The original scrolls of papyrus had no explanatory headings, notes or glossary, and no equivalent of capital letters, italics or quotation marks; there were not even spaces between the words. The *Poetics* was passed down to us by scribes, and eventually monks, who laboriously copied it from a copy of a copy of a copy ... and so on. For many centuries until the Renaissance it had few readers, and few of them could make much sense of it. Moreover, copying a difficult text again and again can easily lead to mistakes. The result is that the *Poetics* is one of the worst preserved texts to reach us from antiquity. Fortunately our increased knowledge of the ancient world means that we are better placed to understand it than in the past.

The *Poetics* survived the collapse of ancient culture in the early Middle Ages more by chance than anything else. We know the work from four sources only. There are two medieval manuscripts in the original Greek, MSS A and B (now in libraries in Paris and Florence). We can also learn about the text from two medieval translations, the first into Arabic (based not on the Greek, but on a Syriac intermediary of which only one page survives), and the second into Latin.

Because of the process of repeated copying explained above, these sources often disagree; deciding what the text originally said can be difficult. I have based my translation on the Greek text established by Rudolf Kassel, which is the standard one in use. But when I came to consider the manuscripts' divergences, I found that I disagreed with Kassel's text more often than I at first expected. This is partly because I think he has not given enough weight to two sources, MS B and the Arabic, whose importance has only been demonstrated relatively recently. Some of the readings I have adopted are new; places where the text presents problems are briefly discussed in the notes. Occasionally copyists have inserted a few words to explain Aristotle's meaning; I have not translated such phrases, but mention them in the notes. Sometimes all the sources have lost a word or a phrase; where this has occurred, material I have inserted to fill the gap is shown by square brackets [ ]. Any gaps which cannot be filled are indicated by asterisks (* * *). All such passages are discussed in the notes.

The *Poetics* is incomplete, since it contains no account of catharsis, comedy and laughter, topics which Aristotle says elsewhere that he discusses there. This is because, as I mentioned above, it originally consisted of two books, the second of which is lost. All three topics are dealt with in a medieval Greek manuscript now in Paris, the so-called *Tractatus Coislinianus (T.C.)*; I have argued elsewhere, from its Aristotelian language, content and structure, that this treatise is in fact a summary of the lost Book II, and accords well with what else we know about that work. A translation of it is included here, together with a hypothetical reconstruction of *Poetics* II, which integrates the known fragments of Book II into the *Tractatus*. Aristotle also presented his views about representation and catharsis in his dialogue *On Poets*. Since the fragments of this work throw light on the *Poetics*, they are newly collected here. Many of them are not easily available in translation, and fragments 3 and 4 are published in English for the first time. Fragments assigned to the *On Poets* only by conjecture are marked with an asterisk, e.g. "frag. *3".

My translation attempts to follow the original Greek closely, with minimal alterations for the sake of natural English. An important term is translated by one English word as far as possible, with one or two variants where this is unavoidable. I have retained the frequent Greek use of definite article plus adjective, because "the laughable" is not quite the same as "humour"; abstract nouns are useful, but too many of them might conceal how simply Aristotle expresses some of his basic concepts. Also, for the sake of clarity, I have filled out many of his frequent ellipses, the source of his extraordinary brevity; the result is less concise but more intelligible. Such supplements are marked with square brackets (the few places where square brackets mark that all the manuscripts have lost some original words are signalled in the notes). I have sometimes divided Aristotle's longer sentences. However, I have not tidied up his occasional unexpected transitions, e.g. sudden shifts from a collective singular to the plural, when he is thinking of a number of instances of something. To alter such features of the *Poetics* would unduly disguise its difficulty.

The explanatory headings, paragraphing and numeration within the translation, e.g. (a), (b) etc., are modern impositions on the text. So are the standard page and line numbers of Immanuel Bekker's 1830 edition of Aristotle's works, which are given in the outer margins (e.g. 53a20), and the numbering of the chapters (boldface in the outer margins). For the sake of convenience, I have omitted the initial 14- in all Bekker references to the *Poetics*; thus 1453a1 has become 53a1. It is impossible

to make these numbers correspond exactly to the lines of the translation: thus 53a5 in the margin signals only that line 53a5 begins somewhere within this line of the translation, and words from 53a4,
commented on under that number, may appear on the same line.
Hence the note numbers may sometimes seem slightly inexact.

8
Notes on the Text

I translate Rudolf Kassel's text of the *Poetics* (Oxford, 1966), except for
the variations listed below. Kassel's reading is given, where necessary,
to the right of the slash marks //. Words or phrases he wishes to delete
or insert are simply accepted, unless indicated below. In the following
list square brackets [ ] signal the *deletion* of words found in some or all
of the sources, and angle brackets ‹ › mark the *insertion* of words
found in neither of the Greek manuscripts (these are often preserved
by the Arabic version). Daggers † † precede and follow words corrupted by the copyists. Changes of punctuation are not listed.

47a29	psilois ē	//	psilois ‹kai› hē
b9	‹anōnumos› tunchanei ousa	//	anōnumoi tunchanousi
b14	‹tous men› elegopoious		
48a15	gar	//	†gas†
a15	Philoxenos, ‹houtō›		
a16	autēi de ‹tautēi› tēi		
a23–4	[ ]	//	†tous mimoumenous†
a24	tautais ‹tais›		
a33	ou	//	ho poiētēs
49b6	Epicharmos kai Phormis	//	[ ]
b29	kai melos	//	[ ]
b37	toutous	//	hous
50a12	ouk oligoi autōn	//	†ouk oligoi autōn†
a13	opseis echoien an	//	†opsis echei pan†
a17–20	kai . . . tounantion	//	[ ]
b12	[ ]	//	†tōn men logōn†
51a9	hōsper . . . phasin	//	†hōsper . . . phasin†
b32	kai dunata genesthai	//	[ ]

52a3	kai mallon	//	[ ]
a35	estin . . . sumbainein	//	✝estin . . . sumbainei✝
b2	eti de	//	epeidē
53a5–6	[ ]	//	eleos . . . homoion
a25	kai pollai	//	kai hai pollai
a35	hautē ⟨hē⟩		
b29	Mēdeian: ⟨estin de gignōskontas mellēsai kai mē praxai:⟩ estin de praxai		
b34	tetarton	//	triton
54a22	andreion	//	andreian
b14–15	hoion ton Achillea agathon kai paradeigma sklērotētos Homēros	//	✝paradeigma sklērotētos hoion ton Achillea agathon kai Homēros✝
55a20	[ ]	//	sēmeiōn
a27	horōnt' ⟨an⟩ ton theatēn	//	horōnta
b7–8	dia tina . . . katholou	//	[ ]
b17	theou tinas	//	Poseidōnos
b31	⟨dēlōsis, lusis d' hē⟩	//	* * lusis d' hē
b31	aitēseōs	//	aitiaseōs
56a2	opsis	//	✝oēs✝
a20	thaumastōn	//	thaumastōs
b8	hē idea	//	hēi deoi
b21	arthron onoma rēma	//	onoma rēma arthron
b36	sullabē, kai	//	✝sullabē kai✝
57a2	pephukuian	//	pephukuia
a2–3	[ ]	//	kai epi tōn akrōn kai epi tou mesou
a5	[ ]	//	mias
a6	*after* phōnēn *insert* hoion to amphi kai to peri kai ta alla *from a7–8*		
a8–9	[ ]	//	ē phōnē . . . phōnōn
a10	mesou, ⟨hoion 'kai' 'oukoun' 'alla'⟩.		
a22	⟨ē⟩ epitaxin		
b1	⟨epeuxamenos Dii⟩	//	* *
b6	glōtta: ⟨to de doru hēmin men kurion, Kupriois de glōtta.⟩		
b11	eidos, ⟨hoion⟩		
b24	[ ]	//	ē
b33	⟨kosmos d' esti * * *⟩	//	* *

58a16	pente, ‹doru pōu napu gonu astu›.		
a17	kai N ‹kai R›		
a29	metaphoran	//	metaphorōn
b10	ankeramenos	//	†an geramenos†
b16	epektetamenōn	//	epōn
59b5–7	pleon . . . Trōiades	//	[ ]
b13	hekateron ‹hekaterōs›		
b16	pantas	//	panta
b36	kai metaphoras ‹kai epektaseis›		
b36	kai ‹tautēi› hē		
60a11	allo ti [ēthos]		
a34–5	an de tethēi, kai . . . atopon	//	†an de thēi, kai . . . atopon†
b17	‹hippon orthōs, hēmarte d' en tōi mimēsasthai di' ›	//	* *
b18	[ ]	//	‹ham'›
b19	[ ]	//	ē
b21	epitimēmata ‹ta›		
b23	‹ei› adunata		
b28	hēmartēsthai	//	[ ]
61a1	houtō	//	oun
a16	ta de	//	to de
a27	ton kekramenon oinon ‹oinon› phasin einai		
b1	eti	//	hoti
b12	dunaton: ‹isōs gar adunaton›		
b14	pros ‹d'› ha		
b14	‹gar luteon›	//	te
b14	ouk alogon ‹alogon›		
b18	luteon	//	kai †auton†
62a4	an eiē. ‹peri dē toutōn lekteon an eiē.›		
a7	epoiei	//	[esti]
a7	āidonta	//	diāidonta
a16	kai tas opseis, di' has	//	di' hēs
b11	mimēseis	//	mimēsis
b19	peri de iambōn kai kōmōidias * * *	//	* * *

At *T.C.* 13, I now read *eisin de pente* instead of ‹pisteis› *pente*.

Poetics I

1. The field of the enquiry

Our topic is poetry in itself and its kinds, and what potential
each has; how plots should be constructed if the composition is
to turn out well; also, from how many parts it is [constituted],
and of what sort they are; and likewise all other aspects of the
same enquiry. Let us first begin, following the natural [order],
from first [principles].

1.1 Poetry is a kind of representation using rhythm, speech and melody

Epic and tragic composition, and indeed comedy, dithyrambic
composition, and most sorts of music for wind and stringed in-
struments are all, [considered] as a whole, representations.
They differ from one another in three ways, by using for the
representation (i) different media, (ii) different objects, or (iii) a
manner that is different and not the same.

Some people use colours and forms for representations, making images of many objects (some by art, and some by practice),
and others do so with sound; so too all the arts we mentioned
produce a representation using rhythm, speech and melody,
but use these either separately or mixed. E.g., the art of [play-
ing] the oboe and lyre, and any other arts that have the same
potential (e.g. that of [playing] the pan-pipes), use melody and
rhythm alone, but the art of dancers [uses] rhythm by itself
without melody; for they too can represent characters, sufferings and actions, by means of rhythms given form.

1

1.1.1 We have no term for "literary representation", whether in prose or verse

But the art of representation that uses unaccompanied words or verses (whether it mixes these together or uses one single class of verse-form) has to the present day no name. For we have no common name for the mimes of Sophron and Xenarchus and the Socratic dialogues, and would not have one even if someone were to compose the representation in [iambic] trimeters, elegiacs or some other such verse. But people attach the word "poet" to the verse-form, and name some "elegiac poets" and others "epic poets", terming them poets not according to [whether they compose a] representation but indiscriminately, according to [their use of] verse. Thus if someone brings out a work of medicine or natural science in verse, they normally call him a poet; but there is nothing in common between Homer and Empedocles except the verse-form. For this reason it is right to call the former a poet, but the latter a natural scientist

rather than a poet. Likewise, if someone produced a representation by intermingling all the verse-forms, just as Chaeremon composed his *Centaur* (a recitation which mixes all the verse-forms), he must still be termed a poet. This, then, is how we should define these matters.

1.2 The kinds of poetry are classified by (a) the media of the representation

Some arts use all the media we have mentioned (i.e. rhythm,

song and verse), like the composition of dithyrambic poems, that of nomes, and tragedy and comedy; they differ because the former use all the media at the same time, the latter [use them only] in certain parts. So these are what I mean by the differences between the arts in the media by which they produce the representation.

1.3 The kinds of poetry are classified by (b) the objects of the representation

Since those who represent represent people in action, these people are necessarily either good or inferior. For characters al-

most always follow from these [qualities] alone; everyone dif-   **48a3**
fers in character because of vice and virtue. So they are either (i)
better than we are, or (ii) worse, or (iii) such [as we are], just as   **5**
the painters [represent them]; for Polygnotus used to make
images of superior persons, Pauson of worse ones, and
Dionysius of those like [us].

Clearly each of the [kinds of] representation we mentioned
will contain these differences, and will vary by representing objects which vary in this manner. For these divergences can arise
in dancing and in playing the oboe and lyre. They can also arise   **10**
in speeches and unaccompanied verse: e.g. (i) Homer [repre-
sents] better persons, (ii) Cleophon [represents] ones like [us],
and (iii) Hegemon of Thasos, who was the first to compose parodies, and Nicochares who composed the *Deiliad*, [represent]
worse ones. [They can arise] likewise in dithyrambs and nomes: **15**
for just as Timotheus and Philoxenus [represented] Cyclopes,
[so] one may represent [people in different ways]. Tragedy too
is distinguished from comedy by precisely this difference; comedy prefers to represent people who are worse than those who
exist, tragedy people who are better.

1.4 The kinds of poetry are classified by   iii
(c) the manner of the representation,
i.e. narrative or dramatic

Again, a third difference among these [kinds] is the manner in
which one can represent each of these things. For one can use   **20**
the same media to represent the very same things, sometimes
(a) by narrating (either (i) becoming another [person], as Homer
does, or (ii) remaining the same person and not changing), or
(b) by representing everyone as in action and activity.

Representation, then, has these three points of difference, as
we said at the beginning, its media, its objects and its manner.   **25**
Consequently, in one respect Sophocles is the same sort of representational artist as Homer, in that both represent good people, but in another he is like Aristophanes, since both represent
men in action and doing [things].

1.4.1 Why "drama" and "comedy" are so named

48a28 This is why, some say, their works are called "dramas", because they represent men "doing" (*drōntas*). For this reason too
30 the Dorians lay claim to both tragedy and comedy. The Megarians here allege that comedy arose during the time of their democracy, and the Megarians in Sicily claim it; for Epicharmus
was from there, though he was not much prior to Chionides
35 and Magnes. Some of the Dorians in the Peloponnese lay
claim to tragedy. They produce the names [of comedy and
drama] as an indication [of their origins]: they say that they call
villages *kōmai* but the Athenians call them *dēmoi*, on the assumption that comedians were so called not from their revelling
(*kōmazein*), but because they wandered around the villages,
48b1 ejected in disgrace from the town. They also say that they term
"doing" *dran*, but that the Athenians term it *prattein*.

Anyway, as for the points of difference in representation,
and how many and what they are, let this account suffice.

iv ## 2. The origins of tragedy, comedy and epic

2.1 The origins of poetry

Two causes seem to have generated the art of poetry as a
5 whole, and these are natural ones.

(i) Representation is natural to human beings from child-
hood. They differ from the other animals in this: man tends
most towards representation and learns his first lessons
through representation.

Also (ii) everyone delights in representations. An indication
10 of this is what happens in fact: we delight in looking at the most
detailed images of things which in themselves we see with pain,
e.g. the shapes of the most despised wild animals even when
dead. The cause of this is that learning is most pleasant, not
only for philosophers but for others likewise (but they share in
15 it to a small extent). For this reason they delight in seeing
images, because it comes about that they learn as they observe,
and infer what each thing is, e.g. that this person [represents]
that one. For if one has not seen the thing [that is represented]

before, [its image] will not produce pleasure as a representa- **48b18**
tion, but because of its accomplishment, colour, or some other
such cause.

2.2 The early development of serious and humorous poetry

Since by nature we are given to representation, melody and **20**
rhythm (that verses are parts of rhythms is obvious), from the
beginning those by nature most disposed towards these generated poetry from their improvisations, developing it little by little. Poetry was split up according to their particular characters;
the grander people represented fine actions, i.e. those of fine **25**
persons, the more ordinary people represented those of inferior
ones, at first composing invectives, just as the others composed
hymns and praise-poems. We do not know of any composition
of this sort by anyone before Homer, but there were probably
many [who composed invectives]. Beginning with Homer [such
compositions] do exist, e.g. his *Margites* etc. In these the iambic **30**
verse-form arrived too, as is appropriate. This is why it is now
called "iambic", because they used to lampoon (*iambizein*) each
other in this verse-form. Thus some of the ancients became
composers of heroic poems, others of lampoons.

Just as Homer was the greatest composer of serious poetry
(not that he alone composed well, but because he alone com- **35**
posed dramatic representations), so too he was first to indicate
the form of comedy, by dramatising not an invective but the
laughable. For his *Margites* stands in the same relation to comedies as do the *Iliad* and *Odyssey* to tragedies. When tragedy and **49a1**
comedy appeared, people were attracted to each [kind of] composition according to their own particular natures. Some became composers of comedies instead of lampoons, but others
presented tragedies instead of epics, because comedy and trag- **5**
edy are greater and more honourable in their forms than are
lampoon and epic. To consider whether tragedy is now fully
[developed] in its elements or not, as judged both in and of itself and in relation to its audiences, is a different topic.

2.3 The development of tragedy

49a10 Anyway, arising from an improvisatory beginning (both tragedy and comedy—tragedy from the leaders of the dithyramb,
and comedy from the leaders of the phallic processions which
even now continue as a custom in many of our cities), [tragedy]
grew little by little, as [the poets] developed whatever [new
part] of it had appeared; and, passing through many changes,
15 tragedy came to a halt, since it had attained its own nature.

(i) Aeschylus was first to increase the number of its actors
from one to two; he reduced the [songs] of the chorus, and
made speech play the main role. Sophocles [brought in] three
actors and scenery.

(ii) Again, as for its magnitude, [starting] from trivial plots
20 and laughable diction, because it had changed from a satyric
[composition], [tragedy only] became grand at a late date. Its
verse-form altered from the tetrameter to iambic verse. For at
first [poets] used the tetrameter, because the composition was
satyric and mainly danced; but when [spoken] diction came in,
nature itself found the proper verse-form. The iambic is the
25 verse most suited to speech; an indication of this is that in
[everyday] speech with each other we use mostly iambic
[rhythms], but rarely hexameters, and [only] when we depart
28 from the intonations of [everyday] speech.

(iii) Again, as for the number of its episodes, and how each of
its other [parts] is said to have been elaborated, let them pass as
described; it would probably be a major undertaking to go
through their particulars.

v ## 2.4 The development of comedy

Comedy is, as we said, a representation of people who are
rather inferior—not, however, with respect to every [kind of]
vice, but the laughable is [only] a part of what is ugly. For the
35 laughable is a sort of error and ugliness that is not painful and
destructive, just as, evidently, a laughable mask is something
ugly and distorted without pain.

The transformations of tragedy, and [the poets] who brought
them about, have not been forgotten; but comedy was disre-
49b1 garded from the beginning, because it was not taken seriously.

For the magistrate granted a chorus of comic performers at a   **49b2**
late date—they had been volunteers. The record of those
termed its poets begins from [a time] when comedy already
possessed some of its forms. It is unknown who introduced
masks, prologues, a multiplicity of actors, etc. As for the com-   **5**
posing of plots, Epicharmus and Phormis [introduced it]. In the
beginning it came from Sicily, and, of the poets at Athens,
Crates was the first to relinquish the form of the lampoon and
compose generalised stories, i.e. plots.

2.5 The nature of epic compared to that of tragedy

Epic poetry follows tragedy insofar as it is a representation of
serious people which uses speech in verse; but they differ in   **10**
that [epic] has a single verse-form, and is narrative. Again, with
respect to length, tragedy attempts as far as possible to keep
within one revolution of the sun or [only] to exceed this a little,
but epic is unbounded in time; it does differ in this respect,
even though [the poets] at first composed in the same way in   **15**
tragedies as in epics. As for their parts, some are the same,
others are particular to tragedy. For this reason, whoever
knows about good and inferior tragedies knows about epics
too. Tragedy possesses all [the parts] that epic has, but those
that it possesses are not all in epic.

3. The nature of tragedy   **vi**

We will discuss representational art in hexameters, and com-   **20**
edy, later. Now let us discuss tragedy, taking up the definition
of its essence that results from what we have said.

3.1 The definition of tragedy

Tragedy is a representation of a serious, complete action which   **25**
has magnitude, in embellished speech, with each of its elements [used] separately in the [various] parts [of the play]; [rep-
resented] by people acting and not by narration; accomplishing
by means of pity and terror the catharsis of such emotions.

49b28   By "embellished speech", I mean that which has rhythm and
melody, i.e. song; by "with its elements separately", I mean
30   that some [parts of it] are accomplished only by means of spoken verses, and others again by means of song.

3.1.1 The deduction of the qualitative parts of tragedy from its nature

Since people acting produce the representation, first (i) the ornament of spectacle will necessarily be a part of tragedy; and
then (ii) song and (iii) diction, for these are the media in which
they produce the representation. By "diction" I mean the con-
35   struction of the [spoken] verses itself; by "song" I mean that of
which the meaning is entirely obvious.

     Since [tragedy] is a representation of an action, and is enacted
by people acting, these people are necessarily of a certain sort
according to their character and their reasoning. For it is because of these that we say that actions are of a certain sort, and
50a2   it is according to people's actions that they all succeed or fail. So
(iv) the plot is the representation of the action; by "plot" here, I
5   mean the construction of the incidents. By (v) the "characters",
I mean that according to which we say that the people in action
are of a certain sort. By (vi) "reasoning", I mean the way in
which they use speech to demonstrate something or indeed to
make some general statement.

     So tragedy as a whole necessarily has six parts, according to
which tragedy is of a certain sort. These are plot, characters,
10   diction, reasoning, spectacle and song. The media in which [the
poets] make the representation comprise two parts [i.e. diction
and song], the manner in which they make the representation,
one [i.e. spectacle], and the objects which they represent, three
[i.e. plot, character and reasoning]; there are no others except
these. Not a few of them, one might say, use these elements;
for they may have instances of spectacle, character, plot, diction, song and reasoning likewise.

3.1.2 Plot is the most important part of tragedy

15   But the most important of these is the structure of the incidents.
For (i) tragedy is a representation not of human beings but of
action and life. Happiness and unhappiness lie in action, and
the end [of life] is a sort of action, not a quality; people are of a

certain sort according to their characters, but happy or the op-   **50a19**
posite according to their actions. So [the actors] do not act in   **20**
order to represent the characters, but they include the charac-
ters for the sake of their actions. Consequently the incidents,
i.e. the plot, are the end of tragedy, and the end is most important of all.

(ii) Again, without action a tragedy cannot exist, but without
characters it may. For the tragedies of most recent [poets] lack   **25**
character, and in general there are many such poets. E.g. too
among the painters, how Zeuxis relates to Polygnotus—Polygnotus is a good character-painter, but Zeuxis' painting contains
no character at all.

(iii) Again, if [a poet] puts in sequence speeches full of character, well-composed in diction and reasoning, he will not   **30**
achieve what was [agreed to be] the function of tragedy; a tragedy that employs these less adequately, but has a plot (i.e.
structure of incidents), will achieve it much more.

(iv) In addition, the most important things with which a tragedy enthralls [us] are parts of plot—reversals and recognitions.

(v) A further indication is that people who try their hand at   **35**
composing can be proficient in the diction and characters before
they are able to structure the incidents; e.g. too almost all the
early poets.

3.1.3 The nature and importance
of tragedy's other parts

So plot is the origin and as it were the soul of tragedy, and the
characters are secondary. It is very similar in the case of paint-   **50b1**
ing too: if someone daubed [a surface] with the finest pigments
indiscriminately, he would not give the same enjoyment as if he
had sketched an image in black and white. Tragedy is a representation of an action, and for the sake of the action above all [a
representation] of the people who are acting.

Reasoning comes third, i.e. being able to say what is possible   **5**
and appropriate, which is its function in the case of the
speeches of civic life and rhetoric. The old [poets] made people
speak like citizens, but the recent ones make them speak like
rhetoricians. Character is that which reveals decision, of what-
ever sort; this is why those speeches in which the speaker de-   **10**
cides or avoids nothing at all do not have character. Reasoning,

50b11 on the other hand, is that with which people demonstrate that
something is or is not, or make some universal statement.

Diction is fourth. By "diction" I mean, as we said earlier,
communication by means of language, which has the same potential in the case of both verse and [prose] speeches.

15 Of the remaining [parts], song is the most important of the
embellishments. Spectacle is something enthralling, but is very
artless and least particular to the art of poetic composition. The
potential of tragedy exists even without a performance and actors; besides, the designer's art is more essential for the accom-

20 plishment of spectacular [effects] than is the poets'.

vii ## 3.2 The nature of plot

Now that these definitions have been given, let us next discuss
what sort of structure of the incidents there should be, since
this is the first and most important [part] of tragedy.

3.2.1 Plot should represent a single complete action of the proper magnitude

We have laid down that tragedy is the representation of a com-

25 plete i.e. whole action which has some magnitude (for there can
be a whole with no magnitude). A whole is that which has a
beginning, a middle and a conclusion. A beginning is that
which itself does not of necessity follow something else, but after which there naturally is, or comes into being, something
else. A conclusion, conversely, is that which itself naturally fol-

30 lows something else, either of necessity or for the most part,
but has nothing else after it. A middle is that which itself naturally follows something else, and has something else after it.
Well-constructed plots, then, should neither begin from a random point nor conclude at a random point, but should use the
elements we have mentioned [i.e. beginning, middle and
conclusion].

Further, to be fine both an animal and every thing which is

35 constructed from some [parts] should not only have these
[parts] in order, but also possess a magnitude that is not random. For fineness lies in magnitude and order. For this reason
a fine animal can be neither very small, for observation becomes
confused when it approaches an imperceptible instant of time;

nor [can it be] very large, for observation cannot happen at the   **51a1**
same time, but its unity and wholeness vanish from the observ-
ers' view, e.g. if there were an animal a thousand miles long.
Consequently, just as in the case of bodies and of animals these
should have magnitude, but [only] a magnitude that is easily
seen as a whole, so too in the case of plots these should have   **5**
length, but [only] a length that is easily memorable.

As for the limit on their length, one limit relates to performances and the perception [of them], not to the art [itself]. If the
performance of a hundred tragedies were required [at one
tragic competition], they would be performed "against the
clock", as the saying goes! But as for the limit according to the
nature of the thing [itself], the larger the plot is, the finer it is **10**
because of its magnitude, so long as the whole is still clear. To
give a simple definition, in whatever magnitude a change from
misfortune to good fortune, or from good fortune to misfortune, can come about by a sequence of events in accordance
with probability or necessity—this is an adequate definition of   **15**
its magnitude.

3.2.2 The unity of plot does not come   viii
from representing a single person

A plot is not unified, as some suppose, if it concerns one single
person. An indefinitely large number of things happens to one
person, in some of which there is no unity. So too the actions of
one person are many, but do not turn into a single action. For
this reason, it seems, all those poets who composed a *Heracleid*, **20**
a *Theseid* or similar poems are in error. They suppose that, because Heracles was a single person, his story too must be a single story. But, just as Homer is superior in other respects, it
seems that he saw this clearly as well (whether by art or by nature). In composing the *Odyssey*, he did not put into his poem   **25**
everything that happened to Odysseus, e.g. that he was
wounded on Parnassus and pretended to be insane during re-
cruitment; whether one of these things happened did not make
it necessary or probable that the other would happen. But he
constructed the *Odyssey* around a single action of the kind we
are discussing, and the *Iliad* similarly.

Therefore, just as in the other representational arts a single   **30**
representation is of a single [thing], so too the plot, since it is a

51a31 representation of action, ought to represent a single action, and a whole one at that; and its parts (the incidents) ought to be so constructed that, when some part is transposed or removed, the whole is disrupted and disturbed. Something which, **35** whether it is present or not present, explains nothing [else], is no part of the whole.

ix

3.2.3 Poetry should represent universals, not particulars

It is also obvious from what we have said that it is the function of a poet to relate not things that have happened, but things that may happen, i.e. that are possible in accordance with **51b1** probability or necessity. For the historian and the poet do not differ according to whether they write in verse or without verse—the writings of Herodotus could be put into verse, but they would be no less a sort of history in verse than they are without verses. But the difference is that the former relates **5** things that have happened, the latter things that may happen. For this reason poetry is a more philosophical and more serious thing than history; poetry tends to speak of universals, history of particulars. A universal is the sort of thing that a certain kind of person may well say or do in accordance with probability or **10** necessity—this is what poetry aims at, although it assigns names [to the people]. A particular is what Alcibiades did or what he suffered.

In the case of comedy this has already become clear. When [comic poets] have composed a plot according to probability, only then do they supply the names at random; they do not, like the composers of lampoons, compose [poems] about partic- **15** ular individuals. In the case of tragedy [the poets] keep to actual names. The reason is that what is possible is believable; we do not believe that what has never happened is possible, but things which have happened are obviously possible—they would not have happened, if they were impossible. Nonetheless even among tragedies some have only one or two well- **20** known names, and the rest made up; and some have not one, e.g. Agathon's *Antheus*. In this [drama] the incidents and the names alike are made up, and it is no less delightful. Conse- quently one must not seek to keep entirely to the traditional **25** stories which tragedies are about. In fact it is ridiculous to seek

to do so, since even the well-known [incidents] are known only   **51b25**
to a few people, but even so everyone enjoys them.

So it is clear from these arguments that a poet must be a composer of plots rather than of verses, insofar as he is a poet according to representation, and represents actions. So even if it
turns out that he is representing things that happened, he is no   **30**
less a poet; for there is nothing to prevent some of the things
that have happened from being the sort of things that may happen according to probability, i.e. that are possible, which is
why he can make a poetic composition about them.

3.3 The kinds of plot

3.3.1 The episodic plot

Among simple plots and actions, episodic [tragedies] are the
worst. By "episodic" I mean a plot in which there is neither
probability nor necessity that the episodes follow one another.   **35**
Such [tragedies] are composed by inferior poets because of
themselves, but by good ones because of the actors. For in composing competition-pieces, they extend the plot beyond its potential and are often compelled to distort the sequence.   **52a1**

3.3.2 Plots that arouse amazement

The representation is not only of a complete action but also of
terrifying and pitiable [incidents]. These arise to a very great or
a considerable extent when they happen contrary to expectation
but because of one another. For they will be more amazing in   **5**
this way than if [they happened] on their own, i.e. at random,
since the most amazing even among random events are those
which appear to have happened as it were on purpose, e.g. the
way the statue of Mitys at Argos killed the man who was the
cause of Mitys' death, by falling on him as he looked at it. Such
things do not seem to happen at random. Consequently plots of   **10**
this kind are necessarily finer.

3.3.3 Simple and complex plots   x

Among plots, some are simple and some are complex; for the
actions, of which plots are representations, are evidently of
these kinds. By "simple", I mean an action which is, as we have

52a15   defined it, continuous in its course and single, where the transformation comes about without reversal or recognition. By
"complex", I mean an action as a result of which the transformation is accompanied by a recognition, a reversal or both.
These should arise from the actual structure of the plot, so it
20   happens that they arise either by necessity or by probability as a
result of the preceding events. It makes a great difference
whether these [events] happen because of those or [only] after
those.

xi   ## 3.4 The parts of plot

3.4.1 Reversal

A reversal is a change of the actions to their opposite, as we
said, and that, as we are arguing, in accordance with
probability or necessity. E.g. in the *Oedipus*, the man who
25   comes to bring delight to Oedipus, and to rid him of his terror
about his mother, does the opposite by revealing who Oedipus
is; and in the *Lynceus*, Lynceus is being led to his death, and
Danaus follows to kill him, but it comes about as a result of the
preceding actions that Danaus is killed and Lynceus is rescued.

3.4.2 Recognition

30   A recognition, as the word itself indicates, is a change from ignorance to knowledge, and so to either friendship or enmity,
among people defined in relation to good fortune or misfortune. A recognition is finest when it happens at the same time
as a reversal, as does the one in the *Oedipus*. There are indeed
other [kinds of] recognition. For it can happen in the manner
35   stated regarding inanimate objects and random events; and one
can recognise whether someone has done something or not
done it. But the sort that most belongs to the plot, i.e. most
belongs to the action, is that which we have mentioned: for
52b1   such a recognition and reversal will contain pity or terror (tragedy is considered to be a representation of actions of this sort),
and in addition misfortune and good fortune will come about in
the case of such events.

Since recognition is a recognition of people, some recognitions are by one person only of the other, when the identity of

one of them is clear; but sometimes there must be a recognition   **52b5**
of both persons. E.g. Iphigeneia is recognised by Orestes as a
result of her sending the letter, but it requires another recognition for him [to be recognised] by Iphigeneia.

3.4.3 Suffering

These, then, reversal and recognition, are two parts of plot. A
third is suffering. Of these, we have discussed reversal and rec-   **10**
ognition. Suffering is a destructive or painful action, e.g. deaths
in full view, agonies, woundings etc.

3.5 The quantitative parts of tragedy   **xii**

Regarding the parts of tragedy, we stated earlier which ones
should be used as elements. The quantitative parts, i.e. the sep-   **15**
arate parts into which it is divided, are as follows: (i) prologue,
(ii) episode, (iii) exit and (iv) choral [part], with this divided into
(a) processional and (b) stationary [song]—these are shared by
all [dramas], and [songs sung] from the stage, i.e. dirges—these
are particular [to some].

    (i) A prologue is a whole part of a tragedy that is before the
processional [song] of the chorus.   **20**

    (ii) An episode is a whole part of a tragedy that is between
whole choral songs.

    (iii) An exit is a whole part of a tragedy after which there is no
song of the chorus.

    (iv) Of the choral [part], (a) a processional is the first whole
utterance of the chorus; (b) a stationary song is a song of the
chorus without anapaestic or trochaic verse; and (c) a dirge is a
lament shared by the chorus and [those] on stage.   **25**

    Regarding the parts of tragedy, we stated earlier which ones
should be used [as elements]; the quantitative ones, i.e the separate parts into which it is divided, are these.

4. How tragedy can best achieve its function

4.1 Plot in tragedy

52b28
After what we have just been saying, we must perhaps discuss next what [poets] should aim at and what they should beware
30
of in constructing plots, i.e. how tragedy will achieve its function.

4.1.1 The deduction of the best change of fortune

Since the construction of the finest tragedy should be not simple but complex, and moreover it should represent terrifying and pitiable events (for this is particular to representation of this sort), first, clearly, it should not show (i) decent men un-
35
dergoing a change from good fortune to misfortune; for this is neither terrifying nor pitiable, but shocking. Nor [should it show] (ii) wicked men [passing] from misfortune to good fortune. This is most untragic of all, as it has nothing of what it should; for it is neither morally satisfying nor pitiable nor terri-
53a1
fying. Nor, again, [should it show] (iii) a thoroughly villainous person falling from good fortune into misfortune: such a structure can contain moral satisfaction, but not pity or terror, for the former is [felt] for a person undeserving of his misfortune,
5
and the latter for a person like [ourselves]. Consequently the outcome will be neither pitiable nor terrifying.

There remains, then, the person intermediate between these. Such a person is one who neither is superior [to us] in virtue and justice, nor undergoes a change to misfortune because of
10
vice and wickedness, but because of some error, and who is one of those people with a great reputation and good fortune, e.g. Oedipus, Thyestes and distinguished men from similar families. Necessarily, then, a plot that is fine is single rather than (as some say) double, and involves a change not from misfortune to good fortune, but conversely, from good fortune to
15
misfortune, not because of wickedness but because of a great error by a person like the one mentioned, or by a better person rather than a worse one.

4.1.1.1 The tragedians' practice confirms this

An indication [that this is so] is what is coming about. At first   **53a17**
the poets recounted stories at random, but now the finest tragedies are constructed around a few households, e.g. about
Alcmeon, Oedipus, Orestes, Meleager, Thyestes, Telephus and   **20**
the others, who happen to have had dreadful things done to
them, or to have done them. So the tragedy which is finest according to the [principles of the] art results from this structure.

4.1.1.2 Critics of this change of fortune are misguided

For this reason, people make the same error when they bring
against Euripides the charge that he does this in his tragedies,
and many of his [tragedies] end in misfortune; for this, as we   **25**
said, is correct. A very important indication [that this is so is the
following]. On stage, i.e. in performance, tragedies of this sort,
if they are done correctly, are obviously the most tragic, and
although Euripides manages badly in other respects, he is obviously the most tragic of poets.   **30**

The second[-best] structure is that which some say is first, the
[tragedy] which has a double structure like the *Odyssey*, and
which ends in opposite ways for the better and worse [per-
sons]. This [structure] would seem to be first because of the
weakness of the audiences; the poets follow the spectators,
composing to suit their wishes. But this is not the pleasure [that   **35**
comes] from tragedy, but is more particular to comedy. There
the bitterest enemies in the story, e.g. Orestes and Aegisthus,
exit as friends at the conclusion, and nobody kills anyone else.

4.1.1.3 Plot, not spectacle, can best   **xiv**
achieve the function of tragedy

That which is terrifying and pitiable can arise from spectacle,   **53b1**
but it can also arise from the structure of the incidents itself; this
is superior and belongs to a better poet. For the plot should be
constructed in such a way that, even without seeing it, someone who hears about the incidents will shudder and feel pity at   **5**
the outcome, as someone may feel upon hearing the plot of the
Oedipus. To produce this by means of spectacle is less artful and
requires lavish production. Those [poets] who use spectacle to
produce what is only monstrous and not terrifying have noth-

53b10 ing in common with tragedy. For we should not seek every [kind of] pleasure from tragedy, but [only] the sort which is particular to it. Since the poet should use representation to produce the pleasure [arising] from pity and terror, it is obvious that this must be put into the incidents.

4.1.2 The deduction of the best type of incidents

Let us consider, then, what sorts of occurrence arouse dread or

15 compassion in us. These sorts of action against each another necessarily take place between friends, enemies or people who are neither. If it is one enemy [who does the action] to another, there is nothing pitiable, whether he does it or is [only] about to do it, except in the suffering itself. Nor [is it pitiable] if the people are neither [friends nor enemies]. But when sufferings hap-

20 pen within friendly relationships, e.g. brother against brother, son against father, mother against son or son against mother, when someone kills someone else, is about to, or does something else of the same sort—these are what must be sought after.

[The poet] cannot undo the traditional stories, I mean e.g. that Clytaemestra is killed by Orestes or Eriphyle by Alcmeon;

25 but he should invent for himself, i.e. use the inherited [stories], well. Let me explain more clearly what I mean by "well".

The action may arise (i) in the way the old [poets] made people act knowingly, i.e. in full knowledge, just as Euripides too made Medea kill her children. Or (ii) they may be going to act,

30 in full knowledge, but not do it. Or (iii) they may act, but do the dreadful deed in ignorance, and then recognise the friendly relationship later, as Sophocles' Oedipus [does]. This is outside the drama; but [they may do the deed] in the tragedy itself, as Astydamas' Alcmeon or Telegonus in the *Wounded Odysseus* [do]. Again, fourth beside these [ways] is (iv) to be about to do

35 something deadly in ignorance [of one's relationship], but to recognise it before doing so. Beside these there is no other way: for the act is necessarily either done or not done, and those who act either have knowledge or do not.

Among these [ways], (i) to be about to act in full knowledge, but not do it, is the worst. For this is shocking and also not tragic, as there is no suffering. For this reason nobody com-

54a1 poses in this way, except rarely, e.g. Haemon against Creon in

the *Antigone*. (ii) To act is second[-worst]. (iii) To act in igno-   **54a2**
rance, but recognise [the relationship] afterwards, is better.
This has nothing shocking in it, and the recognition is astonishing. (iv) The last [way] is the best. I mean e.g. the *Cresphontes*,   **5**
where Merope is about to kill her son, but does not kill him and
recognises him; the *Iphigeneia*, where [it is the same for] the sister and her brother; and the *Helle*, where the son is about to
hand over his mother but recognises her. This is why, as we
said a while ago, tragedies are not about many families. [The   **10**
poets] sought to produce this sort [of effect] in their plots, and
discovered how to not by art but by chance; so they are obliged
to concern themselves with those households in which such
sufferings have happened.

As for the structure of the incidents, and what sort of plots
there should be, let this suffice.   **15**

4.2 Character in tragedy   xv

4.2.1 Requirements for tragic character

Regarding characters, there are four things at which [the poet]
should aim.

(i) First and foremost, the characters should be good. [The
tragedy] will have character if, as we said, the speech or the
action makes obvious a decision of whatever sort; it will have a
good character, if it makes obvious a good decision. [Good
character] can exist in every class [of person]; for a woman can   **20**
be good, and a slave can, although the first of these [classes]
may be inferior and the second wholly worthless.

(ii) Second, [they should be] appropriate. It is possible to be
manly in character, but it is not appropriate for a woman to be
so manly or clever.

(iii) Third, [the character should be life-]like. This is different
from making the character good and appropriate in the way al-   **25**
ready stated.

(iv) Fourth, [the character should be] consistent. If the model
for the representation is somebody inconsistent, and such a
character is intended, even so it should be consistently
inconsistent.

54a29
30
An example of unnecessary villainy of character is the Menelaus in the *Orestes*; of the unsuitable and inappropriate, the lament of Odysseus in the *Scylla*, and the speech of Melanippe;
and of the inconsistent, the *Iphigeneia at Aulis* (the girl who begs
[for her life] does not seem at all like the later Iphigeneia).

4.2.2 Coherence is needed in character and in plot

In the characters too, exactly as in the structure of the incidents,
[the poet] ought always to seek what is either necessary or
35
probable, so that it is either necessary or probable that a person
of such-and-such a sort say or do things of the same sort, and it
is either necessary or probable that this [incident] happen after
that one.

It is obvious that the solutions of plots too should come about
54b1
as a result of the plot itself, and not from a contrivance, as in
the *Medea* and in the passage about sailing home in the *Iliad*. A
contrivance must be used for matters outside the drama—either
previous events which are beyond human knowledge, or later
5
ones that need to be foretold or announced. For we grant that
the gods can see everything. There should be nothing improba-

ble in the incidents; otherwise, it should be outside the tragedy,
e.g. that in Sophocles' *Oedipus*.

4.2.3 How to represent undesirable
traits of character

Since tragedy is a representation of people who are better than
10
we are, [the poet] should emulate the good portrait-painters. In
rendering people's particular shape, while making them [life-]
like, they paint them as finer [than they are]. So too the poet,
as he represents people who are angry, lazy, or have other such
traits, should make them such in their characters, [but] decent
[too]. E.g. Homer [made] Achilles good as well as an example
15
of stubbornness.

4.3 Common types of error in tragedy

[The poet] should guard against these things, as well as against
[causing] reactions contrary to those that necessarily follow
from the art of poetry. In fact one can often make errors in

these; there is a sufficient account of them in my published   **54b18**
work.

4.3.1 The kinds of recognition, and which is best   xvi

We stated earlier what recognition is. As for the kinds of recognition, (i) the first is the least artful, which [poets] make most   **20**
use of from lack of resourcefulness—recognition by signs. Of
these, (a) some are congenital, e.g. "the spear-head that the
earth-born bear", or [the birth-marks like] stars such as Carcinus [made up] in his *Thyestes*. (b) Others are acquired. Of these
(1) some are on the body, e.g. scars, and (2) others are external,
e.g. necklaces, and e.g. [the recognition] by means of the din-   **25**
ghy in the *Tyro*.
    These can be used more or less well; e.g. Odysseus was
recognised from his scar in one way by the nurse, and in another by the swineherds. For the latter recognitions, and all
similar ones, are less artful because of the [means of] proof; but
those that result from a reversal, like that in the "Bath-scene",   **30**
are better.
    (ii) Second are those recognitions made up by the poet, which
is why they are not artful. E.g., in the *Iphigeneia*, how Orestes
makes it known that he is Orestes; for Iphigeneia is recognised
by means of the letter, but he himself says what the poet wants,
not what the plot does. For this reason, this recognition is not   **35**
far from the error we [just] mentioned; Orestes could have
brought some actual objects. Also "the shuttle's voice" in Sophocles' *Tereus*.
    (iii) The third [kind of recognition] is by means of a memory,
when someone reacts to something he sees, like the one in Di-   **55a1**
caeogenes' *Cypriots* where he bursts into tears upon seeing the
painting, or the one in the "Tale told to Alcinous" where Odysseus hears the lyre-player and weeps at his memories, as a result of which they recognise him.
    (iv) Fourth is recognition resulting from an inference, e.g. in
the *Libation Bearers*, on the grounds that "someone like [Electra]   **5**
has come; but there is nobody like [her] except Orestes; it is he,
then, who has come". Or the recognition [proposed by] the
sophist Polyidus concerning Iphigeneia: it would be reasonable,
he said, for Orestes to infer that "his sister was sacrificed, and it
[now] falls to him to be sacrificed himself". Or in Theodectes'

55a9 *Tydeus*, on the grounds that "he came to find a son, but is to die
10 himself". Or the recognition in the *Sons of Phineus*: when the
women see the place they infer their fate, on the grounds that
"they are fated to be killed there, for [the boys] were left to per-
ish there".

There is also a combined recognition resulting from a false
14 inference by the audience, e.g. in *Odysseus the False Messenger*:
14¹ for the fact that [Odysseus could] bend the bow, but nobody
else [could], is made up by the poet and is a premise, and [so is
14² Odysseus'] saying that he would recognise the bow which he
15 had not seen; but the way he is expected to make himself
known by the former means, but does so by the latter, is a [case
of] false inference.

(v) The best recognition of all is that which results from the
incidents themselves, when our astonishment comes about by
means of probable [incidents], e.g. in Sophocles' *Oedipus* and
the *Iphigeneia*: it is probable that Iphigeneia would wish to dis-
patch a letter. For such recognitions alone are without made-up
20 [incidents] and necklaces. Recognitions as a result of inference
are second[-best].

**4.3.2 The poet should visualise the action,
        and feel with his characters**

In constructing his plots and using diction to bring them to
completion, [the poet] should put [the events] before his eyes
as much as he can. In this way, seeing them very vividly as if he
25 were actually present at the actions [he represents], he can discover what is suitable, and is least likely to miss contradictions.
An indication of this is the [contradiction] for which Carcinus
was criticised. His Amphiaraus comes up out of a shrine; this
would have been missed by anyone not seeing it as a spectator.
But [the play] failed on stage, as the spectators were upset
about it.

As far as possible, [the poet should] also bring [his plots] to
30 completion with gestures. Given the same nature, those [poets]
who experience the emotions [to be represented] are most believable, i.e. he who is agitated or furious [can represent] agitation and anger most truthfully. For this reason, the art of poetry
belongs to the genius or the madman; of these, the first are
adaptable, the second can step outside themselves.

4.3.3 The poet should construct
his plots in outline first

As for his stories, both those [already] made up and those he   **55a34**
composes himself, he should set them out as universals, and   **55b1**
only then introduce episodes, i.e. extend them. I mean that he
might investigate what is universal in them in the following
way, e.g. [the story] of Iphigeneia: "a girl has been sacrificed
and disappears in a way unclear to the people who sacrificed
her. She is set down in another country, where there is a law
that foreigners must be sacrificed to the goddess; this is the   **5**
priesthood she is given. Some time later it turns out that the
priestess' brother arrives ..." The fact that the oracle com-
manded him to go there, for some reason that is not a universal, and his purpose [in going], are outside the plot. "After he
arrives, he is captured. When he is about to be sacrificed [by his
sister], he makes himself known [to her]", either as Euripides
or as Polyidus arranged it, "by saying—as would be probable—   **10**
that it was not only his sister's fate to be sacrificed, but his own
too. This leads to the rescue." After this [the poet] should now
supply the names and introduce episodes. Take care that the
episodes are particular [to the story], e.g. in Orestes' case his
madness through which he is captured, and his rescue by
means of the purification.   **15**

In dramas the episodes are brief, but epic is lengthened out
with them. The story of the *Odyssey* is not long: "someone has
been away from home for many years, with a god on the
watch for him, and he is alone. Moreover affairs at home are
such that his wealth is being consumed by [his wife's] suitors,   **20**
and his son is being plotted against [by them]. He arrives after
much distress, makes himself known to some people, and attacks. He is rescued, his enemies annihilated." This is what is
proper [to the *Odyssey*]; its other [parts] are episodes.

4.3.4 The two parts of tragedy: **xviii**
complication and solution

[Part] of every tragedy is the complication, and [part] is the solution. The [incidents] outside [the tragedy] and often some of   **25**
those inside it are the complication, and the rest is the solution.
By "complication", I mean the [tragedy] from the beginning up

55b27 to the final part from which there is a transformation towards
good fortune or misfortune; by "solution", the [tragedy] from
the beginning of the transformation up to the end. E.g. in The-
30 odectes' *Lynceus*, the prior incidents, the capture of the baby
and then its parents' explanation is the complication, and the
[tragedy] from the demand for the death penalty up to the end
is the solution.

4.3.5 The four kinds of tragedy

There are four kinds of tragedy (for we said that its parts too are
of the same number): (i) the complex tragedy, the whole of
which is reversal and recognition; (ii) the tragedy of suffering,
56a1 e.g. the [tragedies called] *Ajax* and *Ixion*; (iii) the tragedy of
character, e.g. the *Women of Phthia* and the *Peleus*; (iv) the fourth
[kind] is spectacle, e.g. the *Daughters of Phorcys*, the *Prometheus*
and [dramas set] in Hades.

4.3.6 The poet should aim to succeed
in all the parts of tragedy

Preferably [the poet] should attempt to have all [the parts]; otherwise, the most important and the majority of them, especially
5 given the way people belittle poets nowadays. Since there have
been poets good at each part [of tragedy], they demand that a
single [poet] surpass the particular good [quality] of each one;
but it is not right to call a tragedy the same [as another] or different according to anything so much as the plot, that is, [plots]
with the same development and solution. Many [poets] de-
10 velop [the plot] well and solve it badly, but one should harmonise both [parts].

4.3.7 The plot should be unified,
not episodic or merely amazing

[The poet] ought to remember what we have often said, and
not compose a tragedy with an epic structure (by an "epic"
structure, I mean one with more than one plot), e.g. if someone
were to compose [a tragedy with] the whole plot of the *Iliad*. For
there, the parts receive suitable magnitude because of the
15 length [of the epic]; but in dramas the result is far from one's
expectation.

An indication [that this is so is the following]: those [tragedi-   **56a16**
ans] who composed a *Sack of Troy* as a whole and not in part like
Euripides, or a *Niobe* and not like Aeschylus, either fail or compete badly, since even Agathon failed in this one respect. In
reversals and in simple incidents, they aim to arouse the amazement which they desire; for this is tragic and morally satisfying.   **20**
This is possible when someone who is clever but villainous is
deceived, like Sisyphus, or someone who is brave but unjust is
defeated. This is even probable, as Agathon says; for it is probable that many things will happen even against probability.

4.3.8 The chorus should relate to the plot

[The poet] should regard the chorus as one of the actors. It   **25**
should be a part of the whole, and contribute to the performance, not as in Euripides but as in Sophocles. In the rest the
sung [parts] belong to the plot no more than they belong to another tragedy. For this reason they sing interludes; Agathon
was first to begin this. Yet what difference is there between   **30**
singing interludes and trying to adapt a speech, or a whole episode, from one [drama] to another?

We have discussed the other elements [of tragedy]; it remains   **xix**
to discuss diction and reasoning.

4.4 Reasoning in tragedy

As for reasoning, what was said about it in my *Rhetoric* should   **35**
be assumed; for this is proper rather to that enquiry. All [the
effects] that have to be produced by speech fall under reasoning. The types of these are (i) demonstration and refutation, (ii)
the production of emotions (e.g. pity, terror, anger, etc.), and   **56b1**
again (iii) [arguments about things'] importance or
unimportance.

In the incidents too [the poet] clearly should use some of the
same elements when he needs to make things [e.g.] pitiable,
dreadful, important or probable, except that there is this difference, that these [effects] should be apparent without a produc-   **5**
tion, but those dependent on speech should be produced by
the speaker and arise from speech. What would be the
speaker's function be, if the element were apparent even without [the use of] speech?

4.5 Diction in tragedy

4.5.1 Delivery is not part of the art of poetry

56b9
10

Among matters related to diction, one kind of investigation is the forms of the diction. Knowledge of this belongs to the art of delivery and to the person with mastery in it. [I mean] e.g. what is a command, what is a wish, a statement, a threat, a question, an answer, etc. No criticism at all made against the art of poetry, that is based on knowledge or ignorance of these [forms], actually deserves to be taken seriously. What error could anybody consider there to be in "Sing, goddess, of the wrath", which Protagoras criticises on the grounds that [Homer] supposes he is making a wish, but is giving an order? (For Protagoras says that telling someone to do something or not do it is an order.) For this reason let us leave this investigation aside, as it belongs to another art and not to that of poetry.

xx

4.5.2 The Parts of Diction

20

The parts of diction in its entirety are as follows: (i) the element [i.e. letter], (ii) the syllable, (iii) the particle, (iv) the conjunction, (v) the name [i.e. noun or adjective], (vi) the verb, (vii) the inflection, (viii) the utterance.

(i) The element is an indivisible sound—not every [kind of] sound, but one from which it is natural for a composite sound to arise. For wild animals too make indivisible sounds, none of
25
which I mean by an element. The types of this [kind of] sound are (a) the vowel, (b) the semi-vowel and (c) the consonant.

(a) A vowel is that which has an audible sound without a contact [between the parts of the mouth]. (b) A semi-vowel is that which has an audible sound with [such] a contact, e.g. *s* and *r*. (c) A consonant is that which has no audible sound in itself with [such] a contact, but becomes audible together with those elements that have a sound of some sort; e.g. *g* and *d*.

30

The elements differ according to the forms of the mouth, the places [in the mouth where they are produced], aspiration, non-aspiration, length, shortness, and also high, low or intermediate pitch. One must investigate the particulars of these matters in works on versification.

35

(ii) A syllable is a non-significant sound composed of a consonant and [an element] which has sound. In fact *gr* without an *a*

is a syllable, and [it is also a syllable] with an *a*, as in *gra*. But the   56b37
investigation of the differences between these also belongs to
the art of versification.

(iii) A particle is (a) a non-significant sound which neither   57a1
precludes, nor brings about, the production of a single significant sound that by nature is composed of several sounds [i.e.
an utterance], and which it is not appropriate to place at the
beginning of an utterance on its own, e.g. *men, ētoi, de*. Or [it
is] (b) a non-significant sound which by nature produces, as a
result of [joining together] several sounds that are significant, a   5
single significant sound [i.e. an utterance], e.g. "about", "con-   6
cerning" etc.   7

(iv) A conjunction is a non-significant sound which makes   6
clear the beginning of an utterance, its end or its dividing-point,   7
and which by nature is placed both at the extremities and in   9
the middle [of an utterance], e.g. "or", "because", "but".   10

(v) A name [i.e. noun or adjective] is a composite significant
sound without [an indication of] time, no part of which is significant in itself. For in double names we do not use [any part]
as being significant in and of itself: e.g. in "Theodore" [i.e. "gift
of god"] *dore* is not significant.

(vi) A verb is a composite significant sound with [an indication of] time, no part of which is significant in itself, just as in   15
the case of names. For "human being" or "white" does not signify when, but "walks" or "walked" signifies this as well, present time in the first case, and past time in the second.

(vii) An inflection of a name or verb is either (a) the inflection
according to the [part] that signifies "of him", "for him", etc.,
or (b) that according to the [part] that signifies "one" or   20
"many", e.g. "person" or "persons", or (c) that according to
the delivery, e.g. according to [whether it is] a question or an
order; for "did he walk?" or "walk!" is an inflection of the verb
according to these kinds.

(viii) An utterance is a composite significant sound, some
parts of which signify something in themselves. For not every
utterance is composed of verbs and names, e.g. the definition   25
of a human being, but there can be an utterance without verbs.
However, an utterance will always have a part that signifies
something [in itself], e.g. "Cleon" in "Cleon walks".

57a28   An utterance can be single in two ways, either (a) by signifying one thing, or (b) by a conjunction of several things. E.g. the

30   *Iliad* is one by a conjunction [of many things], but the definition
of a human being is one by signifying one thing.

xxi   ### 4.5.3 The kinds of names

4.5.3.1 Classified according to quantity,
i.e. single or compound

The kinds of name are (i) single (by "single", I mean that which
is not composed from [parts] that are significant, e.g. "earth"),
and (ii) double. Of the double name, (a) one [kind] is composed
of [a part] that is significant and [a part] that is non-significant,

33¹   except that these [parts] are not significant and non-significant
in the [double] name [itself]; (b) the other [kind] is composed of
[parts] that are significant. There can be a triple and a quadru-

35   ple name, even a multiple one: e.g. most of the names of the
people of Marseilles, "Hermocaicoxanthus, who prays to

57b1   Zeus".

4.5.3.2 Classified according to quality, i.e. usage and form

Every name is either (i) standard, (ii) exotic, (iii) a metaphor,
(iv) an ornament, (v) made-up, (vi) lengthened, (vii) reduced or
(viii) altered.
By (i) "standard", I mean a name which a particular people
uses; by (ii) "exotic", I mean one which other peoples use. Consequently it is obvious that it is possible for the same [name] to

5   be both exotic and standard, but not for the same people. For
6   *sigunon* ("spear") is standard for the Cypriots, but exotic for us;
6¹   and "spear" is standard for us, but exotic for the Cypriots.
7   (iii) A "metaphor" is the application [to something] of a name
belonging to something else, either (a) from the genus to the
species, or (b) from the species to the genus, or (c) from a species to [another] species, or (d) according to analogy.

10   By (a), "from genus to species", I mean e.g. "here stands my
ship": for [the species] lying at anchor is a [part of the genus]
standing. By (b), "from species to genus", I mean e.g. "truly
has Odysseus done ten thousand deeds of worth": for [the spe-
cies] "ten thousand" is [part of the genus] "many", and [Ho-
mer] uses it here instead of "a lot". By (c), "from species to

species", I mean e.g. [killing a man by] "draining out his life		**57b13**
with bronze" [i.e. a weapon], and [drawing water by] "cutting
it with long-edged bronze" [i.e. a bowl]: for here [the poet] calls
cutting "draining" and draining "cutting". Both are [species of		**15**
the genus] "taking away". By (d), "analogy", I mean when *b* is
to *a* as *d* is to *c*; for [the poet then] will say *d* instead of *b*, or *b*
instead of *d*.

Sometimes too [poets] add [to the metaphor] the thing to
which the name relates, instead of what it means. I mean e.g.		**20**
that the wine-bowl stands to Dionysus as the shield does to
Ares: so [the poet] will call a wine-bowl "shield of Dionysus"
and a shield "wine-bowl of Ares". Again, as old age stands to
life, so the evening stands to the day: so [the poet] will call evening "old age of the day", as Empedocles does, and old age
"the evening of life" or "the sunset of life".		**25**

There may be no current name for some of the things in the
analogy, but even so they will be expressed in the same way.
E.g. to scatter seed is to sow, and to scatter radiance from the
sun has no name; but this has the same relation to the sun as
sowing does to the seed. For this reason [the poet] says "sow-
ing god-wrought radiance".		**30**

This manner of [making a] metaphor can be used in another
way too. After terming something by a name that belongs to
something else, one can deny to it one of the things particular
to [that other thing], e.g. if [a poet] called a shield not "wine-
bowl of Ares" but "wine-bowl without wine".

(iv) [An "ornament" is * * *]

(v) A "made-up [name]" is one which is wholly unused by
people, but which the poet supplies himself. There would seem
to be some such names, e.g. "branchers" for "horns" or		**35**
"prayerman" for "priest".

(vi)–(vii) As for lengthened or shortened names, the former is		**58a1**
one which uses a longer vowel than the one particular [to it], or
an inserted syllable. The latter is one some [part] of which has
been shortened. A lengthened [name] is e.g. *polēos* for *poleōs* "of
the city", and *Pelēiadeō* for *Peleidou* "son of Peleus"; a shortened		**5**
[name] is e.g. *kri* [for *krithē*] "barley", *dō* [for *dōma*] "mansion"
and, in "one seeing comes from both [eyes]", *ops* [for *opsis*]
"seeing".

(viii) An altered [name] is when [the poet] leaves some of the appellation [unaltered], but makes up some of it, e.g. "by her righter breast" instead of "right".

4.5.3.3 Classified according to quality, i.e. gender

Among names [in] themselves, (a) some are masculine, (b) some are feminine, and (c) some are in between [i.e. neuter]. (a) Masculine names are those that end in *n, r, s* and the elements that are composed of *s*; there are two of these, *ps* and *x* [i.e. *ks*]. (b) Feminine names are (i) those that end in the vowels that are always long, i.e. in *ē* and *ō*, and (ii) those that end in *a* among the vowels that may be lengthened. Consequently the elements in which the masculine and feminine names end turn out to be equal in number [i.e. three], for *ps* and *x* are composite. No name ends in a consonant, nor in a short vowel [that is always short]. There are only three names ending in *i*, "honey", "gum" and "pepper" (*meli, kommi, peperi*); there are five ending in *u*, "spear", "fleece", "mustard", "knee" and "city" (*doru, pōu, napu, gonu, astu*). The [names] that are in between end in these elements [*a, i* and *u*], and in *n*, [*r*] and *s*.

4.5.4 How diction can best achieve its function

The virtue of diction is to be clear and not commonplace. Diction made up of standard names is clearest, but is commonplace. An example is the poetry of Cleophon and that of Sthenelus. Diction that uses unfamiliar names is grand and altered from the everyday. By "unfamiliar", I mean the exotic [name], metaphor, lengthening and everything that is contrary to what is standard. But if someone makes all [the names] of this sort, [his poem] will be either a riddle or gibberish. If [it is composed] of metaphors, it will be a riddle; if of exotic [names], gibberish. For it is the form of a riddle to use an impossible combination [of names] in saying things that are the case. This cannot be done with the combination of the other names, but is possible with metaphor, e.g. "I saw a man glue bronze on a man with fire", etc. Things [composed] of exotic names are gibberish. [The poet], then, should mix these [two kinds] in some way. The first (e.g. the exotic name, metaphor, ornament and the other kinds we mentioned) will produce that which is not

everyday and commonplace, and the standard name will pro-   **58a33**
duce clarity.

Lengthenings, curtailments and alterations of names make
no small contribution towards making the diction clear and not   **58b1**
everyday. These will produce what is not everyday, because of
their variation from what is standard, as they are contrary to
the norm, but clarity will come from what they have in common   **5**
with the norm.

4.5.4.1 The critics of poetic diction are misguided

Consequently those who criticise this manner of speech and
ridicule the poet [for using it] are not correct to abuse him. E.g.
old Euclides, to show that it is easy to compose if [a poet] is
allowed to lengthen [names] as much as he wishes, composed
as a lampoon in his words "I saw Epichares walking to Mara-
thon" and "not mixing hellebore for him". To use this manner   **10**
in some obvious way is laughable. [The need for] due measure
is shared by all the types [of unfamiliar names]. For [a poet]
who purposely uses metaphors, exotic [names], and the other
kinds unsuitably, with a view to arousing laughter, can accomplish the same [effect].   **15**

How much what is appropriate is superior [to what is inap-
propriate] can be observed, in the case of lengthened [names],
by inserting the [standard] names into the verse [instead]. In
the case of exotic [names], as well as metaphors and the other
forms, someone who substitutes the standard names can see
that what we are saying is true. E.g. when Euripides composed
the same iambic verse as Aeschylus, and substituted only one   **20**
name, an exotic name instead of the usual standard one, his
verse seems fine, but Aeschylus' seems ordinary. For Aeschylus in his *Philoctetes* composed the verse

"the gangrene which eats at the flesh of my foot,"

but Euripides substituted "feasts on" for "eats at". Also, [in the
verse]

"now I am a paltry man, nothing worth and plain",   **25**

suppose that someone substituted the standard names to say

58b27   "now I am a little man, a feeble one and ugly".

Compare too

"setting down a squalid hassock and a paltry table"

with

30   "setting down a nasty hassock and a little table",

or "the headlands bellow" with "the headlands yell".

Again, Ariphrades ridiculed the tragedians on the grounds that they use things which nobody would say in his [everyday] speech, e.g. "without the palace" and not "outside the palace",

59a1   "of thee", "mine own", "Achilles round" and not "around Achilles", etc. Because all such [names] are not among the standard ones, they produce what is not everyday in the diction. But Ariphrades was ignorant of this.

4.5.5 How to use diction appropriately

5   It is important to use each of the [kinds] mentioned suitably, both double names and exotic ones, but the metaphorical [kind] is the most important by far. This alone (a) cannot be acquired from someone else, and (b) is an indication of genius. For to make metaphors well is to observe what is like [something else].

          Among names, double ones are most appropriate for

10   dithyrambs, exotic ones for heroic [verses], and metaphors for iambic verses. In heroic verses all the [kinds] mentioned are useful. In iambic verses, because these represent [everyday] diction as far as possible, those [kinds] of names are appropriate which one can use in [prose] speeches too. These are the standard name, metaphor and ornament.

15   As for tragedy, i.e. representation by means of acting, let this account suffice us.

5. Epic Poetry

5.1 How epic resembles tragedy

5.1.1 The plot of epic should represent a single complete action

As for the art of exposition and representation in verse, it is   **59a17**
clear that, just as in tragedies, [the epic poet] should construct
plots that are dramatic (i.e. [plots] about a single whole action
that is complete, with a beginning, middle [parts] and end), so   **20**
that it will produce the pleasure particular to it, as a single
whole animal does. The constructions [of the incidents] should
not be like histories; in these it is necessary to produce a
description not of a single action, but of a single time, with all
that happened during it to one or more people; each [event]
relates to the others at random. Just as the sea-battle at Salamis   **25**
and the battle against the Carthaginians in Sicily happened at
the same time, but did not contribute to the same end, so too in
sequential [periods of] time one thing sometimes comes about
after another, but from these there comes about no single end.
But this is what the majority, almost, of [epic] poets do.

5.1.1.1 Homer's practice confirms this

For this reason, as we said already, Homer appears marvellous   **30**
compared to the others, in that he did not undertake to put into
his composition even the [Trojan] war as a whole, although it
has a beginning and an end. For the plot would probably have
been too big and not easily seen as a whole; or, if it were moderate in magnitude, [it would have been too] complex in its variety [of incidents]. As it is, selecting a single part [of it], Homer   **35**
has used many of them as episodes, e.g. he diversifies his composition with the "Catalogue of Ships" and other episodes. The
other [poets] compose about a single man, a single time, or a
single action that has many parts, e.g. he who composed the   **59b1**
Cypria and the *Little Iliad*. Consequently one or at most two
tragedies in each case are produced from the *Iliad* and the *Odyssey*; but many [are produced] from the *Cypria*, and from the *Little Iliad* more than eight, e.g. the *Judgment of Arms*, *Philoctetes*,   **5**

59b6   *Neoptolemus, Eurypylus, Vagabondage, Laconian Women, Sack of Troy, Embarkation, Sinon,* and *Trojan Women.*

xxiv   ### 5.1.2 Epic has the same kinds and qualitative parts as tragedy

Again, epic must have the same kinds as tragedy, for [it must be] either (i) simple or (ii) complex, (iii) an epic of character or
10   (iv) one of suffering. Its parts, except for song and spectacle, are the same; in fact it needs reversals, recognitions and sufferings. Again, the reasonings and diction should be fine.

Homer is first and foremost in the use of all of these. In fact each of his poems is constructed in each of the two ways—the
15   *Iliad* is simple and full of suffering, the *Odyssey* is complex (for it is recognition right through) and full of character. In addition, he has surpassed all [others] in diction and reasoning.

5.2 How epic differs from tragedy

Epic differs [from tragedy] in (i) the length of its [plot-]structure, and (ii) its verse.

(i) As for its length, the definition that we stated is sufficient; it should be possible to see at one view its beginning and end.
20   This would be so, if the structures were smaller than the ancient ones, but reached [the length of] the number of tragedies presented at a single hearing.

For extending its magnitude, epic has an [advantage] very particular [to it]. In tragedy, it is not possible for many parts [of
25   the action] to be represented as being done at the same time, but only the part of the actors on the stage. But in epic, because it is exposition, it is possible to put in many parts which are accomplished at the same time; with these—provided they are particular [to it]—the weight of the poem is increased. Consequently epic has this advantage [over tragedy], both (a) for [giving it] splendour, and (b) for diverting the listener and
30   introducing episodes that are unlike [one another]. For likeness [in episodes] is soon boring and makes tragedies fail.

(ii) As for its verse-form, heroic verse has been found appropriate from experience. If anyone produced an expository representation in some other verse-form, or in many, it would obviously be unsuitable. Heroic verse is the stateliest and

weightiest of the verse-forms. For this reason, it most readily   **59b35**
admits exotic names, metaphors and lengthenings—for expository representation exceeds the other [kinds] in this too. But the
iambic and tetrameter verse-forms are [fast-]moving, as the first   **60a1**
is related to action, and the second to dance. It would be still
more odd if someone mixed them, as Chaeremon did. For this
reason, nobody has composed a long structure in any verse
other than the heroic; but, as we said, nature itself teaches
[poets] to choose [the verse-form] that is appropriate to it.

5.3 Common types of error in epic

5.3.1 The best manner of representation in epic

Homer deserves acclaim for many things, but especially be-   **5**
cause he alone among [epic] poets is well aware of what he
himself should do. The poet should say very little himself; for
this is not the way in which [a poet] represents. The other [epic]
poets do the performing themselves right through [the poem],
but represent few [people speaking] and do so rarely. But Homer, after a brief preamble, immediately brings on a man, a   **10**
woman, or some other [person]— and none of them character-
less, but [all] with character.

5.3.2 How best to use improbability in epic

5.3.2.1 To produce amazement

[The poet] should put what is amazing into his tragedies; but
what is improbable, from which amazement arises most, is
more admissible in epic because [the audience] does not see the
person in action. For the passage about the pursuit of Hector   **15**
would obviously be laughable on the stage, with the Greeks
standing still and not pursuing him, and Achilles forbidding
them to do so, but it passes unnoticed in the epic verses. What
is amazing is pleasant. An indication [of this is that] everyone
narrates [stories] with additions, so as to please.

5.3.2.2 To produce false inference

Homer above all has taught the other [poets] to tell untruths in
the right way, that is, [by] a false inference. For if, whenever *p*   **20**

60a21 exists or comes to be, *q* exists or comes to be, people suppose
that if the latter (*q*) exists, the former (*p*) also exists or comes to
be. But this [supposition] is untrue. For this reason, if the former (*p*) is untrue, but it follows from its existence that something else (*q*) exists or comes to be, [the poet] should add it [i.e.

25 *q*]. Because we know that this (*q*) is true, our soul falsely infers
that the former (*p*) exists too. An example of this is the passage
in the "Bath-scene".

5.3.2.3 How to avoid mistakes in using improbability

Impossible [incidents] that are believable should be preferred to
possible ones that are unbelievable, and stories should not be
constructed from improbable parts, but above all should contain nothing improbable; otherwise, it should be outside the

30 plot-structure, like Oedipus' not knowing how Laius was
killed. But it should not be within the drama, like the people
who narrate [the accident at] the Pythian games in the *Electra*,
and the person who comes to Mysia from Tegea without speaking in the *Mysians*. Consequently it is ridiculous to say that the
plot would have been ruined [without the improbability]; such
plots should not be constructed in the first place. But if one is

35 set up, and it appears fairly logical, even an oddity can be admitted. For even the improbabilities in the *Odyssey* over the putting ashore [of Odysseus] would clearly not be tolerable, if an

60b1 inferior poet composed them. But as it is, the poet makes the
oddity disappear by using his other good [qualities] for
embellishment.

5.3.3 How best to use elaborate diction in epic

[The poet] should take great pains with the diction in the slack
parts [of the poem], i.e. those with neither character nor reasoning. For in turn excessively resplendent diction obscures

5 characters and reasonings.

xxv ## 5.4 Questions raised about epic,
and their solutions

As for the questions that are raised [about epic poetry] and their
solutions, it may become obvious to how many kinds they be-

long, and of what sort they are, if we investigate them as   60b7
follows.

5.4.1 Basic principles for finding solutions

(i) Since a poet represents, just like a painter or some other
maker of images, at any moment he is necessarily representing
one of three things, either (a) things as they were or are, or (b)   10
things as people say and think [they were or are], or (c) things
as they should be.

(ii) These things are expressed in diction in which there are
exotic names, metaphors and many modifications of diction; we
grant these to poets.

(iii) In addition, there is not the same [standard of] correctness in the art of civic life as in that of poetry, nor is there in any
other art as in that of poetry. Error in the art of poetry itself is of   15
two sorts, (a) error in the art itself, (b) error in it by coincidence.
For if [an artist] decided to represent [a horse correctly, but
erred in the representation because of his] lack of ability, the
error belongs to the art itself; but if he decided to represent it
incorrectly, and [represented] the horse with both right legs
thrown forward, [it is] an error in the individual art (e.g. one in
medicine or another art of whatever sort), not in the art of po-   20
etry itself.

Consequently one should consider and solve the criticisms
that are among the questions raised [starting] from these
[principles].

5.4.2 The twelve solutions to questions
raised about poetry

5.4.2.1 The six solutions dependent on the art itself

(i) First, some [criticisms should be solved] with reference to the
art itself. [If] impossibilities have been produced, there is an error; but it is correct, if it attains the end of the art itself. The end
has been stated [already, i.e.] if in this way it makes either that   25
part [of the poem], or another part, more astonishing. An example is the pursuit of Hector.

However, if the end [of the art] could. have been brought
about better or no worse [without erring] according to the art

60b28 concerned with these matters, the error is not correct. For [the poet] should, if possible, have made no errors at all.

30 (ii) Again, to which sort does the error belong, to those in the art [itself], or [to those in it] by coincidence? The error is less, if [an artist] did not know that a female deer has no horns, than if he painted without representing [anything].

(iii) In addition, if [the poet] is criticised for representing things that are not true, perhaps he is representing them [as] they should be, e.g. as Sophocles said that he himself portrayed people as they should be, but Euripides portrayed them as they **35** are—there is the solution.

(iv) If [the solution] is in neither of these ways, then [it may be] on the grounds that people say [it is] so, e.g. the [stories] about the gods. These are perhaps neither better [told this way] **61a1** nor true, but are possibly [lies] as Xenophanes thought; yet people say [it is] so.

(v) Some things are perhaps not better [than they should be], but were so, e.g. the passage about the weapons:

"their spears, [set] upright on the butt-spike..."

This was the custom then, as it is among the Illyrians even now.

(vi) As for whether someone's saying or action is fine or not **5** so fine, one must consider not only what was said or done itself, to see whether it is good or inferior, but also the person saying or doing it, and to whom, at what time, by what means and to what end, e.g. whether it is to bring about a greater good, or to avert a greater evil.

5.4.2.2 The six solutions dependent on diction

10 (vii) Some [criticisms] must be resolved by looking at the diction, e.g. by [assuming] an exotic name in "the *oureis* first": perhaps [Homer] means not "mules" but "sentinels". As for Dolon "who was evil in form", [Homer may mean] not that his body was misproportioned, but that his face was ugly; for the Cretans call someone fair of face "well-formed". Also by "mix it **15** purer" [he may mean] not "[mix the wine] stronger", as if for drunkards, but "mix it faster".

(viii) Some things are said with a metaphor, e.g. "all gods and men slept all night long", but [Homer] says at the same

time "but when he gazed at the Trojan plain, [he marvelled at]   **61a18**
the din of flutes and pipes". "All" is said for "many" with a
metaphor; for "all" is a lot. So too "[this constellation] alone has   **20**
no share [in the baths of Ocean]" is said with a metaphor; for
what is best known is "alone".

(ix) [Some questions should be solved] with reference to the
pronunciation, as Hippias of Thasos solved [the question of]
"but grant that he gain his prayer" [instead of "we grant"], and
"part rotted by rain" [instead of "not rotted"].

(x) Some [should be solved] by punctuation, e.g. Empedocles' "at once were things mortal born, that learnt before to be
immortal, and things were mixed, pure before".   **25**

(xi) Some [should be solved] by [assuming] an ambiguity,
[e.g.] in "more of the night has gone", "more" is ambiguous.

(xii) Some [should be solved] with reference to a habit of diction. People call mixed [wine] "wine", whence [Homer] composed "a greave of new-wrought tin" [i.e. of bronze, copper
mixed with tin]; and they call men who work iron "bronze-
smiths", whence his calling Ganymede "wine-pourer of Zeus",
although [gods] do not drink wine [but nectar]. This could also
be [solved] with reference to a metaphor.   **30**

5.4.3 Critics are often misguided

Whenever any name would seem to signify something contradictory, one should consider how many ways it may signify in
the passage, e.g. in "there the brazen spear was held" consider
how many ways it can mean "was stopped there", one way or
another as best one may understand it, according to the exact   **35**
opposite of what Glaucon says.   **61b1**

Again, some people illogically make some prior assumption,
and judging it right themselves make inferences [from it]. If
there is a contradiction to their own supposition, they criticise
[the poet] as if he had said what they think. This has happened
in the case of Icarius. People suppose that Icarius is a Lacedaemonian: so they think it odd that Telemachus does not meet   **5**
him when he goes to Lacedaemon. But perhaps it is as the
Cephallenians say; they say that Odysseus took a wife from
among them, and that [Penelope's father] was Icadius and not
Icarius. It is probable that the question [has arisen] because of
an error [by Homer's critics].

5.4.4 Summary, based on the main kinds of problem

61b9
10
In general, (i) the impossibility should be explained with reference either to (a) the composition, or to (b) [making something] better [than it is], or to (c) opinion. In relation to [the needs of] the composition, a believable impossibility is preferable to an unbelievable possibility. For it may be impossible that there are people like those Zeuxis painted, but [it is] better [so]. For [the artist] should improve on his model.

(ii) Improbabilities [should be explained] with reference to what people say; for one must solve them in this way, and on the grounds that sometimes an improbability is no improbabil-
15 ity: for it is probable that things will happen even against probability.

(iii) Sayings that are contradictory should be considered just like refutations in arguments, as to whether it is the same thing [that is meant], relates to the same thing, or is said in the same way. Consequently [these] must be solved with reference either to (a) what [the poet] himself says or to (b) what a sensible person may assume.

Criticism of improbability and wickedness is correct when, with no necessity at all to do so, [the poet] uses an improbabil-
20 ity, as Euripides uses Aegeus, or villainy, as Euripides uses Menelaus in the *Orestes*.

So the criticisms that people make are of five kinds—that things are impossible, improbable, harmful, contradictory, or incorrect in terms of [another] art. Solutions must be looked for
25 among the items we have stated; there are twelve of them.

xxvi
5.5 A comparison between epic and tragedy

One may be puzzled about which is better, epic or tragic representation.

5.5.1 The argument in favour of epic

If the less vulgar representation is better, and the less vulgar is always that which relates to better spectators, it is very clear that the one which represents in all respects is vulgar. Assum-
30 ing that [the spectators] will not react unless [each actor] adds something himself, they use a lot of movement, like inferior

oboe-players who whirl about if they have to represent a dis-   61b31
cus, and drag the chorus-leader about if they are playing the
Scylla. So tragedy is [a representation] of this sort. Compare too
how the earlier actors regarded those who came after them.
Mynniscus used to call Callippides a monkey, on the grounds   35
that he went to great excesses, and the opinion about Pindarus
was similar. As the later actors stand to them, so the whole art   62a1
[of tragedy] stands to epic. So people say that epic relates to
decent spectators, who have no need of gestures, but the tragic
[art] relates to inferior ones. Therefore, if it is vulgar, clearly it
would be worse [than epic].

5.5.2 Objections to the argument in favour of epic

So let us discuss these matters. (i) First, the charge is not   5
against the art of [tragic] composition but against that of [the
actors'] delivery. For [visual] signs can be overworked even in
reciting an epic, as Sosistratus did, and in singing, as
Mnasitheus of Opus did.

(ii) Next, not all movement is to be rejected, unless dance is
to be too, but [only] that of inferior [people], such as that for
which Callippides was criticised, and others now are, on the   10
grounds that they represent women who are not free born.

(iii) Again, tragedy can produce its own [effect] even without
movement, as epic does. For it is obvious from reading it what
sort [of tragedy] it is. So if tragedy is superior in all other
things, this at any rate does not necessarily belong to it.

5.5.3 Arguments in favour of tragedy

(i) Furthermore, [tragedy is superior] because it has everything
that epic has; for it is even possible to use its verse [in tragedy].   15

(ii) Again, it also has as no small part of it music and spectacles, by means of which its pleasures are constructed very
vividly.

(iii) Next, it has vividness in reading as well as in
performance.

(iv) Again, [it has the advantage] that the end of the repre-   62b1
sentation is in a smaller length. What is more concentrated is
more pleasurable than what is diluted with a lot of time [in per-
formance]. I mean, e.g., [the effect] if someone put Sophocles'
Oedipus into as many epic verses as the *Iliad*.

(v) Again, the epic poets' representation is less unified. An indication [of this is] that more than one tragedy comes from any [epic] representation. Consequently, if they compose a unified plot, it appears either docked, if it is briefly presented, or watery, if it accords with the length [appropriate to] the verseform. [By "less unified"], I mean, e.g., [the effect] if it is composed of several [complete] actions, just as the *Iliad* and the *Odyssey* have many such parts, which have magnitude even in themselves. Yet these poems are as well constructed as [epics] may be, and are, as far as possible, representations of a single action.

So if tragedy is superior in all these ways, and also in [achieving] the function of the art (for tragedy and epic should produce not a random pleasure, but the one we have mentioned), it is obvious that it will be superior to epic as it achieves its end more than epic does.

6. Conclusion of the account of tragedy and epic

So regarding tragedy and epic, in themselves, their kinds and their parts, as to how many there are and how they differ, and what are the causes of doing well or not [in them], and regarding questions raised and their solutions, let this account suffice.

Poetics II

1. The field of the enquiry

Regarding lampoons and comedy . . . ***

The *Tractatus Coislinianus*

(argued to be a summary of *Poetics* II)

1. The kinds of poetry

[The kinds] of poetry are non-representational [and representa-   **1**
tional]. Non-representational [poetry] is divided into (a) historical and (b) educational, which is divided into (i) instructional
and (ii) theoretical.

[The kinds of] representational poetry are (a) narrative and   **2**
(b) dramatic, i.e. enacted. This is divided into (i) comedy and
(ii) tragedy, [to which we can add] (iii) mimes and (iv) satyr-
plays.

2. Catharsis in tragedy

Tragedy reduces the soul's emotions of [pity and] terror by   **3**
means of compassion and dread. It wishes to have a due proportion of terror. It has pain as its mother.

3. The nature of comedy

3.1 The definition of comedy

Comedy is a representation of an action that is laughable and   **4**
lacking in magnitude, complete, [in embellished speech,] with
each of its parts [used] separately in the [various] elements [of
the play; represented] by people acting and [not] by narration;

43

accomplishing by means of pleasure and laughter the catharsis of such emotions. It has laughter as its mother.

3.2 The nature of laughter

5   The laughter of comedy has its structure as a result of (a) diction and (b) incidents.

3.2.1 Laughter from diction

[It arises] from diction in seven ways:

(i) First, from homonymy, e.g. "paying" ["defraying" and "profitable"], and "metre" ["measure" and "verse-form"].

(ii) Second, from synonymy, e.g. "I'm here and am arrived": for this is the same thing.

(iii) Third, from verbosity, when someone [twice] uses the same name.

(iv) Fourth, from paronymy, (a) by addition, when something extraneous is attached to the standard [name, e.g. * *]; and (b) by shortening, e.g. "I'm called Midas the joke" [instead of "joker"]; (c) from a diminutive, e.g. "Socratiddles, Euripidipides" [instead of "Socrates, Euripides"]; (d) from an alteration, e.g. ["the worstest of all"].

[(v) From parody(?), e.g.] "O Clod Almighty" instead of "O God".

[(vi) From metaphor.] This happens [from things similar] in sound or [some other perception, and with] things of the same genus.

(vii) Seventh, from the form of the diction.

3.2.1 Laughter from the incidents

6   Laughter arises from the incidents in two ways. (i) First, from deception, e.g. Strepsiades believing that the story about the flea was true.

(ii) Second, from making [something] like [something else]. Making something like something else is divided into two in its use, [making something] (a) like something better, e.g. Xanthias [made to resemble] Heracles, or (b) like something worse, e.g. Dionysus [made to resemble] Xanthias.

[It also arises]

(iii) from the impossible.

(iv) From the possible and inconsequential.

(v) From things contrary to expectation.

(vi) From making the characters tend to be wicked.

(vii) From using vulgar dancing.

(viii) When someone who has the power [to decide] lets go the most important things and takes those most inferior.

(ix) When the argument is disjointed and lacking any sequence.

3.3 The objects of comic laughter

Comedy differs from abuse, since abuse details without concealment the bad [qualities and actions] attaching to people, but comedy requires the so-called innuendo. 7

The joker wishes to expose errors of soul and body. 8

3.4 Catharsis in comedy and tragedy

There wishes to be a due proportion of terror in tragedies and of the laughable in comedies. 9

4. The parts of comedy

4.1 The qualitative parts of comedy

The elements of comedy are plot, character, reasoning, diction, song and spectacle. 10

(a) Comic plot is one which is structured around laughable actions. 11

(b) Characters of comedy are the buffoonish, the ironical and the boasters. 12

(c) The parts of reasoning are two, general statement and proof. There are five [kinds of artless proof]: oaths, agreements, testimonies, ordeals and laws. 13

(d) Comic diction is common and popular. The comic poet should assign his characters their ancestral dialect, and himself the local one. 14

15   (e) Song is particular to [the art of] music; hence [the poet] will need to take his starting-points complete in themselves from that [art].
             (f) Spectacle supplies * * as a great need to dramas.
16   Plot, diction and song are observed in all comedies, reasonings, character and spectacle in [not] a few.

4.2 The quantitative parts of comedy

17   There are four parts of comedy: (a) prologue, (b) choral [part], (c) episode and (d) exit.
             (a) A prologue is a part of a comedy that is up to the entry of the chorus.
             (b) A choral [part] is the song sung by the chorus, when it has sufficient magnitude.
             (c) An episode is the [part] between two choral songs.
             (d) An exit is the [part] uttered at the end by the chorus.

4.3 The three kinds of comedy

18   [The kinds] of comedy are (a) old, which goes to excess in the laughable; (b) new, which abandons this, and inclines towards the grand; and (c) middle, which is mixed from both.

A Hypothetical Reconstruction
of *Poetics* II

(based on the *Tractatus Coislinianus* and the fragments of *Poetics* II)

1. The field of the enquiry

Our [next] topic is lampoons and comedy, [and what potential each has; how many kinds of the laughable there are, of what sort they are, and how they should be used if the composition is to turn out well; also, from how many parts comedy is constituted, and of what sort they are; and likewise all other aspects of the same enquiry. Let us begin again, following the natural order, from first principles.]

1.1 The kinds of poetry are classified   1
according to (a) representation

[As we said,] poetry is of two kinds, non-representational and representational, [depending on whether the name "poet" is applied according to representation, or merely according to the media used, i.e. song and verse. The non-representational kind is divided into] (a) historical and (b) educational (whether this is for instruction or theoretical investigation). [As we said, even when someone puts such works into verse, he is not rightly called a poet according to representation.]

47

2

1.2 The kinds of poetry are classified according to (b) the manner of the representation

[Representational poetry is divided according to the manner in which the representation is produced, into] (a) narrative [like epic], and (b) dramatic, i.e. enacted [like comedy and tragedy.]

1.3 The kinds of poetry are classified according to (c) the objects of the representation

[Dramatic poetry, as we said, represents people doing things, and these people and their actions are either good or inferior. The difference between] comedy and tragedy [is that the former aims to represent people as worse, the latter as better, than they are: we may add] mimes and satyr-plays. [So let this account of representation, its points of difference, and how many and what they are, suffice.]

3

2. The function of tragedy

[Just as I showed that tragedy and comedy arose from causes natural to man, so too they arose by nature for an end, namely the catharsis of human emotions. We have already seen how this is accomplished in tragedy. If it is properly constructed,] tragedy reduces the soul's emotions of [pity and] terror by means of compassion and dread, [which are aroused by the representation of pitiable and terrible events. By "reduces", I mean that] tragedy aims to [make the spectator] have a due proportion [i.e. the mean] of [emotions of] terror [and the like, by arousing these emotions through the representation. Tragedy, like epic, has as its end the catharsis of these emotions, which gives rise to the pleasure proper to tragedy.] It has, [as one might say, emotions of] pain as its mother. [As for how catharsis works in comedy, and how this differs from tragedy, I shall explain below when we have looked at the nature of the laughable. But now let us discuss comedy, taking up the definition of its essence that results from what has been said.]

3. The nature of comedy

3.1 The definition of comedy   4

Comedy is a representation of an action that is laughable and lacking in magnitude, complete, [in embellished speech], with each of its parts [used] separately in the [various] elements [of the play]; [represented] by people acting and [not] by means of narration; accomplishing by means of pleasure and laughter the catharsis of such emotions. It has laughter, [so to speak,] as its mother.

[I explained what each of these things means when tragedy was defined.]

3.2 The qualitative parts of comedy may be deduced from the laughable

[Since the function of comic representation is to represent the laughable, we must next consider from how many kinds] laughter has its structure, [i.e. how the pleasure that is particular to comic representation arises.] Laughter arises from (a) diction and (b) incidents.

3.2.1 The laughter of comedy comes from (a) diction   5

Laughter arises from diction in seven ways.

(i) First, [it arises] from homonymy, [when the same name has two or more meanings,] like "paying": [this means "defraying" and "profitable";] e.g. "metre", [which Aristophanes puns on in the *Clouds*.]

(ii) Second, from synonymy, when two or more names have the same meaning, like "cloak", "wrap" and "mantle"; e.g. "I'm here and am arrived", which is the same thing, [as Aristophanes jokes in the *Frogs*.]

(iii) Third, from verbosity, when someone [twice] uses the same name [with the same meaning].

(iv) Fourth, from paronymy, [when the standard name is in part the same and in part altered.] Paronyms are divided into those (a) by addition, when something extraneous is attached to the standard [name, e.g. "infamonous" instead of "infamous"]; and (b) by shortening, [when something is removed from the standard name,] e.g. "I'm called Midas the joke" [instead of "joker". Also] (c) from a diminutive, [when the standard name is lengthened or curtailed to trivialise something and make it laughable,] e.g. "Socratiddles, Euripidipides" [for "Socrates" and "Euripides" in Aristophanes. Again,] (d) from an alteration, [when the standard name is in part left unchanged and in part made up, e.g.] "the worstest of all" [instead of "the worst"].

[(v) Again, laughter arises from parody, when one name is pronounced instead of another,] e.g. "O Clod Almighty" instead of "O God".

[(vi) Again, from metaphor. By "metaphor" I mean, as we said, the transference of names from things similar] either in sound or [in appearance or potential or some other perceptible quality, especially if ugly but not painful or destructive; one should not transfer a name from something too dissimilar, but use] something of the same genus [or similar by analogy, otherwise it will be a riddle but not a metaphor.]

(vii) Seventh, from the form of the diction. [By this I mean e.g. what is a command, or what is a wish; this belongs to the art of delivery.]

[These then are the seven kinds of the laughable that arise from diction, and it necessarily follows that diction is an element of comic representation.]

6   ### 3.2.2 The laughter of comedy comes
         ###   from (b) the incidents

Laughter [also arises] from the incidents [on the stage,] in two ways. [As I said in the *Rhetoric*, a major cause of amusement is making something like something else, and the accompanying deception of expectations. Obviously this can happen in the incidents.]

(i) [Laughter arises] first from deception, e.g. Strepsiades believing that the story about the flea was true [in Aristophanes' *Clouds*,] and (ii) secondly from making [something] like [something else]. Making something like something else is divided into two in its use: (a) making something like something better [than it is], e.g. [the slave] Xanthias [disguised as the hero] Heracles [in Aristophanes' *Frogs*,] or (b) making it like something worse, e.g. [the god] Dionysus [disguised as the slave] Xanthias [in the same play].

[Other kinds of the laughable are errors in serious poetry, which can be used inappropriately on purpose to arouse laughter, as we said. Laughter arises] (iii) from the impossible, [or] (iv) from the possible and inconsequential, [i.e. the improbable; these are effective if they accomplish the function of the representation, i.e. the arousal of laughter; otherwise they are errors even in comedy. It also arises] (v) from things contrary to expectation. [From this it will be clear that the representation of the action or structure of the incidents is also useful for arousing laughter, and it necessarily follows that this is an element of comic representation.]

[Laughter also arises] (vi) from making the characters incline to be wicked [without this being necessary or probable; this is of course an error in tragedy. Comedy represents persons who are inferior to us, as we said, but not in every kind of wickedness. What sort of people they are may be revealed] (vii) by their use of vulgar dancing [like the cordax, or] (viii) [by bad decision, e.g.] when someone who has the power [to decide] lets go the most important things and takes those most inferior. [Hence character too is a part of comic representation; but so also is reasoning, since actions are caused by the reasoning as well as the characters of the people acting. Therefore laughter can also arise] (ix) [from reasoning,] when the argument [for an action] is disjointed and lacking any sequence. [These, then, are the kinds of the laughable arising from the incidents.]

[For this reason the elements of all comic representation are necessarily four, diction, plot, character and reasoning. Comedy is superior to lampoon in this, since it has song and spectacle also.]

3.3 The function of personal abuse in comedy and lampoon

[Again, comedy and abuse in verse, i.e. lampoon, differ in the representation of people. As we said in the *Rhetoric*, the elements of the laughable are people, words and deeds.] Comedy is superior to abuse, since abuse details without concealment the bad [qualities and actions] attaching to people, but comedy

7

requires the so-called innuendo. [Whereas abuse represents how actual people like Alcibiades do behave, comedy, in its essential nature to which it has attained, aims to represent how people may behave in general; this is why, as we said, comic poets now use made-up names for their characters, and do not abuse real people as the writers of lampoons do.]

8   [Even so, there is a place for jokes in comedy, since vice should be reproached, and a joke is a concealed reproach of an error. In both comedy and lampoon,] the joker wishes to expose errors of soul and body [in his victims, and this arouses laughter, provided that the error is not painful or destructive to the victim or others.]

9   ## 3.4 The function of tragedy and comedy compared

[Now that we have considered the laughable and its parts, we should explain what we stated above about the function of comedy, i.e. the catharsis of pleasure and laughter. Just as the function of tragedy is to arouse pity and terror through the representation of pitiable and terrifying actions, which come about through an error that is painful or destructive in some way, so too the function of comedy is to arouse pleasure and laughter through the representation of laughable actions, which also come about through an error, though not a painful or destructive one. Each kind of poetry aims to purify that part of the soul concerned with these emotions. By seeing a representation of terrifying things happening to others, one will learn to feel terror in the right way, for the right reason, to the right extent and so on; this will be accomplished by the catharsis of the emotion of terror.]

[This applies not to the painful emotions only, but to the pleasant ones as well. Just as] in tragedies [the poet] aims to produce a due proportion of terror [in the souls of the spectators, so too] in comedies there is to be a due proportion of the laughable. [So much for the function of tragedy and comedy.]

4. The parts of comedy   10

4.1 The qualitative parts of comedy, and how they should be used

The elements of comedy are, [as we have shown, six:] plot, character, reasoning, diction, song and spectacle. [These are the   14
same as the elements of tragedy, and, as in tragedy, two of them refer to the media of the representation (i.e. diction and song), one to the manner (i.e. spectacle), and three to the object of the representation (i.e. plot, character and reasoning). There are no others except these.]

4.1.1 Plot in comedy   11

Comic plot is one which is structured around laughable actions. [We have said of what sort these are. The action should be structured in accordance with probability, unless the comedy achieves its aim better by using impossibilities and improbabilities, as we have seen.]

4.1.2 Character in comedy   12

[Comedy represents characters who are inferior to ourselves, i.e. worse than we are: therefore comic characters are those who are somehow in error in soul or body. Typical] characters of comedy are the buffoonish, the ironical, and the boasters. [Each of these diverges from the mean, and therefore deserves not praise but reproach. As we said in the *Ethics*, the buffoon errs in humour, as he will make any joke, even against himself, to please another, but an ironical person jokes to please himself. This is why we say that buffoonery is more suited to a slave and less to a free citizen than is irony. But even the ironical man errs, just as does the boaster in the opposite way; the first understates the truth, the second overstates it. Both, then, are liars, but the boaster seems more worthy of blame. But, as we said, not every kind of bad character is appropriate, but only those that are not painful or destructive.]

4.1.3 Reasoning in comedy   13

The parts of reasoning are two, [as we said, namely] general statement and proof. [These are explained in the *Rhetoric*. In particular the comic poet should use the proofs that do not depend on art:] there are five [of these]—oaths, agreements, testimonies, ordeals and laws.

4.1.4 Diction in comedy

[We have already discussed diction and its parts, and how laughter arises from it.] Comic diction is common and popular. [Therefore it uses standard names and metaphors more than exotic names, since it is closer to everyday speech than is tragedy. In tragedy the characters all speak in the same way, but in comedy the diction should be appropriate.] The comic poet should assign his characters their own ancestral dialect, and himself the local one. [Thus the Boeotian in Aristophanes' *Acharnians* uses his own dialect, but the poet in the parabasis uses the local Attic dialect.]

15

4.1.5 Song and spectacle in drama

[The last two elements of comedy are shared with tragedy but not with epic, and as we passed over them before we will mention them now.] Song, [i.e. speech, rhythm and melody,] is particular to [the art of] music [and not to that of poetry.] Hence [the poet] will need to take his starting-points complete in themselves from that [art.] Spectacle [belongs still less to the art of poetry, but is enthralling. It] supplies, as a great benefit to dramas, [both tragic and comic, the masks, scenery and costumes.]

16

4.1.6 The qualitative parts of comedy
are not equally important

[Of these elements,] plot, diction and song are observed in all comedies, but reasonings, character and spectacle in [not] a few. [If there is no plot, there is no representation of an action, but an action can be represented without including the character and reasonings of those acting. Spectacle is least particular to the art of poetry, as the nature of a comedy can be apparent even when it is read. But a comedy could not exist without the means of representation, since each comedy consists of spoken verses and choral song in its separate parts. Preferably one should try to have all the elements; otherwise, as many as possible of them. So much for the parts of comedy that one should use as elements.]

4.2 The quantitative parts of comedy   17

The [quantitative] parts of comedy, [i.e. the separate parts into which it is divided,] are four: (a) prologue, (b) choral [part], (c) episode and (d) exit.

(a) A prologue is a [whole] part of a comedy that is up to the entry of the chorus.

(b) A choral [part] is the song sung by the chorus, when it has sufficient magnitude.

(c) An episode is the [whole] part [of a comedy] that is between two [whole] choral songs.

(d) An exit is a [whole] part [of a comedy] uttered at the end by the chorus.

[These, then, are the quantitative parts of comedy, i.e. the separate parts into which it is divided.]

5. The three kinds of comedy compared   18

[Comedy is superior to lampoon, as we stated. But comedy did not at once relinquish the form of the lampoon, but developed little by little to attain its nature.] The old comedy goes to excess in the laughable [as does the buffoon, since he desires to please everybody, including vulgar people.] The new comedy abandons this, and inclines towards the grand [or serious; but there should be jokes and laughter in comedy. Therefore] the comedy intermediate [between these is left,] which is mixed from both, [e.g. the comedies of Aristophanes. This kind is the best.]

[Regarding comedy and lampoon, then, and indeed poetry as a whole, in themselves, their kinds and their parts, as to how many there are and how they differ, and what are the causes of doing well or not in them, let this account suffice.]

The Fragments of the *On Poets*

The definition of poetry
according to representation

1(a) Therefore are we not to say that, even though they are not in verse, the so-called mimes of Sophron are [prose] speeches and representations, or the Socratic dialogues of Alexamenus of Teos, the first that were written?

1(b) Dramatic dialogues were written even before Plato by Alexamenus of Teos.

1(c) The first to write dialogues was Alexamenus of Styrea or Teos.

2 The form of his [i.e. Plato's] dialogues is between poetry and prose.

The objects represented in tragedy,
epic, lampoon and comedy

*3.1 ... [not] those who are acting, [but narrates(?) the] actions of people acting ...

*3.2 ... all these things [are] with a view to those who are acting ...

*3.3 Some [poets] attempted to humanise tragedy.

*3.4 ... the achievement of perfection in diction and incidents, but abandonment ...

*3.5   Archilochus and Aristophanes represented more human actions.

*3.6   Pauson made laughable representations.

*3.7   ... representation in the grander [manner] ... sharing in the emotion ... Sophocles ...

Tragedy is superior to epic

*3.8(a)   In tragedy the narrative is [done] only with messengers, and what is enacted is in the other [parts], but in epics there is narrative only.

*3.8(b)   Narrative must be added as a part of the dramatic.

*3.9(a)   [Tragedy is superior to epic, since epic only] has the heroic line instead of those of tragedy; for it [i.e. tragedy] is composed of all the verse-forms.

*3.9(b)   [Tragedy] uses every verse-form.

*3.10(a)   Everything that is in it [i.e. epic] is also in tragedy, but the opposite does not hold.

*3.10(b)   Those [elements] that are in tragedy are in epic too.

Tragedy achieves its function through speech, not song

*3.11   Tragedy may reasonably be thought to have [a kind of] song of its own, as it represents songs to the oboe.

*3.12   [The] composition of nomes, if they are not in articulated [speech], has its end in sound and noises [only]. But since [in tragedy] there are words set to melody, they will have the end of the representation in speech as well.

*3.13   As we say actors relate to the composers of tragedy, and epic reciters to the composers of epic, [so] singers relate to the composers of songs.

*3.14   Tragedy produces its entire effect in speech alone.

*3.15   He manages the [choral] parts and the song with a view to the action.

*3.16   [He composes] songs inferior to nobody's.

*3.17   The [parts] that are shared belong to the same art.

*3.18   Not even Dicaeogenes composed inferior songs.

Catharsis is the function of tragedy, epic and comedy

Testimonia A–D.

A(i) Aristotle, *Politics* VIII 5.1339b42–1340a27:

However, we must investigate whether perhaps this [i.e. the utility of music for relaxation] has not come about by coincidence, and the nature of music is more honorable than accords with the need [for relaxation] which we just mentioned. We should not only share in the common pleasure from it, which everyone can perceive—for music has a kind of natural pleasure, for which reason its use is welcome to [people of] all ages and all characters—but should see whether in some way it contributes to the character and the soul. This would be clear, if we become of a certain sort in character by means of it.

Actually, the fact that we do become of a certain sort [because of music] is obvious for many reasons, especially the songs of Olympus. For it is agreed that these arouse the soul to ecstasy, and ecstasy is an emotion of the character connected with the soul. Again, when listening to representations everyone comes to share in the emotion, even apart from rhythms and songs themselves.

Since music happens to belong among pleasant things, and virtue is concerned with feeling delight correctly and loving and hating [correctly], clearly one should learn, and become habituated to, nothing so much as judging correctly, i.e. feeling delight in decent characters and fine actions. Rhythms and songs contain especially close likenesses of the true natures of anger and mildness, bravery, temperance and all their opposites, and of the other [traits of] character: this is clear from the facts—we are moved in our soul when we listen to such things. Habituation to feeling pain and delight in things that are like [the truth] is close to being in the same state regarding the truth [itself]. E.g. if someone delights in looking at the image of something for no other reason than because of its shape, it must necessarily be pleasant for him to look at the thing itself, the image of which he is looking at.

1340a1

5

10

15

20

25

A(ii) Aristotle, *ibid*. 7.1341b32–1342a18:
We accept the division of songs proposed by some people en-
gaged in philosophy into songs relating to (a) character, (b) ac-   **1341b35**
tion and (c) ecstasy, as well as their proposal that the nature of
the melodies particular to each of these varies according to the
type [of song] involved. We can therefore state that the art of
music should be used not for a single beneficial purpose only,
but for several. In fact it should be used (a) for education and
(b) for catharsis (what we mean by catharsis, we shall state simply now, but more clearly in the *Poetics*), and thirdly (c) for en-   **40**
tertainment, for both rest and relaxation from tension.

It is therefore obvious that one must use all the [kinds of]   **1342a1**
melodies, but not use them all in the same way. (a) Those most
related to character must be used for education, but (b) those
related to action and to ecstasy must be used for listening to
while others play them. For the emotion that arises violently in   **5**
some souls exists in all, but differs in its degree, e.g. pity and
terror, as well as ecstasy. Some people tend to be taken over by
this agitation [of the soul], but we can see that, as a result of the
holy songs they use to rouse the soul to a frenzy, they settle
down as if they have attained healing, i.e. catharsis. It follows   **10**
that this very same thing happens to people who are prone to
[an excess of] pity, terror and emotion in general, and to the
rest [of us] to the degree that each participates in such [emo-
tions], and a sort of catharsis and relief, accompanied by pleas-   **15**
ure, comes about for everyone. Likewise cathartic songs too
afford people harmless delight. For this reason, those performers who are concerned with music for the theatre must be allowed to use such melodies and songs.

B Iamblichus, *On the Mysteries* I 11:
The potentialities of the human emotions that are in us become
more violent if they are hemmed in on every side. But if they
are briefly put into activity, and brought to the point of due
proportion, they give delight in moderation, are satisfied and,
purified by this means, are stopped by persuasion and not by
force. For this reason, by observing others' emotions in both
comedy and tragedy, we can check our own emotions, make
them more moderate and purify them.

C(i) Proclus, *Commentary on*
Plato's "Republic" I, p. 42:
Why does he [i.e. Plato] not accept tragedy and the comic art in
particular, when these conduce to the expiation of the emotions? For it is neither possible to shut these out entirely, nor
again safe to indulge them. The emotions need some timely exercise; if this is provided by listening to these [kinds of poetry],
it frees us from being troubled by them in the future.

C(ii) Proclus, *ibid.* p.49:
It has been objected that tragedy and comedy are expelled
[from Plato's "Republic"] illogically, if by means of these [kinds
of poetry] it is possible to satisfy the emotions in due measure,
and, by satisfying them, to keep them tractable for education,
by treating the ache in them. Anyway, it was this that gave Aristotle, and the defenders of these [kinds of] poetry in his dialogue against Plato, most of the grounds for their accusation
[against him]. We will refute this [objection], in accord with
what preceded, as follows ...

C(iii) Proclus, *ibid.* p.50:
We too will say that the statesman should arrange for some
vomitings of the emotions we mentioned, but not so that we
intensify our clinging to them, but the opposite, so that we bri-
dle them and restrain their stirrings fittingly. Those kinds of poetry, then, with their immoderation in calling forth the
emotions we mentioned, as well as their diversity, are far from
being useful for the expiation [of the emotions]. For expiations
[of things] consist not in excesses [of them], but in restrained
activities—which bear little resemblance to the things which
they expiate.

D(i) Olympiodorus, *Commentary on*
Plato's "First Alcibiades" p. 54:
Aristotelian catharsis cures evil with evil, and, by the conflict of
opposites, leads to due proportion [in the emotions].

D(ii) Olympiodorus, *Commentary on*
Plato's "Gorgias" p. 172:
Those who wish tragedy to be admitted [into Plato's "Repub-
lic"] make the defence that it should be admitted, first because

it represents heroic incidents, and secondly because it does not let our emotions remain enflamed within us, but calls them forth and expels them.

Fragments.

*4.1 ... these ... unemotional ... tragedy ... these ... the one ... relating to other people, we said ... makes terrifying ..., but the other ... all ... they work out ... what must ... some less ... compositions of this sort, so that ...

*4.2 ... about ... poetry ...as ... as if of the ... action(?) ... if also ... to be ... alone ... conversing ... I say ... poets and ... being ... fine ...

*4.3 ... [a] complete d[rama] ... arises ... an art ... of some sort, to be ... tragic catharsis of pity, i.e. c[atharti]c of pitiable things. If(?) ... of things relating to other people, poetry ... of a complete ... of a complete drama ... equal ...

*4.4 ... [the] virtues of poets ... displays [in the] story the ca[tharsis] of errors ... with [the] correction ... some manner ... not the pleasing ... to consider the errors of [poe]ts ... The same thing, on the one hand ... an error to recount ... tragedy ... nor to recount untruths such as ... composing ...

*4.5 ... of some sort, and reveals another art, and indignation, as ... much ... the things that are said against good poets ... But ... is by no means ..., he says, it being possible to err ... representational ... of disgrace itself ... [correct] the error with a small correction ... foolish(?) ...

*4.6 Folly is present in the wisest of souls, and intemperance in the most temperate. Likewise there are terrors in brave souls and jealousies in magnanimous ones. It is possible to observe, regarding the ... [pleasures(?)], during sleep ... in drunkenness, in fevers ... and [in the] emotions [of the soul] ...

*4.7 [We have concluded from] what we have agreed [that] a poet represents a complete action. It must be understood that poetry is useful with regard to virtue, purifying, as we said, the [related] part [of the soul]. It must be added that every art can become [the origin] of what is best among the things that are in them [i.e. the arts] by nature ... for the sake of ... this ... and produces catharsis ...

Faults in poetry

Testimonium E.
Aristotle, *Poetics* 54b15–18:

[The poet] should guard against these things [i.e. faults in plot and characterisation], as well as against [causing] reactions contrary to those that necessarily follow from the art of poetry. In fact one can often make errors in these; there is a sufficient account of them in my published work.

Fragments.
*5 ...[e.g.] costume [and diction], and represents [these things in] both [ways], and seeks what is appropriate [by these means.] The appropriate is proportionate(?) ... [*Scraps of 61 short lines follow.*] [He] who is above all able to render it exactly is above all a good poet. This is why Homer is good, and Sophocles too. He is able to invent, in diction, character and reasoning, what Andromache would say on seeing her husband being dragged, and how she would say it. But some poets do not represent the person they propose to, but someone else, and represent him well. We have in our midst an example that gives an idea of this. So too in his "lament of Odysseus" Timotheus may be representing someone, and knows what someone is like, but [gives] Odysseus [an inappropriate character ...]. [*30 lines lost.*] ... ruin, who ... of a certain sort ... being appropriate ... clashed ... is established ... rhythm ... like ...

*6.1 The poet who maintains about an equal level in plots, in the making of other characters and in diction is the best.
*6.2 Diction and incidents are about equally necessary.

7 Euripides says that the sons of Thestius came with the left foot unshod; at any rate he says

> "Unsandalled were they on the leftward foot,
> shod on the other, so their knees were light."

In fact the Aetolians have exactly the opposite custom. They are shod on the left foot, but leave the right foot bare. I suppose one should keep light the foot that leads, not the one that lags.

Literary history

8　Socrates had as his detractors Antilochus of Lemnos and Antiphon the seer, just as Pythagoras had Cylon of Croton. Syagrus was Homer's while he lived, and Xenophanes of Colophon was after his death. Cercops was Hesiod's detractor while he lived, and after his decease the afore-mentioned Xenophanes was. Pindar's was Amphimenes of Cos, Thales' was Pherecydes, Bias' was Salaros of Priene, Pittacus' were Antimenidas and Alcaeus, Anaxagoras' was Sosibius and Simonides' was Timocreon.

9　On the island of Ios, at the time when Neleus son of Codrus led the colonisation of Ionia, a local girl became pregnant by one of the spirits who dance with the Muses. In shame (because of the weight in her belly) at what had happened, she went to a place called Aegina. Pirates raided it, enslaved the afore-mentioned girl and took her to Smyrna, then under Lydian control. They made a present of her to the Lydian king, Maeon by name, who was friendly towards them. He fell in love with the girl and married her for her beauty. She, lingering by the river Meles and seized by birth-pangs, gave birth to Homer by the river. Maeon adopted the child and raised him as his own, since Critheis had passed away straight after giving him birth. After a short while he too passed away. As the Lydians were hard-pressed by the Aeolians, they decided to leave Smyrna. When their leaders announced that whoever wished to go with them should leave the city, Homer, being still an infant, said that he was willing to be a hostage (*homēros*) himself. Therefore, instead of Melesigenes ["born by the Meles"], he was named Homer. When he had grown up, and had already acquired a reputation for his poetry, he enquired of the god [i.e. Apollo at Delphi] who his parents were and where they were from. The god replied:

"The isle of Ios is your mother's land; it will
receive you dead. Beware the riddle of young men!"

There is reported to be another oracle to this effect:

"Blessed and unhappy! You were born to both.
You seek your country; know your mother's home
(but not your father's) is an isle by Crete
not near, not far from Minos's broad land.
On this it is your fate to end your days
When from boys' lips you hear nor understand
A song in crooked words beyond intelligence.
Your lot, to have two fates of life, the first
Dark with twin suns, the other like the gods'—
Alive and dead, but ageless still in death."

A short time later, after sailing to Thebes for the Cronia (a musical festival they hold), he came to Ios. There he sat on a rock and watched some fishermen sail in. He asked them if they had caught anything. They had caught nothing, but had been catching their lice because the catch was so bad. So they replied:

"What we caught we left, what we didn't catch we have,"

expressing with this riddle that they had killed and left behind the lice they had caught, but still had on their clothes the lice they did not catch. Homer, unable to interpret this, died of despair. The people of Ios gave him a splendid burial and put the following inscription on his tomb:

"Here earth covers the holy head
of godlike Homer, singer of heroes."

10　Empedocles is Homeric and clever in expression, as he is metaphorical and uses the other things that succeed in the art of poetry. He wrote, among other poems, a *Xerxes' Crossing* and a *Hymn to Apollo*, but a sister of his burnt these later, the *Hymn* by mistake, but the poem on the Persians deliberately, because it

was unfinished. [Aristotle] says generally that he wrote tragedies too and political works.

*11   The earliest [poet] to write an elegiac poem seems to
have been Callinus. Aristotle adds besides as poets of this sort
Antimachus   of   Colophon,   Archilochus   of   Paros,   and
Mimnermus of Colophon. In their number belongs Solon, the
distinguished lawgiver.

*12   Aristotle thinks he [i.e. the poet Alcman] was a Lydian.

*13   Pindar says that the dithyramb was invented at Corinth.
Aristotle says that Arion began this [kind of] song; he was first
to lead the chorus in a round dance.

*14(a)   Both [tragedy and comedy] were invented among the
Athenians, as Aristotle says. For it was there that human beings
first appeared, which is why the finest and most serious learning bears witness to this city. Arion of Methymna introduced
the first tragic drama, as Solon says in his *Elegies*.
*14(b)   Comedy came from Sicily originally—for Epicharmus
and Phormus were from there—but was developed more finely
at Athens. Sicyonian poets were the inventors of tragedy, but
Athenians perfected it.

*15(a)   We pay no attention to Aristotle, who says that [in
tragedy] at first the chorus entered and sang to the gods; Thespis discovered the prologue and speech, Aeschylus the third
actor and high boots, and what more there is than this we owe
to Sophocles and Euripides.
*15(b)   In tragedy long ago, the chorus at first staged the en-
actment, but later Thespis devised an actor to give the chorus a
rest; Aeschylus [devised] a second one, but Sophocles [devised]
the third and brought tragedy to completion.

*16   Aristotle says that Susarion began it [i.e. comedy].

Notes to *Poetics* I

47a8–13 In his opening paragraph Aristotle sketches out the main points of the investigation that will follow. For its characteristic emphases compare 60b6–7, the introduction to questions raised about epic, and 62b16–19, the end of the *Poetics*.

47a8 "poetry in itself" Literally "the art of poetry in itself", since "poetry" (*poiētikē*) is really short for "the art of poetry" (*poiētikē technē*). The actual title of the *Poetics, Peri poiētikēs*, thus means 'On [the art of] poetry'. Aristotle refers to the essential nature of poetry as REPRESENTATION: see below 47a13–b24.

"its kinds" "Kind" (*eidos*) is an Aristotelian technical term for "species" as opposed to "genus", e.g. at 57b8 (where I translate it as "species"). However, Aristotle also uses "kind" to mean the four types of tragedy (55b32), and its parts too (52b14, 56a33); in fact he often uses "kind", "part" and "element" (*eidos, meros* or *morion*, and *idea*) interchangeably in the *Poetics*. See Glossary under ELEMENT, and the note on 56a37.

For Aristotle, the vital first step in examining a topic is to seek a DEFINITION by means of a division according to its GENUS and differentia, i.e. the DIFFERENCES that distinguish its SPECIES from one another. This is the method he pursues in the paragraphs that will follow. The various "species" of the genus poetry are what we call its "genres"; Aristotle will discuss in detail tragedy, epic and comedy, leaving aside lyric poetry, which he assigns to SONG and therefore neglects in the *Poetics* (see on 49b34).

47a9 "potential" (*dunamis*). For Aristotle, the natural POTENTIAL of something is realised in its ACTIVITY or actuality (*energeia*). Thus the potential of a tragedy exists even when it is a script sitting on a shelf, but that potential is realised in its performance, when it achieves its FUNCTION (*ergon*); see on 53b11. Likewise the potential of the tragic genre as a whole is realised in the actuality of its historical development (see 49a7–15). For a more detailed account of potentiality see *Metaphysics* V 12.

"how plots should be constructed" This looks forward to 50b21–52a21, and especially 52b27–54a15. Plot is singled out for special mention because it is in Aristotle's view fundamental to the function of tragedy.

47a10 "composition" (*poiēsis*) This is from the verb *poiein*, "to do", "fashion" or "make", which I often translate "compose" or "produce". Thus a poem (*poiēma*) is a "thing made", a poet (*poiētēs*) is a "maker" (cf. on 51b27), and poetry (*poiētikē*) is the "art of making". So for the Greeks "poetry" suggests craftsmanship and production rather than creativity or originality; the art of poetry, like that of rhetoric, is classed by Aristotle among those arts concerned with production, like carpentry, where the end or aim is something outside the art itself, i.e. the product, and not only the process involved in making it. Thus in the art of boat-building the end is a boat, not the process of building it; so too in poetry the end is the poem, not the process of composing it. See *Ethics* I 1.1094a4.

"how many parts . . . and of what sort" Tragedy has both QUALITA-TIVE and QUANTITATIVE parts, and there are several of each. It also has the "complication" and "solution", as well as its four "kinds" (see 55b32).

47a11 "it is [constituted]" "It" must mean either "each kind of poetry" or "the composition"; but the parts of tragedy in general, and those of *a* tragedy in particular, are in theory the same, even if in practice not all tragedies contain all the QUALITATIVE parts (see on 50a12).

47a12 "following the natural [order]" Literally "according to nature". Aristotle proceeds from first principles, i.e. from that aspect of poetry that applies to all of it, REPRESENTATION; he then eliminates the lyric genres by distinguishing their MEDIA of representation, and comedy by the OBJECTS it represents, and so focusses on the serious genres he intends to study, i.e. epic and tragedy. The same procedure is followed in the *Tractatus Coislinianus* (*T.C.*) 1–2, where it is used to focus on comedy. Compare *Physics* I 7.189b31, "it is in accord with nature to discuss first the things that are shared, and only then to investigate those particular to each".

47a13–b28 The genus REPRESENTATION (*mimēsis*), which Aristotle proceeds to subdivide, is in fact that type of representation which as its MEDIA uses RHYTHM, WORDS and MELODY. REPRESENTATION as a whole is a larger entity, including e.g. instrumental music and dancing, which he explicitly excludes (even though they produce the same effect), or mimicking sounds and painting, which he does not discuss at all except as an analogy, e.g. at a18–20. Thus Aristotle uses REPRESENTATION in both a broad sense, and the narrow sense of "literary representation": compare the use of "error" to cover both "error" and "accident" at *Ethics* V 8.1135b12–18, and that of "poetry" to cover "representational" and "non-representational" types at *T.C.* 1–2. For my translation of *mimēsis* as "representation" rather than "imitation", see the Introduction (section 4) and the Glossary.

47a14 "dithyrambic composition" The DITHYRAMB was a type of choral ode, originally sung in honour of Dionysus, the god of wine and wildness: see on 49a10.

47a17 "media, objects, manner" Aristotle has no abstract nouns for these terms, but makes do with adverbs and adjectives, literally "by representing either in other things, or other things, or otherwise": the abstracts are indispensable in translation.

47a20 "by art . . . by practice" For art (*technē*), see Glossary. Some painters achieve their results because they know the principles of their art, others do so by trial and error.

"do so with sound" The text distinguishes these people from poets and musicians. Most probably Aristotle means popular entertainers who used their voices to represent the sounds of animals, machines or natural phenomena. Plato compares their performances to those of the poets (*Republic* III 397A), so Aristotle may be making a point against his teacher here.

47a23 "separately or mixed" Drama alternates spoken verses with sung portions, but choral lyric uses all MEDIA together. See on 49b25.

47a24 "oboe" The ancient *aulos* had a reed, and resembled an oboe in register; the usual translation "flute" is misleading.

"lyre" The guitar is the closest modern equivalent of the ancient cithara or lyre. Aristotle means simply "music for woodwind and strings", singling out the two types of instrument that were highly evolved in his time.

47a26 "[uses]" A copyist who did not understand the sense supplied "they represent" instead, which was inserted into the Greek text. The Arabic version preserves the original.

47a27 "characters, sufferings and actions" These correspond to the four types of tragedy and epic—those predominantly portraying character, suffering or action (the latter subdivided into simple and complex actions) at 55b32, 59b7, and to the three types of music at *Politics* VIII 7.1342b32 (see the notes on 55b32–56a3 and *On Poets* Testimonium A(ii)). Dance can have the same effect as poetry, but is distinguished from it by the MEDIA employed. Both Plato (*Laws* II 655D) and Aristotle (*Politics* VIII 5.1340a39) see character as a major object of musical representation; and in the *Ethics* (e.g. II 6.1107a5), good character involves attaining the mean with reference to our emotions and actions. "Sufferings" (*pathē*) can also signify "emotions", as both are things we experience; the emotions are defined at *Ethics* II 5.1105b21–3 as "desire, anger, fear . . . generally the things which pleasure or pain follow".

"rhythms given form" This is usually taken to refer to rhythm and gesture, but Aristotle means that the rhythms dancers follow are given form in the postures or figures they adopt.

47a28–b24 Aristotle in effect complains that the Greeks of his time had no word for "representational literature", regardless of whether it is in prose or verse; for him, the latter distinction matters less than that between work that is "representational" and "non-representational" (the same distinction that is made in the *Tractatus Coislinianus* 1–2—see notes there). To show what he means, he suggests that certain prose genres really belong in this category (compare *On Poets* frag. 1), and certain works in verse do not. Some scholars alter the text to make Aristotle regret the lack of two names, one for prose fiction, and another for fiction in verse; but this is unnecessary and confusing (see Note on the Text). Aristotle wants a term that will cover literary representation (*mimēsis*), from mime to Homer. Plato noted the lack of a suitable term in his late work, the *Sophist* (267D).

47a28 "art of representation" This is supplied. An ancient reader thought Aristotle meant "epic" here, and therefore supplied "epic" instead, which entered the Greek text. The Arabic lacks it, which proves it spurious.

47a29 "unaccompanied words" Literally "bare words", i.e. prose.

"verse" I have used this term, interchangeably with "verse-form", to translate *metron*, literally "measure" and normally rendered "metre". This does not mean the concept of metre itself, which Aristotle calls RHYTHM, but measured units of rhythm, i.e. verses: see 48b21. It has the further sense of "spoken verses", and does not include verse set to music, which is instead called SONG.

47b9 "no name" This is lost in the Greek, but preserved in the Arabic, and was also in the text used by the Byzantine scholar John Tzetzes.

47b10 "mimes of Sophron and Xenarchus" A prose representation of everyday or low life, such as Sophron and his son Xenarchus composed at Syracuse in the second half of the fifth century. Even though mime is a prose genre, Aristotle cites it as a prime example of REPRESENTATION (*mimēsis*).

47b11 "Socratic dialogues" Aristotle pointedly juxtaposes dialogues involving Socrates, such as Plato wrote, with mimes (as also at *On Poets* frag. 1). For his denunciation of literary representation, Plato had used a literary form resembling mime, i.e. he wrote representational literature, even though it was not in verse; worse still, dialogues, like mimes, are dramatic in form. Aristotle also stated that Plato's works are close to poetry (*On Poets* frag. 2). A pupil of Aristotle's reports that Plato was fond of Sophron's mimes—a strange contrast to his denunciation of *mimēsis*. It is important to bear in mind that there was as yet no prose fiction, except for these two genres.

47b12 "even if someone were to compose the representation in [iambic] trimeters" English cannot convey the connexion, obvious in Greek, between "compose" (*poiein*) and "poet" (*poiētēs*). Even if these kinds of prose representation were put into verse, we would have no name for them *qua* representation, but only according to the verse-form, a far less important factor. Compare 51b2, on how Herodotus' *Histories* would be no less a history if someone put it into verse.

47b14 "elegiac poets . . . epic poets" Whereas epic poets composed only in the hexameter, elegiac poets composed in couplets which alternate the hexameter with a shorter line, the elegiac pentameter.

47b15 "indiscriminately" Literally "commonly".

47b18 "Homer" Homer, the great epic poet active in eastern Greece circa 750–725, was regarded by Aristotle as author of not only the *Iliad* and *Odyssey*, but also the comic poem *Margites* as well; thus he was in a way the originator of both tragedy and comedy (see 48b34). He was, for Aristotle, far superior to the other epic poets (51a16–30, 59a30–b16). See also *On Poets* frag. 9.

"Empedocles" This speculative natural-scientist and mystic (circa 492–433) set out his theories in hexameter verse. Elsewhere Aristotle grants that he had excellent literary abilities (*On Poets* frag. 10), especially in his metaphors; but his work was not representational in Aristotle's sense, which is the crucial question.

47b21 "Centaur" The early to mid fourth-century tragedian Chaeremon composed this dramatic work in mixed metres, for recitation not acting; this is why it is literally called a "rhapsody", which was normally a part of an epic recited at one performance (a "rhapsode" was a reciter of epic: see Plato, *Ion*). It certainly contained hexameters. Even though Chaeremon adheres to no single verse-form in his *Centaur*, whose very title alludes to its hybrid form, he is still a composer of representational literature, like Sophron and Plato, who use no verse-form at all. See also 60a2 and *Rhetoric* III 12.1413b8ff., where Chaeremon is praised for being highly effective when read.

47b25 "song" This means words sung to music, and therefore includes MELODY (above, a22), just as "verse" includes the spoken words (above, a29).

47b26 "nomes" Like DITHYRAMB, the nome was a lyric poem sung by a choir. These differ from tragedy and comedy because they are sung throughout, whereas Greek drama alternates spoken with sung portions. See also *On Poets* frag. *3.12.

47b29 "differences" Another of Aristotle's technical terms; a DIFFER-ENCE is that which distinguishes different SPECIES of the same GENUS from one another (cf. 48a12). See Glossary under DEFINE.

48a1 "people in action" Literally, "those doing things". Aristotle's concept of ACTION has a strong moral content; it means a purposeful action, resulting from a DECISION, for which its agent is to some degree responsible. Good and bad decisions are fundamental expressions of CHARACTER, which differs by VIRTUE and VICE. Aristotle takes it for granted that literature deals with human action in the fullest, moral sense.

48a2 "good" This epithet (*spoudaios*), which I have also had to translate as "serious", connotes a person we should take seriously in both social and moral terms. Its two opposites are "inferior" (socially and morally), and "laughable".

48a5 "such [as we are]" No genre, at least in verse, had as yet represented characters exactly "like us": had Aristotle lived to see the New Comedy of Menander, he might have cited it as an example.

"Polygnotus" Little is known of these artists, except for Polygnotus of Thasos (active ca 475–447), greatest painter of the fifth century. Aristotle draws the same contrast between the Athenian caricaturist Pauson (late fifth century) and Polygnotus at *Politics* VIII 5.1340a36, where he says that the young ought not to look at Pauson's pictures, but rather at those of Polygnotus and other painters good at representing character (i.e. who represent good character). See also the notes on 50a26–9, *On Poets* frag. *3.6 and Testimonium A(ii), 1341b34.

48a7–16 Aristotle leads up to his central distinction between tragedy and comedy by noting that the same distinction is seen in other types of REPRESENTATION, including some outside literature altogether.

48a7 "[kinds of] representation" Literally "representations".

48a11 "speeches and unaccompanied verse" Literally, "words and bare verse". This is often understood as "prose and unaccompanied verse"; but all the examples Aristotle gives are poets. He means only to stress the contrast between purely instrumental music, and literary genres where speech predominates.

48a12 "Cleophon" An Athenian fourth-century tragic poet whose ludicrous diction is mentioned in the *Rhetoric* (III 7.1408a15); see also on 57b33 and 58a20.

"Hegemon" Hegemon of Thasos composed epic burlesques, i.e. parodies of Homer in hexameters, in late fifth-century Athens; Nicochares was a slightly later comic poet—his *Deiliad* was a "tale of cowardice", to match the *Iliad*, the "tale of Ilium".

48a15 "Timotheus" Timotheus of Miletus (ca 450–360) and Philoxenus of Cythera (ca 435–380) were dithyrambic poets who both composed lyrics about the monstrous Cyclops Polyphemus, the latter to caricature the Sicilian tyrant Dionysius I; presumably Timotheus depicted the monster in a more serious manner. Timotheus is mentioned again at 54a30, 61b32, and *On Poets* frag. *5.

The text is in a mess here. After "just as" the sources, except the Arabic, had a few letters that make no sense; I emend them to "for", but this may be wrong and something else may have been lost, possibly a poet's name and what he represented, or merely a scribe's explanation that the Cyclopes were giants. "So" is preserved by the Arabic only. See Note on the Text.

48a16 "precisely this difference" So the Arabic: the Greek has "the difference itself" (see Note on the Text). For examples of inferior comic character-types see *T.C.* 12.

48a20–24 Aristotle divides the genres by their MANNER of representation into narrative and dramatic, and then subdivides narrative into pure narration, and narrative which includes speeches (e.g. the Homeric epics). The same main division into narrative and dramatic is presupposed later (a25–8), and is also found at *T.C.* 1–2. Plato, placing his emphasis on the idea of representation as impersonation, has a three-way division into narrative, dramatic and mixed (e.g. Homer): see *Republic* III 392D-394D. Such a division in Aristotle would contradict the basis of his system; but this passage is not written clearly enough to avoid giving rise to the view that he is simply echoing Plato.

48a21 "another [person]" Literally "another thing". Aristotle has been talking about the OBJECTS of the representation, but shifts suddenly at a23 to speaking of persons.

48a23 "everyone" Literally "all the persons". They are specified as "those being represented" or "those representing". I have deleted this, as it is an explanation by a copyist, like "they represent" at 47a26. See Note on the Text.

48a25–7 Tragedy (Sophocles) and comedy (Aristophanes) differ from epic (Homer) in the MEDIA of the representation (verses mixed with song, not unaccompanied verses), and in their MANNER (narrative not dramatic), but tragedy is like epic because both represent "good" or "serious" people (*spoudaioi*: see on 48a2).

48a26 Sophocles, 497–406, was regarded both in his time and by Aristotle as the greatest tragedian Athens produced; his *Oedipus the King* clearly played a considerable part in shaping Aristotle's theory of tragic plot.

48a27 Aristophanes, ca 445–385, the greatest writer of comedy in fifth-century Athens, is infrequently mentioned in Aristotle's extant works; therefore it is often thought that Aristotle disapproved of Aristophanic comedy ("Old Comedy"). If so, it is very odd that here he names him alongside Sophocles and Homer, whom he acknowledges as the masters of the first two genres dealt with in the *Poetics*. It is in fact not surprising that the analysis of humour in the *Tractatus Coislinianus* 5–6, and that of comedy in general, is based on Aristophanes.

48a28 "in action and doing [things]" These synonyms lead into a digression on the Dorians' claim to have originated drama, on the grounds that its name is Dorian; the digression concludes with a return to this point (see on b1).

48a30 "the Dorians" The Dorians, who were fabled to have conquered the Peloponnese under the leadership of Heracles' descendants, spoke a different dialect from the Athenians and were their traditional enemies.

48a31 "the Megarians here" Megara was a Dorian city immediately west of Athens; it enjoyed a democracy early in the sixth century, after the overthrow of the autocrat Theagenes. Presumably the democracy allowed free speech, and therefore comic abuse, to flourish. Although Aristotle credited one Susarion with inventing comedy in some way (see *On Poets* frag. *16), he may have rejected the view that Susarion was from Megara (some said he was from Icaria, the village outside Athens where Thespis, the founder of tragedy, came from). Aristotle probably thought that both comedy and tragedy evolved at Athens, though under Dorian influence (*On Poets* frag. *14). But Megarian comedy was still going strong in his time (see *Ethics* IV 2.1123a24).

48a32 "the Megarians in Sicily" Megara Hyblaea near Syracuse was a Sicilian colony of the Megara near Athens; its inhabitants said Epicharmus was born there (see next note), a claim Aristotle accepts.

48a33 "Epicharmus" Epicharmus, one of the most celebrated of ancient comic poets and "inventor" of Dorian comedy, was active at Syracuse probably from the later sixth century until his death, at an advanced age, around 467 B.C. Many of his plays were burlesques on mythological topics; only fragments survive. Plato put him on the same level as Homer (*Theaetetus* 152E).

The text describes him as "the poet". This must be a note made by a copyist when Epicharmus had ceased to be a household name (compare 56a30). See Note on the Text.

48a34 "Chionides and Magnes" These were the earliest major comic poets in the official record at Athens. Chionides was probably victor when comedy was first instituted at the Dionysia, the great Athenian early summer festival of drama, in 486. Magnes' earliest victory known to us was in 472. Little of either survives. The text should say that Epicharmus lived "not long before" them, but the "not" has fallen out.

"some of the Dorians in the Peloponnese" "Of the Dorians" is supplied. In his discussion of the origins of tragedy, Aristotle does not

refer to these claims, but may have done so in the *On Poets*. See on
49a10 and *On Poets* frags. *13–14.

48a36 "they call villages *kōmai*" In fact "comedy" derives from
kōmos "revel", as Aristotle clearly knows; compare the riotous "phallic
processions" in which it originated (49a11).

48b1 "they term 'doing' *dran*" This etymology of "drama" is correct,
but the word was not limited to the Dorian dialects: Aristotle himself,
writing in Attic prose, uses *dran* as a synonym for *prattein* "do", e.g.
a28, 49b26 (in the definition of tragedy). Although Aristotle disagrees
with the Dorians' claims from etymology, as this shows, it does not
necessarily follow that he thought that they had no basis in literary
history (see on 49a10). It is notable that the Dorians offer no etymology
of "tragedy", literally "goat-song", and neither does Aristotle. There is
slight evidence that the prize for the best tragedy was a goat, which
might explain the name; or it might be owed to an early association of
tragedy with dancers dressed as half-animal satyrs (see on 49a20).

48b4–19 "Two causes seem to have generated the art of poetry" The
first is people's instinct for representation (*mimēsis*); the second is the
pleasure people derive from representations produced by others. Thus
the first relates to artists, the second to audiences; both were needed
for poetry to arise. Aristotle proves his second point by a formal argument. That man also has instincts for melody and rhythm (b20) is a
further minor consideration, parallel to his instinct for representation.

Aristotle's metaphor is one of birth, and similar biological metaphors
appear several times below (e.g. "generated" at b23).

48b4 "as a whole" As opposed to the specifics of how the genres
evolved, to be given at b25 onwards.

48b5 "representation" Poetry is still discussed in the context of REP-
RESENTATION in general: see on 47a13–b28. Aristotle soon introduces an
analogy from the visual arts (b10).

48b9 "representations" Literally "things represented" (so too at
b18). Greek has separate words for representation as a process, and for
an actual representation of an object.

48b10 Aristotle is thinking of diagrams of human and animal bodies,
used in his lectures on biology: he refers to the pleasure we get from
such diagrams, even of the most unpleasant creatures, in *On the Parts
of Animals* I 5.645a11. Here he adds the further point, essential to his
redefinition of "representation" against Plato, that we derive pleasure
from *recognising* the object represented, however displeasing it is in actuality: see also *Rhetoric* I 11.1371b4. This is because recognition is a
form of learning, and learning is pleasant. The idea of aesthetic distance is implicit here: see Introduction, Sections 4–5.

48b13 Aristotle thinks most people regard the highest good as the life of enjoyment, not of learning (*Ethics* I 5.1095b14), although he himself disagrees (*Ethics* X 7–8): but even such people derive pleasure from learning, which proves that man is by nature a rational animal. Cf. *Metaphysics* I 1.980a22, "everyone by nature desires knowledge".

48b17 The PLEASURE from learning and recognition is the true pleasure we obtain from representation as such; if we do not recognise the object represented, we merely obtain another kind of pleasure, that based purely on the senses and not on cognition.

48b20–49a9 In this section Aristotle explains first, how serious and humorous kinds of poetry arose; second, why they have different verse-forms; and third, how Homer formed the link between epic and lampoon on the one hand, and tragedy and comedy on the other. Aristotle's conclusions here are clearly based on reasoning from first principles rather than from literary history, since there was no solid information about the growth of literature down to Homer's time.

48b20–6 Melody and rhythm seem added as an afterthought, since they were connected historically with poetry. Poetry arose by nature from those by nature most gifted; and its genres arose from the characters of those composing improvisations. Aristotle says nothing here of divine inspiration or poetic madness, an omission that eloquently attacks Plato's views on the point. Nor does he identify any particular individual who invented poetry, as the Greeks often did. Poetry is a purely natural phenomenon.

48b21 "**verses are parts of rhythms**" I.e. "segments of rhythm"; see on 47a29.

48b25 "**i.e. those of fine persons**" Literally "and those of such", where "and" means "i.e.", as often. If the actions of fine persons were always fine, there would be no scope for tragedy.

48b27 "**invectives**" These are abusive poems or LAMPOONS, the opposite of poems in praise of gods (hymns) or human beings ("encomia"). "Satire" is a later equivalent. In fact lampoons, aimed at the vices, minor and major, of PARTICULAR individuals, are not poetry in the full sense, since they are insufficiently UNIVERSAL: see 51b11–15, T.C. 7. They are the earliest and worst stage in the development of comedy.

48b30 The lost *Margites* ("*Madman*") ascribed to Homer was a comic burlesque in a mixture of epic hexameters and iambic trimeters, telling the deeds of a ridiculously inadequate hero; the only long fragment to survive tells of a nocturnal misadventure with a piss-pot. Aristotle sees this poem as prefiguring comedy in two respects—its use of direct speech, and its mockery of a fictitious character with harmless faults: see b38, and further 49a34–7.

48b31 "as is appropriate" Iambic verse is closer to ordinary speech, and is thus suited to less dignified content: see 49a23–8, *Rhetoric* III 8.1408b32. The hexameter is naturally more elevated: see 59b31–60a1.

"iambic" This etymology is incorrect; both terms derive from *iambos*, which is of uncertain meaning.

48b33 "the ancients" Aristotle has in mind Homer on the one hand, and Archilochus of Paros (active ca 650), a composer of violently abusive lampoons, on the other. Even if the latter's main victims, Lycambes and his daughters, were really fictitious, antiquity took his poetry at face value. See further on *On Poets* frags. *3.5 and *11. Aristotle wrote a work called *Problems in Archilochus, Euripides and Choerilus* in three Books, but we know nothing about it.

"heroic [poems]" Hexameter epics, so called from their usual content; there were also hexameter hymns and didactic poems.

48b34 "serious poetry" Literally "serious things", i.e. poetry about "serious" people and actions.

48b35 "dramatic representations" Homer used direct speech more than the other epic poets: see on 60a5–11. Alternatively, this could refer to his plots, which are unified like those of drama (see 59a18–20, 30–7). Aristotle is less careful to spell out Homer's relation to tragedy, no doubt because he regards it as obvious, whereas Homer's relation to comedy is not.

48b37 "the laughable" This is defined below at 49a34–7, and exemplified at *T.C.* 5–8.

48b38–49a2 Aristotle regards Homer's poems as somehow transitional between the non-dramatic and the fully dramatic genres, because of their use of direct speech, and, in the case of the *Margites*, because this poem contained only the laughable, not abuse like the lampoons. But at b29–30 the *Margites* was mentioned as if it were a lampoon. Unfortunately for Aristotle's theory, it seemed older than the oldest known lampoons, those of Archilochus, which Aristotle regards as more primitive in form; hence perhaps his inconsistency. Thus we obtain (for the other sources of comedy and tragedy see next note):

lampoon › *Margites* › comedy ‹ phallic songs

hymn › epic › tragedy ‹ dithyramb and satyric poem

49a2–6 Tragedy and comedy correspond to epic and lampoon in content, but are greater genres in form (*schēma*), which explains why poets abandoned the older genres. Aristotle does not mean that drama derives from Homer in terms of form; in fact tragedy and comedy grew out of choral songs with a solo leader (see a10–13).

49a8 "its elements" Aristotle may refer to the QUALITATIVE and QUANTITATIVE PARTS of tragedy. But since he implies below (a15) that tragedy has attained its essential nature in formal terms, he may mean instead the four "kinds" of tragedy (see on 55b32–56a3).

"judged both in and of itself and in relation to its audiences" Some developments, fully compatible with the essential nature of tragedy, may prove unacceptable to its audiences. Conversely at 53a33 Aristotle criticises the spectators' weakness for happy endings, and tragedians who cater to their taste. The same distinction is made at 51a6–11.

49a10 "tragedy [arose] from the leaders of the dithyramb" The leaders of the DITHYRAMB were its poet-composers, who taught the song and dance-steps to the chorus, and led the performance in person, just as the earlier tragedians did (until Sophocles, who, as the story goes, had a poor voice). Archilochus refers to leading the dithyramb himself. Apparently the "leaders" began to perform solo verses between the choral sections. Aristotle's statement has been much contested, on the supposition (which contradicts his remark at 49a38) that all this is sheer hypothesis on his part; but he certainly had more evidence than we do, and does not say that tragedy arose from the dithyramb pure and simple. Elsewhere we hear of the "tragic manner" being invented by the dithyrambist Arion at Corinth (ca 600), and "tragic choruses" being transferred from the cult of the hero Adrastus to that of the god Dionysus at Sicyon around the same date (Herodotus V 67.5); an Epigenes of Sicyon is called inventor of tragedy (see on *On Poets* frag. *13). Both Sicyon and Corinth were Dorian cities in the Peloponnese, and early tragedy seems to have been just such a fusion of epic content with choral song as Herodotus' words would lead us to expect. How much of this was known to Aristotle is uncertain; for his attitude to the Dorian claims to have invented tragedy and comedy see on 48a31. The evidence suggests to me that he thought that both genres did arise in Dorian areas but were developed and perfected in Athens (see *On Poets* frags. *13–16 with notes). Unfortunately it did not suit his purpose to go into detail; the entire passage (to a31) is very condensed.

49a11 "comedy from the leaders of the phallic processions" Processions of revellers following the phallus, in honour of Dionysus, were common in many cities even after Aristotle's time. The processions were accompanied by much scurrility, as is appropriate to a fertility-rite. Such a celebration was still part of the Athenian Dionysia: see Aristophanes, *Acharnians* 241–79.

49a15 "attained its own nature" In Aristotle's teleological view, the tragic form grew like a living organism until it reached its END or goal, when its potential was fully realised. "Nature is an end; such as each thing is when its development has been completed, this we call its nature, e.g. a man, a horse, a house" (*Politics* I 2.1252b32). Cf. *Physics* II 1, *Metaphysics* V 4.

49a15–31 The account of the evolution of tragedy in terms of form (*schēma*) has three aspects: (i) the MANNER and MEDIA of its staging, which relates to three of its QUALITATIVE PARTS (spectacle, song and diction, a15–19); (ii) changes in the grandeur and seriousness of two of these parts (plot and diction, a19–28), and (iii) its QUANTITATIVE PARTS (episodes, a28).

49a16 Aeschylus, ca 525–456, was eldest of the three great tragedians, and the first tragedian whose work survives. Of his trilogies the *Oresteia* is the sole complete example. His addition of a second actor made true dramatic dialogue possible; this makes him, more than anyone else, responsible for tragedy's "attaining its own nature". But Aristotle has surprisingly little to say about him, perhaps because the chorus is still far more prominent in his plays than in his successors'.

49a18 "three actors" "Actors" is supplied. See further *On Poets* frag. *15.

"scenery" Literally "scene-painting". Painted panels offered the only means the Greeks used to elaborate the basic stage set, with its central door and steps down to the circular orchestra or dance-floor.

49a19–24 Three points about primitive tragedy are made: it had trivial (literally "small") PLOTS, humorous DICTION, and trochaic verses instead of iambic. Thus it had the same three indispensable elements (PLOT, SONG and DICTION, i.e. spoken verses) as early comedy (b8), and indeed comedy in general (*T.C.* 16); see also on 50a12. That tragedy had a non-serious origin is paralleled in the development of Japanese *kabuki*.

49a19 "magnitude" This cannot refer only to the length of the plays, since this is specified at a28; it possesses connotations of "grandeur" (see Glossary).

49a20 "became grand at a late date" The process was completed by the time of Aeschylus.

"satyric [composition]" The satyr-play proper was a drama performed after three tragedies at the Dionysia, the four plays occupying in all one day. Its chorus consisted of satyrs, hairy, lustful, drunken, lazy and cowardly attendants of Dionysus with animal traits. It certainly had "trivial plots and humorous diction", as we see from the extant examples (Euripides' *Cyclops*, Sophocles' *The Trackers* and Aeschylus' *The Fishermen*—the last two fragmentary). It has nothing whatever to do with satire. Satyr-play was widely believed to have been added to the Dionysia by Pratinas of Phlius (a Dorian town near Corinth), no later than ca 490, perhaps because tragedy was felt to have come to have "nothing to do with Dionysus", as the proverb went. It is not clear whether Aristotle derives tragedy from satyr-play, or only from something like satyr-play. There is no evidence that tragedy derived from it directly, and many believe that this remark cannot be reconciled with his remarks about tragedy's relation to DITHYRAMB above (a10). Tragedy apparently shared with satyr-play and dithyramb a common ancestry in Dionysiac ritual, and this is surely what Aristotle means. See further the notes on *On Poets* frags. *13–*14.

49a21 "tetrameter" The trochaic tetrameter was a "running" metre, used for dance, including the comic dance, and for recitative to the oboe: see 59b37, *Rhetoric* III 8.1408b36. Iambic metre was more suited to speech: see on 48b31. This transition is also mentioned at *Rhetoric* III 1.1404a31, quoted in the note on 59a12. By "diction" (*lexis*) Aristotle means all the words spoken as opposed to sung.

49a28 "episodes" An EPISODE is originally a unit of dramatic action between choral songs, initiated by the entry of another character: see Glossary.

49a32–7 The summary of comedy's development begins with the difference between comedy and its spiritual ancestor the lampoon, based on the nature of the laughable: this is because comedy aims to arouse laughter, but the lampoon righteous indignation. Aristotle does not define comedy here, since he specifies only one of its points of DIFFERENCE; see the definition at *T.C.* 4. Instead he states a restriction on the OBJECTS it represents—not persons with all kinds of vices, as lampoon does, but only those vices which are not painful or destructive. Pain and destruction are in fact features of tragic SUFFERING, as defined at 52b11. Plato at first equated the object of laughter in comedy with what is bad (*Republic* V 452D), but later identified it as ignorance about themselves in those who cannot harm us (*Philebus* 49B-C).

49a32 "as we said" At 48a17, and compare 48a27, b26.

49a34 "what is ugly" Ugliness has both physical and moral connotations, although the comic mask illustrates only the physical side. Comic error is both bodily and mental: see *T.C.* 8 with note.

"the laughable" LAUGHTER is in fact the EMOTION at which comedy aims, like pity and terror in tragedy (see on *T.C.* 9). This general definition covers the various distortions of DICTION, INCIDENT, CHARACTER and REASONING given as sources of laughter at *T.C.* 5–6.

"a sort of error" Tragic ERROR is painful and destructive for the person who errs; comedy depends on ERROR of precisely the opposite kind, including physical defects for which people can hardly be held responsible.

49a37–b9 The account of comedy's evolution in terms of form (*schēma*) resembles that of tragedy, since it deals with (a) the MANNER and MEDIA of staging comedy, i.e. spectacle (masks), diction (actors) and song (chorus), like a15–19; and (ii) the introduction of PLOT, with which compare a19–28. As in the case of tragedy, DICTION, SONG and PLOT are the absolute essentials (cf. *T.C.* 16). Aristotle's lack of information about who made the innovations in staging does not necessarily prove him ignorant of comedy's origin itself (cf. a11–13).

49b1 "comedy . . . was not taken seriously" A typical joke; who but a philosopher would take comedy seriously anyway?

"granted a chorus" The playwrights submitted their plays to the Athenian *archon* or presiding magistrate, who selected those to be staged and "granted them a chorus", i.e. put a wealthy citizen in charge of the costuming and rehearsal of the chorus.

49b2 "a late date" Comedy was introduced to the Dionysia in 486, which was therefore the date when the official lists of playwrights and their plays began. See on 48a34.

49b3 "those termed its poets" I.e. those popularly called poets. There is some question about whether these playwrights were properly poets in Aristotle's view, since they were not yet producing representations of UNIVERSALS with plots, but remained within the form of the lampoon which attacked real individuals (PARTICULARS); see on b8, and 51b11–15.

49b4 "masks, prologues, a multiplicity of actors" These items are in both logical and chronological order. For the Greeks, masks were fundamental to dramatic representation (thus the comic mask is used to illustrate the laughable at a36). The prologue implies the first actor; a multiplicity of actors is needed for dramatic action of any complexity. Compare *On Poets* frag. *15.

49b6 "Epicharmus and Phormis" On Epicharmus, see on 48a33; little is known of his contemporary Phormis. The Arabic omits this phrase, and says instead "to leave out all the words that are abbreviated". Some take this as a sign that the poets were named in an abbreviated marginal note, which subsequently entered the text. But the phrase is supported by a parallel passage in a later writer who knew the *On Poets*, and says (without naming Aristotle) "comedy came from Sicily originally—for Epicharmus and Phormus were from there" (Themistius, *Oration* XXVII 337B = *On Poets* frag. *14(b)). Here Phormis is called (correctly?) Phormus.

49b7 "Crates" Crates belongs to the generation after Chionides and Magnes (48a34); he was active ca 450–430. Fragments of his comedies survive.

49b8 "generalised stories, i.e. plots" Literally "universal stories and plots", with "and" for "i.e." Poetry deals with UNIVERSALS, not with PARTICULAR actions and individuals, in contrast to history or lampoon.

This distinction will be insisted upon at 51a36–b32. PLOT itself is a "generalised story" (51b5–11).

49b9 Since tragedy resembles epic in that both are serious genres, and comedy in that both are dramatic genres, Aristotle could proceed to study tragedy in relation to either. In *Poetics* I he chooses the first pair, but in the *Tractatus Coislinianus* the focus is on the second.

49b9–20 Epic was already perfected by Homer, so Aristotle does not discuss its development. Instead he indicates briefly how tragedy and epic are similar, and can therefore be judged by the same criteria. This is why he later uses examples from epic even when discussing tragedy, e.g. 51a19–30, 54b2, b26. His discussion relates mainly to the three points of generic difference set up at the outset, and is expanded further in the account of epic at 59a17–60b5, and the comparison between the two at 61b26–62b15. Cf. *On Poets* frags. *3.8–10.

49b9 "Epic poetry follows tragedy" Literally "followed", i.e. in logic and certainly not in time. The past tense suggests the nuance "as we have said already".

49b10 "representation of serious people" On "good" or "serious" people (*spoudaioi*) see on 48a2, and generally 48a1–18. The same word is used for "good" tragedies at b17.

"speech in verse" The Greek MSS have "verse with speech" or a corruption of it, but all VERSE has words anyway (see on 47a29). See Note on the Text.

49b11 "single verse-form" Hexameter verse is the only metre of epic, whereas tragedy used various verse-forms, even in the spoken sections. See 47a28–b9, *On Poets* frag. *3.9.

"narrative" See 48a19–29, *On Poets* frag. *3.8.

49b12 "length" This refers to the duration of the time represented, not to the length of the performance, although there is obviously some correlation between these. Epic can, if it wishes, tell of a family curse extending over generations, and such topics are standard in Aeschylus' trilogies; but from Sophocles onward the tragic action tends to be concentrated into a single day. Despite Aristotle's reluctance to generalise too dogmatically, his observation was elevated into the principle of Unity of Time by Renaissance theorists and dramatists. For further discussion of "length", in relation to plot- structure and length of performance, see 51a6–15, 59b17–31, 62a18–b3. Aristotle's use of the term is not entirely consistent: see Glossary.

49b14 "at first" This point about the use of time in early tragedies is true of the trilogies of Aeschylus (but not, usually, within the individual plays that constitute them).

49b16 The QUALITATIVE PARTS are meant here; epic, like tragedy, has plot, character, diction and reasoning, but lacks song and spectacle (see 59b10, 62a14, *On Poets* frag. *3.10).

49b20 "representational art in hexameters" Epic; compare "the art of exposition and representation in verse" (59a17). Aristotle is not concerned with hexameter verse that is not representational, e.g. that of Empedocles: see 47b13–20. The promised account of epic appears at 59a17–60b5.

"comedy" This was discussed in *Poetics* II: compare *Tractatus Coislinianus* 4–18 below, and my reconstruction of *Poetics* II.

49b23–8 "taking up the definition of its essence that results from what we have said" The ESSENCE of tragedy is stated in terms of its GENUS, which is REPRESENTATION, and its points of DIFFERENCE from the other kinds of poetry, i.e. its MEDIA, OBJECTS and MANNER. The definition is thus based largely on the opening sections, but parts of it still require explanation.

(i) That tragedy is a REPRESENTATION was stated at 47a13; that it represents an ACTION was implied at 47a28. (ii) The ACTION is SERIOUS because it is enacted by the SERIOUS or "good" characters whom tragedy represents: the term for "serious" and "good" is the same, implying an ACTION we take seriously morally and socially (see on 48a2). Compare also 48b25. (iii) That tragedy has MAGNITUDE (or "grandeur") was implied at 49a19–21; both this, and the meaning of a "complete action", will be explained at 50b23–51a15. (iv) Its MEDIA (rhythm, speech and melody) were stated at 47b24–8, where it was also implied that they are found separately, not all at once; see further 49b28–31. (v) Its QUALITATIVE and QUANTITATIVE PARTS (elements) will soon be explained (b32–6, 52b14–27). (vi) Its MANNER (dramatic not narrative) was noted at 48a23–8.

Only CATHARSIS is left obscure; it is peculiar that it is not explained in *Poetics* I at all. Aristotle promises at *Politics* VIII 7.1341b38 that the *Poetics* will discuss it, so the discussion was surely in the lost part of the *Poetics* (compare *T.C.* 3, 9).

The definition of comedy in *T.C.* 4 is (necessarily) very similar, since it too follows from the opening sections of the *Poetics*.

49b25 "embellished speech" Literally "seasoned speech", a metaphor from cookery; see on 50b16.

"each of its elements" Song and spoken verses are meant, as stated at b29–31; Aristotle means only that the plays alternate between these, according to the QUANTITATIVE PART of the play that one is in, e.g. an EPISODE is in spoken verse, or a CHORAL PART is in song (see 52b14–25).

49b27 "pity and terror" The best tragedy should inspire PITY and TERROR (fear), and Aristotle discusses at length how to do so (52a1–11, a38, b28–54a15). But the arousal of these emotions is the means to a further END, catharsis.

"catharsis" See Introduction, Section 5, and Glossary; also *T.C.* 3, 9, and *On Poets* Testimonia A–D and frag. *4.

49b28 "such emotions" "Such" is used (as in English) to recapitulate terms that have preceded without repeating them. Pity and terror at least are meant; but other passages suggest that other painful and disturbing EMOTIONS are included. Compare 56b1, "pity, terror, anger and suchlike" (of the emotions to be aroused by the reasoning); *Rhetoric* II 1.1378a22; *Politics* VIII 8.1342a12, where those who feel "pity, terror and the emotions in general" may undergo catharsis. Likewise comedy accomplishes the catharsis of the pleasant emotions: see on *T.C.* 4. For "emotions" (*pathēmatōn*), MS A and the Latin have "lessons" (*mathēmatōn*) by mistake.

49b29 "rhythm and melody, i.e. song" Literally "... and song"; but since song is diction plus rhythm plus melody (47a22), "and" must stand for "i.e.", unless the phrase is a scribe's explanation, as many scholars believe. Yet Aristotle's own wording at 47b25 is hardly more precise.

49b30 "[spoken] verses" See on b25.

49b31–50a14 Aristotle now deduces the six QUALITATIVE PARTS of tragedy from its definition; this is done in approximately the ascending order of their importance. From the MANNER of the representation he deduces spectacle; from the MEDIA, song and diction; from the OBJECT, an ACTION carried out by people, he deduces plot, character and reasoning. The relation between these and the six parts is made explicit at 50a10–12.

49b31 "the ornament of spectacle" Basically SPECTACLE means "the visual element", and in one sense is therefore fundamental to dramatic representation, in that we watch the performers on stage; in another sense, that of an elaboration of the visual element in costume etc., their appearance is of minor importance—hence "ornament" here. Aristotle reluctantly concedes that, because of this first sense, SPECTACLE may be an integral part of tragedy. The reason for his reluctance will become apparent later, when he has to defend tragedy against the grave charge that its element of spectacle makes it vulgar (62a5–14). See below on 50b19, 53b1–11.

49b34 "diction" See also 50b13–15, and the detailed analysis at 56b20–59a16. DICTION denotes only the spoken words, whether in verse or not; words set to music are subsumed in "song".

"song" See on b29, and the Glossary for POTENTIAL. SONG is dismissed with equal brevity at 50b15 and *T.C.* 15. There is no specific discussion of song or SPECTACLE in the *Poetics*, but song at least was dealt with in the *On Poets* (frags. *3.11–18).

49b36–50a7 We move from the external features of the representation to its internal features, PLOT, CHARACTER and REASONING. The PLOT is the course of the ACTION; ability to understand a situation is a function of REASONING, but one's reactions to it depend on CHARACTER. Moreover, at *Ethics* II 3.1105a28–33, Aristotle says that a human action cannot be described in moral terms without reference to the ethical dispositions of the agent, especially his deliberate DECISION, which depends on his CHARACTER and REASONING. So the agents in the play should display CHARACTER and REASONING. The syntax of this passage is difficult, as it is not clear where the "since"-clause is resumed by the "therefore"-clause. The new solution offered in this translation is that it follows at once; this depends on putting "these people" for "whom" in the MSS (see Note on the Text). Others think the "therefore"-clause begins at 50a2 or even 50a7, and that much of what Aristotle says in between is a parenthesis, not a continuous argument.

49b36–7 "action ... enacted ... acting" There is a word-play in the Greek here, which I have attempted to convey in the translation.

49b38 "actions are of a certain sort" There follows here, in all sources, the disconnected sentence "two things are by nature causes of actions, reasoning and character". This is a later reader's marginal explanation of the previous sentence, which has entered the text; compare the note on 50b9.

50a2 "they all succeed or fail" Tragedy deals with human success and failure, happiness and unhappiness (see 51a13); these lie in action, since we act to obtain our END or goal, HAPPINESS, which is itself an action (see on a16–23).

50a4 "plot" PLOT, being the representation of the action itself, is therefore for Aristotle most basic to literary representation as a whole.

" 'plot' here" Literally "this plot". Aristotle specifies his meaning precisely here, because *muthos* sometimes has another sense in the *Poetics*, "story" (e.g. 53a37, b7, 22): see Glossary under PLOT.

50a5 "incidents" This translates *pragmata*, literally "things done", as against *praxis*, "action (in progress)". See Glossary under ACTION.

"characters" CHARACTER is that which determines the quality of the person acting, and is not used simply to mean a person who appears in a play or story, as often in English. See the other definition at b8, and the Glossary.

50a6 "reasoning" Rather than define REASONING, Aristotle gives its two main branches, the establishment of proof and the statement of general propositions, as also at b11; he expands this at 56a36–b2. Compare the discussion at *Ethics* VI 2.1139a17–b5. The verbal expression of reasoning belongs properly to rhetoric: see 56a34–6.

50a8–14 Aristotle now lists the six parts and signals their relationship to the MEDIA, OBJECTS and MANNER of tragic representation, even though not all tragedies have them all, as he explains later (see on a25).

50a8 "tragedy as a whole" The six QUALITATIVE PARTS belong essentially to tragedy; not all tragedies have them all, just as essentially people have two legs, but some unfortunately do not. Editors' translation of this as "every tragedy", and their failure to grasp this point, has caused much confusion (see on a12 below).

"necessarily" This follows from the definition of tragedy and the intervening deduction of its QUALITATIVE PARTS.

50a9 "according to which tragedy is of a certain sort" Since "parts" used alone could also refer to the QUANTITATIVE PARTS, Aristotle specifies that he means the QUALITATIVE ones. There is probably a connexion with his later classification of particular tragedies in terms of their most prominent qualities: see on 55b32–56a3.

"plot, character, . . . song" The parts are listed in (approximate) descending order of importance, which is also the order in which they will be discussed (but spectacle and song will be omitted altogether, unless the discussion at *T.C.* 15 applies to tragedy as well).

50a12 "Not a few of them" I.e. "very many tragedians". The passage has been much misunderstood. "Not a few" is an even stronger expression than "many"; so Aristotle corrects his overstatement with "one might say", as often in Greek with statements about quantity. Not all tragedians are equally competent in handling all the QUALITATIVE PARTS, and some even omit some of them entirely, as Aristotle says regarding CHARACTER (see on a25): likewise Zeuxis' painting "contains *no* character" (a28: my italics). One should strive to include all the parts (56a3–7); if one element predominates, a particular type of tragedy will result, e.g. one of character (55b32–56a3). In *T.C.* 16 we find that only PLOT, DICTION and SONG are seen in all comedies; these are the absolute essentials for tragedy also, if we leave aside SPECTACLE in its most basic sense (see on 49a19–24, b31).

50a13 "elements" (*eidos*) Literally "species". Aristotle has several words for PART or ELEMENT, and uses them indiscriminately in the *Poetics*: see on 56a37 and Glossary.

"they may have . . . " This is based on a new emendation. The MSS say "spectacle has all, character . . . song and reasoning", but spectacle can hardly be held to subsume all the other parts. Most scholars insert one letter into the text so it says "[drama] as a whole has . . . " or "every [drama] has . . . ", to pick up the similar statement at a8, but the supplement "drama" is rather difficult. The solution followed in this translation is based on an idea of my own, namely, to alter "has all" (*echei pan*) to "they can have" (*echoien an*), which makes Aristotle say that tragedians may succeed in including all six parts to an equal degree: compare 56a3–7.

50a16–23 This is Aristotle's main argument for the primacy of plot. It depends on an analogy between actual human conduct and its representation. In life, people aim at an END (*telos*) that is an ACTION. (For Aristotle, ACTION includes what we may think of as states, e.g. contemplation or happiness.) The end at which people aim is HAPPINESS, whatever they think *that* is (see *Ethics* I 4.1095a13ff.), and they succeed or fail because of their actions, not because they are of a certain quality or sort, i.e. character. Since tragedy represents action and life, it must represent people acting to attain the end for man, happiness, which is itself an action; so the actors act to represent the action and not to display their characters.

If we agree with the premises, this is a convincing argument. Aristotle goes on to deduce from it that the structure of the actions, plot, is the end of tragedy. Given that tragedy is the representation of an action, not of people of a particular character, it is not surprising that the part of tragedy that represents the action—plot—will be its most important. This was already implied by the parallelism between the definitions of tragedy and of plot.

Because Aristotle combines the perspective of the *Poetics* with that of the *Ethics* here, many scholars have found it easier simply to excise a17–20, making the passage run " . . . of action and life; so they do not act . . . ". But this leaves him with only subsidiary arguments for the primacy of plot, and his main argument is perfectly clear.

50a17 "Happiness and unhappiness" So MS B. MS A reads "of unhappiness. Happiness . . . ".

50a18 "quality" (*poiotēs*) This is literally "sort-ness", from *poios* "sort"; this equivalence is important for the argument about "people of a certain sort" which follows.

50a21 "the incidents, i.e. the plot" Literally "and the plot". These are synonymous, as at 50a4.

50a25 "without characters" Aristotle does not of course mean that a play could exist without people to perform the actions: but it could exist without the ethical dispositions of those involved in the actions being made at all clear. Compare 60a11. Many translate "deficient in character", which obscures Aristotle's point; like Zeuxis' paintings, these tragedies have *no* character.

"recent [poets]" Apparently those of the fourth century, whose works are almost entirely lost. It is clear that Aristotle does not regard their dramas as progress in the right direction.

50a27 "Zeuxis", from Heraclea in S. Italy, was a renowned painter active ca 435–390 B.C.; he is mentioned again at 61b12. For his predecessor Polygnotus see above on 48a5.

50a29–33 A series of speeches full of characterization, fine diction and reasoning (the other three main qualitative parts) will not achieve the FUNCTION of tragedy, which properly arises from plot (cf. 53b1–14). The function of tragedy is to produce the pleasure proper to it, caused by the arousal and catharsis of pity, terror and the like emotions by means of representation, as stated in the definition at 49b27, implied at 52b29, and restated at 52b29. See Introduction, Section 5.

50a29 "well-composed in diction and reasoning" This is based on an emendation: the sources have "and instances of diction and reasoning that are well composed", perhaps rightly.

50a33 "enthralls" This expression was originally very strong, as it comes from the idea of raising and controlling the spirits of the dead; but by Aristotle's time ENTHRALMENT has become a standard metaphor for the effect of poetry.

50a34 "reversals and recognitions" These are explained below (52a20–b8).

50a37 "almost all the early poets" It is not clear whether this means tragedians down to Aeschylus, or the early poets of epic, who are contrasted with Homer for the same reason at 59a30–b7. Epic is often cited for illustrations elsewhere, even when tragedy is ostensibly the topic.

50a38 "plot is the origin and as it were the soul of tragedy" For Aristotle, the SOUL "is as it were the origin of living things" (*On the Soul* I 1.402a6). Without soul, they degenerate into mere formless matter, as corpses do. PLOT, as it is the dynamic principle or CAUSE which gives tragedy its form, is equally fundamental.

50a39–b20 "The characters are secondary" Aristotle lists the six parts in descending order of importance, but supplies arguments for the order of the first three only (PLOT, CHARACTER and REASONING; character is defined out of sequence at b8). He takes it as self-evident that there is no other part of tragedy which might be most important.

50a39–b3 In this comparison with painting the image outlined in black and white is compared to plot, the chaotic splodges of color to character, fine diction etc. used with no sort of ordering principle, as at 50a29–33. The former produces the intellectual pleasure of recognition of form, the latter more purely sensory pleasures of perception (the same contrast is also drawn at 48b15–19).

50b4 "reasoning" See on 50a6.

50b6 "civic life" In Greek this is *politikē*, the art of living in society, a broader concept than our "politics". In fact *politikē* is concerned with the good of the whole community (*polis*), and ethics is one of its main subdivisions (see *Ethics* I 2.1094a27–b11). But "rhetoric" had already acquired some connotations of the unscrupulous manipulation of opinion for political purposes. Thus Aristotle may again be criticizing the tragedians of his own time (possibly including Euripides, who set this fashion).

50b9 "decision" A DECISION is a deliberate choice made by a person of mature intellect (i.e. REASONING), in accordance with his settled CHARACTER and with an END, ACTION, in view (see *Ethics* III 2.1111b4ff., 1112a15, VI 2.1139a31ff.). It is basic to Aristotle's theory of action. After "of whatever sort" the MSS, but not the Arabic, have "in which it is not clear whether he is deciding or evading". This is an explanation of the next sentence, added by a later scribe: compare the note on 49b38.

50b12 "Diction" After this the MSS, but not the Arabic, have "of the speeches", a later reader's addition to distinguish their DICTION from that of sung lyrics; but "diction" means "spoken words" only, whether in verse or not, and not those of songs (see on 49b34).

"as we said earlier" At 49b34.

50b15–20 Aristotle does not trouble to define SONG and SPECTACLE. They have a place in his theory, but not an important one (see on 49b34).

50b16 "embellishments" Literally "seasonings", a metaphor from cooking. At *Ethics* IX 10.1170b29 the point is made that one does not need much seasoning to make food taste. Compare *Rhetoric* III 3.1406a18, where Aristotle complains that a rhetorician uses flowery epithets "not as a seasoning but as a main dish". Cf. 49b25 above.

50b19 This distinction between the skills needed by a playwright and those needed by a designer of sets, stage properties (props) and costumes is more obvious now than it was in Aristotle's time, when playwrights still produced their own dramas and very rarely wrote only to be read, as Chaeremon did. Compare Aristotle's remarks about using spectacle, rather than plot, to produce an emotional impact, where he is emphatic that the effect of tragedy should not depend on performance, but should be perceived when it is read, a common practice by his time (53b1–11, cf. also 62a12).

50b21 "these definitions" I.e. those of the parts of tragedy.

50b23 "we have laid down" At 49b25. Aristotle first explains what he means by "a whole" or unity (b25–34), then "a certain magnitude" (b34–51a15), deriving them from his general theory and then applying them to tragedy.

50b26 "beginning" This is the same word as "origin" above (a38).

50b30 "either of necessity or for the most part" This is later rephrased as "what is necessary or probable", by which Aristotle means that which tends to happen most often in a statistical sense (compare

Posterior Analytics II 12.96a8ff.); this, to audiences, is expected and may thus seem almost inevitable.

50b31 "A middle" This does not mean that a whole can have only one middle part: epic has several (59a20), and so does tragedy (its EPISODES).

50b32 The concept of a unified PLOT linking the parts of a work of representational literature, with incidents bound together by logical probability if not necessity, is fundamental to Aristotle's poetic theory. As is evident from what follows, the parallel with a living creature is in turn basic to this concept. This idea is in Plato's late work, *Phaedrus* (264C, 268D).

50b35 It is not enough to have a beginning, a conclusion and a middle: they must be in the right order.

50b37 "fineness lies . . . " With this definition of beauty compare the *Parts of Animals* I 5.645a23ff., where the functional organisation of the whole animal towards its END is that which makes the philosopher perceive beauty even in repugnant creatures; but the underlying principle of wholeness has a basis in Aristotle's wider philosophy. Compare *Metaphysics* XII 3.1078a36, "the most important forms of the beautiful are order, proportion and limitation".

"magnitude" As at 49a19, this has the positive connotations of "grandeur". Thus at *Politics* VII 4.1326a25ff. the finest city is the most populous that is not too large to be managed. In the case of animals the right size is relative to the ideal observer. So too for plots—one must be able to take it in as a whole. Memory in the case of plot corresponds to observation in the analogy from biology.

50b38 "an imperceptible instant of time" Aristotle believed there is a connexion between the size of an object and the time it takes to observe it (*Physics* IV 13.222b15).

51a5 "length" This is used interchangeably with "magnitude", but lacks its positive associations.

51a6 "limit" There are two kinds of limit on the length of literary works—those set by conventions of performance and the ability of the audience to pay attention, and those determined by the nature of the art-form itself. The word translated "limit" also means "definition", and the ambiguity is evident from a9 onwards.

"perception" At 54b16 this denotes the reaction produced among the audience by the staging of the play.

51a7 The convention at Athens was to perform three tragedies and a satyr-play on each day of the tragic competition: were it the norm to stage a hundred instead, as Aristotle remarks with humorous exaggeration, they would have to be timed with water-clocks (as speeches in the law-courts were, to give equal time to both sides of the case).

51a9 "as the saying goes" Literally "as they say now and then"; the Arabic has "as we are accustomed to say . . . ". The phrase has almost always been thought to mean "as people say the tragedians once did", and is therefore found incomprehensible, because tragedies were never timed to waterclocks. But "against the clock" is simply a colloquial expression also found in comedy; Aristotle signals the joke by excusing himself for using it here.

51a13 The important idea that plot involves a change of FORTUNE is first introduced here, but compare the mention of happiness as the end of human action at 50a17–20.

51a16–35 Aristotle now draws a practical conclusion: as plot should represent a single complete action, representations of the diverse acts of a single person lack unity.

51a17 "in some of which there is no unity" A characteristic understatement: many of the things we do are not part of the same action.

51a17–8 "the actions of one person" Aristotle mentions "actions" to make clear that "happen to one person" in the previous sentence implies not only things done to someone, but also his or her actions.

51a20 *Heracleid . . . Theseid* There were several epic poems about the Dorian hero Heracles and his many exploits. We know hardly anything about epics on the Athenian hero Theseus, who was credited with a series of exploits to match Heracles'.

51a22 "story" This is the same word as "plot", but here means merely a series of incidents, whether or not they are interconnected (so also b24, 53a18, a37, b22, 56a11, and Glossary).

51a23–29 This praise of Homer, and criticism of the other epic poets, is expanded at 59a18–b7.

51a24 "whether by art or by nature" As Homer was (and remains) the earliest Greek poet whose work survives, Aristotle leaves it in doubt whether his excellence was owed to skill in traditional poetic techniques or simply to natural talent. Now that we can discern something of traditional oral epic before Homer, it is clear that it came from both.

51a25 "everything that happened to Odysseus" Literally "all that happened to him". Aristotle gives as examples the two earliest "recorded" events in Odysseus' life—his wounding by a boar when he was sixteen, and his feigned insanity upon being recruited to fight at Troy, which both happened long before the *Odyssey*'s plot begins. Previous commentators, not realising that a chronological sequence underlies these examples, have been perplexed by the fact that the second one is narrated in a flashback at *Odyssey* XIX 392ff. But Aristotle means that Homer did not simply relate the events of Odysseus' career (whether connected with each other or not) in chronological order, as a biographer or chronicler would, but narrates a single action, the hero's return, as Aristotle summarises it at 55b17–23. Anything that is not part of this single action is merely incidental, like the story of Odysseus' wounding.

51a30 "a single representation is of a single [thing]" Aristotle has not established that this general proposition applies to the other arts he has in mind, which are presumably music, dance, sculpture and especially painting.

51a32 "its parts (the incidents)" Literally "the parts of the incidents".

51a35 "disturbed" The Arabic has "destroyed".

51a36–b32 From his discussion of plot (50a15–51a35) Aristotle draws a conclusion that bears on his whole theory of poetry, and also affects how poets should compose. It is in PLOT, the representation of a single complete ACTION, that the essence of POETRY lies: the coherence of the action counts for more than whether it really happened. PARTICULAR events, such as history deals with, are normally less tidy than the UNIVERSAL events dealt with in poetry, which is why poetry is more worthy of philosophical analysis than is history. Only incidentally do tragedians represent historical events and real people—such events are suitable for plots only if they contain clear patterns of cause and effect. They might as well invent the names and events. This argument demolishes the popular idea that poets are poets because they write in verse, which Aristotle had already attacked at 47b13–23.

51a38 "probability or necessity" Compare 51a13.

51b2 Herodotus, ca. 484–427 B.C., the indefatigable traveller and researcher from Halicarnassus, wrote up what he had learned in his *Histories* or "researches", which deal with peoples and events of the period 560–479, and culminate in the Persian Wars with the victories of the Greeks at Salamis and Plataea. A rather popular epic poem about these wars, the *Persica* by Choerilus of Samos (active ca. 400), was based on Herodotus. Aristotle quotes Choerilus elsewhere (*Rhetoric* III 14.1415a4,16), compares him adversely to Homer regarding similes at *Topics* VIII 1.157a16, and even wrote a book on him (*Problems in Archilochus, Euripides and Choerilus*, now lost). No doubt he was thinking of Choerilus here and at 59a21–9, where he restates this comparison of poetry and history.

51b5 Aristotle calls poetry "more philosophical" because it gives us a more generalised view of human nature and action than does history; it tells us what people of a certain type are likely to do or must do in a particular set of circumstances (UNIVERSALS), whereas history only tells us what Mr. Smith did on a certain day (PARTICULARS). It follows that even comedy is more important than history. Plato regarded poetry as concerned with particulars (*Republic* X 597B–598A).

"more serious" I.e. "more important".

51b6 Poetry only "tends" to deal with universals, because in both epic and tragedy the main heroes were, or were thought to be, historical figures (e.g. Achilles or Odysseus).

51b7–11 Aristotle digresses to give examples of what are meant by UNIVERSAL and PARTICULAR in the context of human action; this is not a true philosophical definition. Contrast *On Interpretation* 7.17a39, "by a universal I mean that which is by nature predicated to a number of things, by a particular that which is not, e.g. 'man' is a universal, 'Callias' a particular."

51b11 Alcibiades, ca. 450–404, was a brilliant but irresponsible Athenian politician and general.

"did or suffered" This could also be rendered "did or had done to him".

"In the case of comedy this has already become clear" Comedy moved away from the mockery of prominent real individuals like Socrates to that of stock types, such as we already find in the later comedies of Aristophanes. Aristotle evidently considered this an advance (cf. 48b37, 49b7): in this respect comedy is ahead of tragedy. According to a (probably apocryphal) story first attested much later, Alcibiades had a law passed to prevent comic poets from ridiculing citizens by name. If this story was known to Aristotle, it explains his sequence of thought here.

51b12 "only then do they supply the names" For the implied procedure of first drafting a plot and then filling in the characters' names, see 55b12.

51b14 "lampoons" See on 48b27.

51b18 "they would not have happened . . . " This apparently obvious remark is perhaps ironic, if Aristotle intends a joke at b32 (see note).

51b19 "only one or two well-known names" Euripides' *Helen* and *Electra*, for example, contain major characters who are pure inventions.

51b21 Agathon was an innovative Athenian tragedian active in the last fifteen years of the fifth century; little of his work survives. Aristotle was interested in him (cf. 56a18–30), and often quotes his verses (e.g. *Ethics* VI 2.1139b9, 4.1140a19). Nothing is known of the plot of the *Antheus*, unless it is the same as the tale of an Antheus of Halicarnassus, murdered by the woman who vainly loved him, which Aristotle narrated somewhere (frag. 556R.). See also on 56a18, a23, a27.

51b26 "known only to a few people" Although the names of the major heroes were well-known, there is no reason to disbelieve Aristotle's statement that the details of their stories were known only to a minority, and could thus be adapted and modified without causing displeasure.

51b27 "these arguments" "Arguments" is supplied. Aristotle probably means the whole discussion of plot that has preceded. His analysis of it leads in effect to a reassertion of its importance, for reasons additional to those given at 50a15–b4. It is the first and greatest part not only of tragedy, but of poetry itself.

51b27 "composer" Literally "poet". The word-play is untranslatable, as the word for "poet" means literally "maker".

51b28 "a poet according to representation" Cf. 47b15. The Greek literally says "a maker according to *mimēsis*": so this sentence would seem violently paradoxical to people like Plato who argued that poetry, far from being a productive or useful activity, was simply an "imitation" of the particulars of actual life. Aristotle has tacitly reinterpreted *mimēsis* as "representation", and contends instead that the REPRESENTATION allows us a clearer view of the UNIVERSALS of human action than do human actions themselves (see on 51a36–b32).

51b30 "things that have happened" This is not primarily a reference to tragedies about recent historical events—there were few of these, the most famous of which is Aeschylus' *Persians*. Aristotle means stories of the heroic age, like the Trojan War, which most Greeks regarded as history not myth, though Aristotle himself has well-justified reservations. Here he wrily observes that *many* of the things that are supposed to have happened must be probable and within the bounds of the possible (and are therefore believable, cf. b16)—but not all of them are. Aristotle is poking fun at those who accepted everything that was narrated about the heroes of the traditional tales.

51b32 "i.e. that are possible" This is omitted accidentally by the Arabic, and deliberately by modern scholars; they have not seen that Aristotle is ironically drawing a paradoxical conclusion from his preceding statement that many of the heroes' actions, which the Greeks would call events "that have happened", are actually possible. Unless the phrase is ironic, there is a contradiction with b18 above, and it should simply be deleted. See Note on the Text.

51b33–52a11 This paragraph continues the theme of unity in plot and action, but also introduces two new points—the different types of plot, and the arousal of PITY and TERROR.

51b33 The basic meaning of EPISODE is a scene introduced by the entry of a new character; from this it comes to mean an act or scene in a play, and by extension a scene in other types of poem. Because of playwrights' frequent use of irrelevant scenes, the adjective "episodic" acquired the bad connotations explained here.

"episodic [tragedies]" This supplement seems better than "actions" here and at b35. Once again Aristotle equates plot with tragedy.

51b37 "competition-pieces" Literally "things for performance", which in the Greek world of course implies competition. Whereas bad poets insert irrelevant episodes because of their lack of ability, good ones do so to let the actors produce a *tour de force*. Aristotle makes a similar comment at *Rhetoric* III 12.1413b8–12: "in diction . . . the [style] best for delivery is suited to performance . . . This is the reason why actors seek out dramas of this sort, and poets actors of this sort."

52a1–11 Aristotle has almost concluded his analysis of the structure of plot. But it is not enough to have the right structure, if the right emotions are not elicited from the audience. Comedy, for instance, has similar structural requirements (cf. 51b13) but an opposite emotional impact. Thus Aristotle reintroduces the concepts of PITY and TERROR from the definition of tragedy (49b27), which will constitute a major theme down to 54a15; and he shows that plots involving AMAZEMENT (i.e. with REVERSAL and RECOGNITION) best arouse these emotions, so that simple plots, which by definition do not have reversals and recognitions, are inferior to complex plots which do. He says that reversals inspire amazement at *Rhetoric* I 11.1371b10.

52a1 "The representation . . . " Literally "since the representation . . . ", but because "since" is not resumed until "consequently" at a10, I have left it untranslated.

52a3 "to a very great or a considerable extent" Editors delete "or a considerable", but the expression is paralleled at *Posterior Analytics* I 9.76a21, and the qualification is appropriate: surprise is not the only way to arouse these emotions, as Aristotle is well aware.

52a7 "the statue of Mitys" The providential punishment of the murderer of Mitys of Argos happened some time before or around 374 B.C.

52a11–21 Complex plots are distinct from simple ones because they have the parts Aristotle defines in the next paragraph, before he discusses the nature of the tragic change of fortune. He continues to emphasize the need to avoid episodic plot-construction.

52a22 REVERSAL (*peripeteia*) is distinct from the change of fortune (*metabasis*) that is seen in the course of any complete tragedy. It is clearly a more sudden change in the events, present only in complex plots.

"actions" Literally "things being done"; MS B has "people in action", but although the action must involve people's intentions, it is the result of the action relative to their intentions that is reversed, not their intentions in themselves.

"as we said" I.e. from good fortune to misfortune or *vice versa* (cf. 51a12–14). Alternatively, Aristotle may mean 52a4, events which happen "contrary to expectation but because of one another".

52a24 Aristotle's first example of reversal is from Sophocles' *Oedipus the King* 925–1053, where a messenger comes from Corinth to Thebes to bring Oedipus the news that his "father" King Polybus is dead and that he, Oedipus, has succeeded to the throne. The messenger thinks, naturally enough, that this is good news. When Oedipus refuses to go to Corinth, for fear of sleeping with his mother, Merope, the messenger tries to rid him of his fear by revealing that he is not actually the son of Polybus and Merope; but this in fact causes even greater tension, and ultimately leads to the revelation of Oedipus' true identity.

Aristotle's summary telescopes the details of this, but is not inaccurate, as is sometimes claimed. The claim has been supported by *Rhetoric* III 14.1415a19–21 which reads "the tragedians too reveal the topic of the drama, if not immediately, like Euripides, at least somewhere in the prologue, like Sophocles' 'my father was Polybus'" (*Oedipus* 774). But this slip does not, surely, prove that Aristotle did not know at all well the play he cites so often.

52a27 Aristotle's second example is from the lost *Lynceus* by his friend, the distinguished rhetorician and successful tragedian Theodectes (ca. 400–334), to whom he dedicated an early treatise on rhetoric. It is intended to illustrate the fact that a reversal can lead from illfortune to good as well as the reverse; for Aristotle, an unhappy ending is not essential to tragedy (see 54a4–9). The *Lynceus* was about the daughters of King Danaus of Argos, who ordered them to murder their new husbands. Only Hypermestra dared disobey, and spared her husband Lynceus. She gave birth to a boy, Abas; upon finding out Danaus demanded Lynceus' death, but as a result of an unknown sequence of events was put to death himself. Aristotle discusses this play again at 55b29–32.

52a29 "as a result of the preceding actions" Literally "from the things that had been done". Events previous to the climactic scene where Lynceus was led off to his execution must have motivated his rescue and Danaus' demise. Thus the reversal accords with probability or necessity, as it arises from the plot.

52a30 "as the word itself indicates" In English as in Greek, the words recognition ("anagnōrisis"), ignorance ("agnoia") and knowledge ("gnōsis") are related. This "change from ignorance to knowledge" is parallel to the "change of the actions to their opposite" that is REVERSAL.

52a31 "and so to either friendship or enmity" Literally "towards either friendship . . . ". The word translated "friendship" (*philia*) is much stronger than in English; it has connotations of kinship by blood, marriage or ties of hospitality, and "enmity" suggests the violent breach of such kinship, as in the examples that follow. A recognition in tragedy usually reveals that your apparent enemy is a long-lost friend or relative, or *vice versa*. The discovery is of a fact, not an emotion. Thus Oedipus finds out that the apparent enemy of the state, who killed his predecessor (and father) King Laius, is actually a very close kinsman indeed—himself! This question of friends and enemies is explored at 53b15–22, and that of ignorance and knowledge at 53b27–36.

52a31 "defined in relation to good fortune" Many characters in a play may be minor characters, whose recognition of others does not matter because we are not concerned with their happiness: for example, the Corinthian messenger's recognition of Oedipus is unimportant, whereas Oedipus' self-recognition is, since he has been defined as fortunate. Others translate "destined for good fortune" (i.e. by the playwright).

52a32 During the scene of reversal in *Oedipus the King* lines 925–1053, Jocasta recognises that Oedipus is her son, as is clear from her words at 1054–1072, which immediately precede her suicide. Oedipus himself does not discover his identity until the end of the next scene (1182ff.).

52a33–b3 Although recognition usually applies to persons, it can also apply to objects (e.g. tokens left with an abandoned baby), chance events (e.g. overhearing something) or actions (e.g. whether somebody did or did not do something). But the kind accompanied by a reversal belongs most firmly to the plot, and is the best. Aristotle lists the types of recognition, with more examples, at 54b19–55a21.

52a35 "happen in the manner stated" I.e. where there is a change from ignorance to knowledge, revealing friendship or enmity (a30–2). Aristotle is usually misunderstood as saying that he has already mentioned recognition of inanimate objects or random events, which he has not, and the passage is thought to be garbled in the MSS, but there is only a minor corruption (see Note on the Text).

52a38–b3 Aristotle gives two reasons why a combined reversal and recognition belongs most to the plot or action. (i) It will evoke pity and terror, the emotions which the action represented in tragedy (i.e. the plot) aims to evoke. (ii) It will bring about the change of fortune which a tragedy must contain. (Kassel prints an unnecessary emendation, changing "and in addition" to "because": see Note on the Text.)

52b3–8 Recognition of persons is the most important kind, and can be mutual or limited to one side.

52b6 In Euripides' *Iphigeneia in Tauris*, one of his last plays, Iphigeneia, obliged as a priestess in a barbarian land to sacrifice shipwrecked Greeks, decides to save one and send him back to Greece with a letter and a verbal message to her brother Orestes. As one of the group is Orestes himself, this leads at once to his recognizing her (760–87). Then, to prove his own identity to her, he tells her about a piece of her own weaving (795–826). See also 54b31, 55a18, b3–15, where Aristotle summarises the plot.

52b10 "suffering" No translation of this word, *pathos*, can fully convey its meaning—a violent deed done to someone (the complement of "action"); moreover *pathos* also means "emotion". It was perhaps a technical term of the contemporary theatre, as "reversal" and "recognition" may have been. A *pathos* is at least potentially, if not actually, present in all tragic plots, whereas comedy avoids what is painful or destructive (cf. 49a35).

52b12 "deaths in full view" It is usually thought that this means "deaths on the stage", and the objection is raised that Greek tragedy tends to narrate such events in a messenger-speech rather than show them on stage (there are, in fact, hardly any such deaths in extant tragedy). But there is nothing about the stage here, and at 59b11 we are told that epic too should have such events. Since these cannot be on stage in epic, a violent deed narrated in a messenger-speech must also count. Elsewhere Aristotle speaks of using language to "put something before one's eyes", e.g. by vivid metaphors (*Rhetoric* III 10.1411a25–1412a10); this is what his expression here refers to. It applies to the agonies, woundings etc. also.

52b14–27 This analysis of the QUANTITATIVE PARTS of tragedy concludes the explanation of the nature of tragedy, which began with its definition at 49b24, followed by the deduction of its QUALITATIVE PARTS and the discussion of the greatest of them, PLOT, and its parts (the "parts of plot" lead into these "parts" by an easy transition of thought). The QUANTITATIVE PARTS of which single tragedies are constituted were already mentioned at 47a10 and 49b26, and implied at 50a9 (see note); two of them, prologue and episode, have already been named (49b4, 48a28). Thus they are an important part of Aristotle's analysis (compare the quantitative analysis of comedy at *T.C.* 17). This section had been rejected as spurious by many scholars, because it is thought to interrupt Aristotle's argument (which it does not) and to be inconsistent with the practice of fifth-century tragedy. But it should be remembered that Aristotle was writing with fourth-century tragedy in mind as well, and we know far less about the latter than he did.

52b14 "we stated earlier" I.e. at 49b31–50a14.

52b15 "elements" I.e. the QUALITATIVE PARTS, which can be used, it seems, as "elements" of tragedy of a particular type, e.g. one based on character (see on 55b32–56a3). But poets should try to include all parts alike (cf. 56a3–7), which is why Aristotle says "which parts should be used". As we saw at 50a12, not all poets succeed in using all of them.

52b17 "with this divided into" Literally "and of this".

52b18 "shared by all [dramas]" Literally "common to all"; the noun to be supplied is masculine or neuter, and so cannot be "tragedies".

"[songs sung] from the stage, i.e. dirges—these are particular [to some]" Much expanded: literally, "particular are those from the stage and dirges". Since there is no separate definition below of "songs sung from the stage", I interpret "and" as "i.e.": see on b24.

52b19–21 Aristotle defines first the three spoken parts of tragedy, in a system strongly recalling his division of a WHOLE into a beginning (prologue), middle (episodes) and end (exit—cf. 50b26–31); then he defines its three sung parts. He takes for granted the definition of the choral part as a whole, just as he never troubles to state that the three spoken parts are all in spoken verse, what he calls "diction". His definitions are very schematic, no doubt because he is generalizing about hundreds of plays.

52b19 "a whole part of a tragedy" Each part should be a WHOLE in itself, with a well-marked beginning, middle and end.

52b20 "episode" This is equivalent to our "act". In the fifth century the number of EPISODES in the middle of a play is not fixed, but hovers around four; in fourth century tragedy it may have been set at three, as in New Comedy (counting the prologue and "exit" as acts, this is the origin of the five-act play). For the meaning of "episode" see on 51b33.

"between whole choral songs" This excludes minor choral songs that did not serve as act-divisions; see *T.C.* 17(b).

52b21 "exit" The original meaning of this term (*exodos*) was probably the closing words sung or chanted by the chorus as it departed at the very end of the play—often a very brief piece: see on *T.C.* 17(d).

52b22 The "processional" song (*parodos*) is performed by the chorus as it enters the circular orchestra ("dance-floor") below the stage. Such songs included marching-metres (anapaestic and trochaic verses, although in the fifth century the latter were limited to comedy), which were chanted rather than sung. This is probably why Aristotle calls the *parodos* an "utterance" (*lexis*), and excludes anapaests and trochees from the other purely choral songs. Aristotle mentions the processional song of comedy in the *Ethics* (IV 2.1123a23).

"the first whole utterance of the chorus" The MSS have "the first utterance of the whole chorus", an easy error. The *parodos* is a whole like the prologue or episode; compare "whole choral songs" above.

52b23 "stationary song" The *stasimon*, or choral song between episodes, was probably so called because it was sung after the chorus had reached its *station* in the orchestra, although some may have thought it was because the chorus remained stationary while it was sung. In the fifth century tragic choruses certainly danced these songs—although the comic poet Plato (active ca 420–390) complains that instead of dancing well, choruses "now do nothing, but stand there fixed like dummies and howl" (frag. 130K.).

"without anapaestic or trochaic verse" I.e., probably, without chanted verse, such as is particularly suited to marching or dancing (as trochaic verse is said to be at 49a23); for there are instances of passages in these metres being sung in *stasima*. See above on b22.

52b24 "dirge" The *kommos* or lament, so called from beating the breast (*koptein*), is a lyric sung alternately by the actors on stage and the chorus in the *orchestra* below it. To judge from the lack of a definition of "songs from the stage", stage arias performed by actors in dialogue with the chorus also belong under this heading, even if they are not laments. In fact more than half of the lyric dialogues in tragedy are not laments at all.

"and [those] on stage" Another possible rendering is "i.e. [sung] from the stage".

52b25–7 The virtual repetition of b14–16 serves to mark off this analysis as a unit; "as elements" is lost in the MSS here, and is supplied from there.

52b28 "After what we have just been saying" I.e. down to perhaps 52b13, with the intervening material on the QUANTITATIVE PARTS regarded as a digression. After discussing the nature and importance of PLOT, and what plots to aim at and avoid, Aristotle now begins a long discussion of how best to achieve the FUNCTION of tragedy, by using the four main qualitative parts of tragedy and by avoiding error in the composition. As plot is so vital to tragedy, he treats these parts in the order (1) plot (53b1–54a15, including a digression on spectacle); (2) character (54a16–33); (3), after a discussion of avoiding error, reasoning (56a33–b19); (4) diction (56b20–59a14).

52b29 "i.e. how tragedy will achieve its function" Literally "and how . . . ". Tragedy achieves its FUNCTION through plot first and foremost. For the "function" of tragedy, the arousal of pity, terror and the like emotions, see on 50a29–33 and 53b11.

52b31 "the construction of the finest tragedy should be not simple but complex" Aristotle has not said outright that simple plots are inferior to complex ones, but this is the point of his argument at 52a1–11; complex plots, with reversal and recognition, can arouse pity and terror far more powerfully (cf. 52b1), and reversal and recognition are the most enthralling parts of a play (50a33–5).

52b32 "moreover it should represent" I.e. the plot should represent events that arouse pity and terror. This is implicit in the definition of tragedy itself at 49b27. Epic belongs to the same kind of representation (see on 62b12–15).

52b34–53a17 Aristotle now shows what sort of ACTION, i.e. change of FORTUNE, will arouse the proper emotional response. There are four theoretical possibilities, which actually happen in life: (i) the fall of a good person into misfortune; (ii) the rise of a bad person into good fortune; (iii) the good fortune of a good person; (iv) the misfortune of a bad person. Aristotle shows that none of these types of person and situation, so simply formulated, arouses the response that is needed.

We find (i), the unexplained misfortune of a decent person, simply disgusting—this produces no catharsis; (ii) the good fortune of a bad character is the opposite of tragic, and is likewise repugnant to our moral sense; (iii) the good fortune of the good may satisfy our moral sense, but cannot arouse pity or terror (this case is so obvious that Aristotle leaves it out); (iv) the misfortune of a bad character satisfies our moral sense, but cannot arouse pity or terror (unless he has substantial redeeming qualities—see 56a21–3).

Bad characters are excluded because of the nature of PITY and TERROR—we pity those who suffer undeservedly, and feel fear for people who are like ourselves (we do not of course perceive ourselves as evil). But one would have thought that the ruin of decent people is precisely what tragedy represents. Simplistically formulated, it does; but such a formulation is too simplistic for Aristotle, who is anxious to rebut Plato's charge that tragedy is morally offensive, as it shows the ruin of good men. His rebuttal has two aspects, both vital to his view of tragedy. (i) The ruin of a very good man (or a very bad man) is not the proper subject for a tragedy—the person who is ruined should be a more average character, although better rather than worse (so he is "like ourselves"), so that we will feel terror rather than outrage. (ii) The disaster must not come about at random and without explanation, but must have a cause—an "error" (*hamartia*), whose results are out of proportion to its importance, but flow from it according to probability or necessity. In this case we will feel pity, and not outrage, because we feel pity for *undeserved* suffering.

52b34 "decent men" "Decent" is a synonym for "good", and cannot mean "perfect": to suppose it does is an illegitimate solution to this problematic statement. The point is surely that the decent man must not be ruined without cause. Yet below Aristotle qualifies the opposite character as "thoroughly villainous", and says the intermediate charcter must not be "superior [to us] in virtue and justice", which lends support to the view that to be consistent he *ought* to have written "perfectly good men" here.

52b36 "shocking" This term (*miaron*) means "filthy" or "disgusting". It is opposite in one sense to *catharsis*, "cleansing" or "purification" (see Introduction, Section 5), and in another to *to philanthrōpon*, "that which satisfies our sense of what is humane", i.e. "morally satisfying" (what we call "poetic justice"). The ancients (perhaps rightly) were pleased not only at well-deserved success, but also at well-merited disaster, such as the suitors' destruction at the end of the *Odyssey* (see also on 56a21). Another view holds that *to philanthrōpon* means "compassion", even for those who deserved their misfortune; this is based on the usual meaning of *philanthrōpia*, "kindliness" or "tenderheartedness". But general sympathy with suffering, in Aristotle's moral theory, should involve indignation at those who wantonly make others suffer, and satisfaction at seeing them punished. His sympathies lay less with criminals than with their victims (see *Rhetoric* II 9.1386b8–15 on *nemesis*, i.e. proper indignation at evil).

53a4 TERROR and PITY are more extensively discussed in the *Rhetoric* (II 5.1382b26–1383a12, 8.1385b11–1386b7). There PITY is defined as "a painful feeling at an obviously destructive or painful evil that is not deserved" (II 8.1385b13f.) It is often felt for someone like oneself (1386a25). But its essential difference from TERROR is that the suffering is distanced from the person who feels the emotion. To illustrate this, Aristotle tells the story of a man who did not weep when his own son was led off to execution, but wept for his old friend (1386a18ff.). In the case of his son, the pain he felt was too close to himself for him to feel pity. As spectators of a good tragedy we can feel both pity, because the characters suffer undeservedly, and terror, because we experience their suffering as our own. This paradox inherent in tragic REPRESENTATION is presumably the source of much of its power and (as Aristotle believed) value.

53a4–5 "the former is [felt] for . . . , the latter for" In the original text Aristotle took for granted that we know which emotion is which, and did not make it explicit. As at 50a1, an ancient reader inserted an explanatory phrase, "pity for the undeserving, terror for the like", which entered the text except in MS B (see Note on the Text).

53a7 "the person intermediate between these" I.e. between good and bad. Aristotle has no term for the "hero" of a literary work; but the concept is not alien to his thought, as here he thinks of a single person. Many tragedies were named after their most prominent character.

53a10 "error" The term *hamartia* means "error" or "mistake", and not a "flaw" of character; it is pardonable, in contrast with "vice and wickedness". Aristotle is excluding vice as the cause of the hero's fall, although he later notes that the fall of an admirable but morally flawed character arouses pity and terror, but *also* satisfies our sense of justice

(56a21–3). The hero of the only surviving tragedy Aristotle cites as an example of *hamartia*, Oedipus, suffers for the consequences of his error in thinking that he knew the identity of his parents. (The old theory that he is punished for an alleged "tragic flaw" of character, the hasty temper which he displays against Creon, is wrong; Sophocles uses this scene to reveal his human imperfections.) In *Ethics* V 8, Aristotle distinguishes error from accident as follows: "acts committed in ignorance are when someone acts without understanding to whom, or what, or with what, or with what purpose his action is done; as when he thinks he is not hitting, or not with this object, or not this person, or not for this purpose. When the harm comes about contrary to reason, it is an accident, but when it is not contrary to reason, but without wickedness, it is an error. Someone is in error when the origin of its cause is in himself, but he is in an accident when its origin is outside himself" (1135b12ff.). A crime of passion is an injustice in Aristotle's definition, but it is still an error (b22) when contrasted with a premeditated crime.

"Error" means the same here; it provides the probable or necessary link between a person's original good fortune and the disaster that overtakes him. His misfortune is not an accident (which would break the chain of causes in the plot, and produce the wrong emotions in the audience), nor is it a well-merited punishment (which would also arouse the wrong emotional response), but the result of actions performed with the best of intentions; as such, of course, it will best stir up our sympathies. Compare *Ethics* III 2.1110b31: "it is ignorance, not of principle but of facts, that makes such an action involuntary, and allows us to pity and forgive the doer." Comedy is based on error of an opposite, painless kind (49a34).

"a great reputation and good fortune" The heroes of myth were all of high social status, which makes their fall the more spectacular. Such status is an important part of the misfortune or good fortune which is in question here.

53a11 In Sophocles' *Oedipus the King*, Oedipus finds out that he unknowingly killed his father and married his mother. She commits suicide, and he blinds himself. Thyestes is well known for seducing the wife of his brother Atreus, for which Atreus took the terrible revenge of serving him his own children's flesh at a feast. This unsavory tale, dramatised in Sophocles' lost *Thyestes*, does not exemplify innocent errors. Sophocles' lost *Thyestes at Sicyon* told a more suitable story. Thyestes had unknowingly committed incest with his daughter Pelopia; years later, when he is about to be killed by their son, Aegisthus, the boy's parentage is revealed. Pelopia commits suicide, and Aegisthus kills Atreus instead.

53a12–23 Aristotle recapitulates the important conclusions he has reached from theoretical reasoning about the emotions, notes some additional implications they have, and then argues that this is confirmed by the fact that tragedies are now confined to the families whose stories match his conclusions.

53a13 "single rather than double" Aristotle has not explained these terms (which are not to be confused with "simple" versus "complex" plots), and remembers to do so only at a31–3. A single plot ends with everyone in the same state of good or ill fortune; a double one ends well for the good and badly for the bad, like the "poetic justice" seen at the end of the *Odyssey*. Aristotle disfavours this type because it satisfies our moral sense, but does not arouse pity and terror (see on 52b36).

53a14 The best tragic plot involves a change to misfortune, not the converse. This has not been explicitly proved, but it is hard to see how a play with a *general* movement towards a happy ending could arouse pity and terror. Plays with an eventual happy ending are discussed at 54a4–9.

53a16 "a great error" The mistake that causes disaster should not be too trivial, because the ensuing calamity would seem too great to preserve the logical connexions between the incidents of the plot.

"a better person rather than a worse one" Although the tragic hero should not be perfect, he or she should on balance be better than the average, so that we fear for a person we feel to be like ourselves, and we also pity his undeserved misfortune. Compare 48a1–18, on how tragedy and epic represent "good", "serious" people: see also 56a21–3.

53a17 As elsewhere, the development of the genre provides a proof of conclusions reached on a theoretical basis: cf. 50a37.

53a19 "finest" This is omitted, probably by accident, in the Arabic.

53a20 "Alcmeon . . . " Of the heroes mentioned, Oedipus and Thyestes were discussed above (53a11). Alcmeon and Orestes both killed their mothers to avenge their fathers (see 53b24, b33); Meleager and Telephus killed their uncles by accident. With the exception of several plays about Orestes, none of the numerous dramatizations of these stories survive; precisely how they exemplify Aristotle's pattern is not clear, except that they all illustrate the dreadful events among family members that will be the topic at 53b15–22.

53a23–b11 Those who criticise Euripides' unhappy endings, and those who prefer a double ending, happy for the good and unhappy for the bad, both make the mistake of seeking from tragedy the arousal of an emotion (moral satisfaction) not proper to it. The same is often true of those poets who use spectacle as a substitute for plot to arouse emotion. The sequence of thought is difficult; perhaps Aristotle is already borrowing from his account of error in poetry in the *On Poets* (see on 54b19–55a21).

53a24 The plays of Euripides (ca 484–406 B.C.), the radical Athenian tragic poet, enjoyed tremendous popularity after his death, despite his relative lack of success during his lifetime. Eighteen of his plays survive. For Aristotle's mixed opinion about him, see next note and on a29.

53a25 "many of his [tragedies]" There is no evidence that Euripides used unhappy endings more often than the other tragedians, and Aristotle obviously admired his *Iphigeneia in Tauri*, which has a happy ending. We must assume that his work was renowned for a number of especially unhappy endings, as Aristotle's praise of his success in them suggests. MS B says "most" instead of "many" (see Note on the Text).

53a27 "On stage and in performance" More freely "In dramatic contests".

53a27 "most tragic" I.e. best at arousing pity and terror. Compare "most untragic" at 52b37; "not tragic" at 53b39.

"if they are done correctly" All plays require a good production to be properly appreciated, so Aristotle must mean "if rightly handled *by the poet*".

53a29 "although Euripides manages badly in other respects" Aristotle criticises Euripides' plots at b29, 54b1, b31, 61b20; his characters at 54a28, a32, 61b21; and his choruses at 56a27. "Although": literally "even if", but with the nuance "as is in fact the case".

53a30–9 The *Odyssey* is cited because, at the end, the evil suitors are killed and Odysseus and his adherents triumph (compare the summary at 55b16–23). The citation shows that this entire argument applies just as much to epic as to tragedy. The double ending seems better because it is more popular.

53a30 "structure" This is deleted by some editors, who supply "tragedy" instead, from a22; it seems awkward to say "the second-best structure . . . is that which has a double structure". However, Aristotle may be equating the plot with the work itself, as often (see on 59b21, 60a28).

53a35 Tragedy, comedy and the horror-show (b10) all produce different kinds of pleasure, according to the different emotions they arouse. Aristotle does *not* say that comedy aims at satisfying our moral sense, only that such an emotional response is more appropriate to comedy: there not even the villain, let alone the hero, suffers. On the emotions aroused by comedy, see on *T.C.* 4.

53a37 "Orestes and Aegisthus" No specific play may be referred to here; at least, no comedy on this topic survives, although the comic poet Alexis wrote an *Orestes*, and many comedies were on mythologi-

cal topics. The distinguishing feature of this version of Orestes' encounter with his hated step-father, whom he usually kills, is that there
is no SUFFERING (*pathos*); compare b39—"it is not tragic, as there is no
suffering"; at 49a35 the things we laugh at are said to be "not painful
or destructive". Aristotle is already thinking of friendship and enmity,
which he will discuss further at b15–22.

"story" The same word as "plot" (*muthos*), but it does not bear the
sense of our "myth"; most Greeks regarded the heroes as historical
characters. So again at b7, 22.

53b1–54a15 After putting the emphasis on the CHARACTER of those
involved in the plot, to establish what type of character will best arouse
in us the tragic emotions, Aristotle now turns to the type of ACTION
that will best achieve this purpose. He introduces this (b1–11) by arguing that our emotions are better aroused by the plot itself than by spectacle (costumes, masks, scene-painting etc.).

53b1–11 Aristotle uses two arguments to show that it is better to
arouse pity and terror by means of plot than by means of SPECTACLE. (i)
The latter is less artistic, i.e. less germane to the art in question, poetic
composition: it is the province of scene-painters, costume-designers
etc. (so 50b17–20). (ii) Some poets overdo the effect: their productions
are not only terrifying but monstrous, which produces a pleasure alien
to tragedy. We are not told what this pleasure is: presumably it is the
pleasure we get from a horror-movie. The next sentence may supply a
hint: tragedy should produce the pleasure that comes from pity and
terror *via representation*. Monstrosities on stage are *themselves* horrible.
Compare 48b10, where Aristotle remarks that we enjoy seeing images
of things that are themselves revolting. To put it in modern terms, excessive realism detracts from maintaining aesthetic distance.

Why Aristotle chooses to bring up spectacle here is unclear. Perhaps, as I suggested in the note on 53a23–b11, he is already drawing
from the *On Poets'* account of error in poetry; or perhaps he still has in
mind Euripides' success on the stage, and the weakness of the audience. Euripides is often criticised in Aristophanes' plays for using costume (kings in rags) to arouse pity (e.g. *Frogs* 1063). Other sources
report that Aeschylus brought monstrosities onto the stage (*Life of Aeschylus* 7).

53b5 "shudder" This synonym for "feel terror" reminds us that the
EMOTIONS have a physical component (e.g. that of pity is weeping, that
of being amused is laughter). Aristotle makes this very clear at *On the
Soul* I 1.403a4ff. Thus he could say that laughter is the *emotion* aroused
by comedy (see further on *T.C.* 9).

53b7 "the plot of the Oedipus" Others translate "the story of Oedipus", but Aristotle's point is that it is the arrangement of a story as a

PLOT that should arouse pity and terror. Another possibility is that he means the play when read, not acted; this is what is left when spectacle is subtracted.

53b8 "lavish production" Literally "the work of a *choregus*", the wealthy citizen who sponsored the tragedy financially and was responsible for training and equipping the chorus, and for the spectacular costumes.

53b11 "use representation to produce . . . terror" Literally "produce the pleasure from pity and terror by means of representation". This phrase makes clear a very basic question. Tragedy does not work by producing pity and terror in the way they are normally produced in us, i.e. when we ourselves or our loved ones suffer or expect to suffer. We have enough of such experiences in our own lives. Instead, the tragic emotions are aroused by a *representation* of others' sufferings; when the representation ends, the cause of our feelings ceases to exist. This is what is cathartic in tragedy, and shows that Aristotle's theory of representation is an essential complement to his theory of CATHARSIS. See Introduction, Section 5.

53b15–22 Aristotle now establishes that the tragic deed or "suffering" (*pathos*) should occur between FRIENDS, not enemies or neutrals. On the sense of "friends", which is much stronger than in English, see on 52a31. Violence between such people is very disturbing, and arouses pity as well as terror. Compare *Rhetoric* II 8.1386a11: "pity is aroused when, in a quarter whence some good ought to come, something evil happens". Contrariwise, violence between enemies does not arouse pity in us, though the deed itself arouses terror.

Aristotle also introduces the idea that impending suffering, whether or not it actually happens, stirs our feelings: cf. *Rhetoric* II 8.1386b1 "things that have just occurred, or are imminent, are more pitiable". The character who "is about to" do the deed of violence does not necessarily *intend* to do it (a frequent misinterpretation), in the proper sense of acting with full knowledge of the circumstances. This idea leads up to Aristotle's preference for the ending where disaster is narrowly averted (54a4–9).

53b15 "arouse dread or compassion" These synonyms for terror and pity recur in the *Rhetoric* (III 16.1417a13), where they are aroused by an epic narrative, and the *Tractatus Coislinianus* (3), where they are specifically the emotions of tragedy; cf. "shudder and feel pity" at b5. All the violent deeds Aristotle enumerates arouse terror, and interest will now focus on discovering which arouse pity.

53b22–6 The poet can and should remodel the traditional stories about violence in the family while continuing to use them; thus each of the three major tragedians reworked the traditional story of Orestes, producing vastly different plays. A poet is to be a composer of *plots* (51b27). But in tragedy one cannot undo the essentials of such stories, e.g. by reconciling Orestes with Aegisthus (cf. 53a7). For the examples see on 53a20.

53b22 "stories" See on 53a37.

53b27–37 Aristotle now sets up four possibilities, according to whether the violent deed takes place or is averted (for the play to be a tragedy, the deed must be present at least potentially), and whether the doer fully knows what he is doing, or finds out later. He arranges these in ascending order of excellence.

53b27 The fact that doing the deed in full knowledge is characteristic of the "old [poets]" is, for Aristotle, evidence that it is an inferior type of plot-structure. Euripides is surely not included among the "old poets", although the Greek could mean "Euripides too [among them]". In his *Medea* (431 B.C.), the oriental princess, after much agonising, deliberately kills her children to punish her husband Jason for deserting her.

53b29 "Or they may be going to act, in full knowledge, but do not do it." This sentence is lost in the other sources, but preserved in the Arabic.

53b32 "outside the drama" Oedipus' slaying of his father Laius and incest with his mother Jocasta occurred years before the day the *Oedipus the King* represents.

53b33 In Astydamas' lost *Alcmeon*, Alcmeon killed his mother without out knowing her identity. Astydamas, the most prolific tragedian of the fourth century, won fifteen victories between 372 and ca 340 B.C. Aristotle does not mention him elsewhere.

Telegonus, son of Odysseus by the witch Circe, was sent by her in quest of his father, and fatally wounded him in ignorance of his identity, which he learned only when it was too late. The play, by Sophocles, is lost.

53b34 "fourth" "Third" is in all the MSS, yet (if the Arabic is to be trusted) three possibilities have already been mentioned. See Note on the Text.

53b37–54a9 Aristotle now arranges these four types of action among family members and friends in ascending order, according to the desirability of their emotional impact.

(1) Knowingly planning an act of violence, but not carrying it out, is the worst type, because the breach of proper behaviour is shocking and not tragic either (i.e. there is no pity or terror), since there is no deed of violence.

(2) Knowingly committing an act of violence is less bad; we infer that this, although shocking, at least arouses pity and terror as well.

(3) To commit the deed without full knowledge and find out afterwards is better; the element of shock is absent, the recognition is amazing and (evidently) the deed arouses pity and terror.

(4) Best of all is to find out just in time to avert the deed of violence. Aristotle does not explain why this is better, but it accords with his wish to answer Plato's charge that tragedy depicts deeds of violence which arouse emotions that should instead be repressed. Aristotle counters that these emotions should be aroused, but that this can be accomplished even without the deed of violence actually being represented.

It is often thought, wrongly, that this contradicts Aristotle's earlier argument that tragedy must depict a change of fortune from good to bad (53a12–17). In terms of the general movement of the plot, tragedy certainly must depict such a change if pity and terror are to be aroused. But a play where the deed of violence is narrowly averted, if most of it is suitably harrowing, can have this same effect.

54a2 In Sophocles' *Antigone* King Creon's son Haemon, betrothed to Antigone, tries to kill his father, who is responsible for her suicide.

"To act is second[-worst]" Aristotle offers no example, as he has already cited Euripides' *Medea* (53b29).

54a4 Examples of the third type, including Oedipus, were given at 53b31–4.

54a5 Euripides' lost *Cresphontes* told how Cresphontes, son of Merope and a king of Messenia, was smuggled out of the country as a child when a usurper killed the king and forcibly married the queen. A reward was offered to whoever killed Cresphontes, who therefore returned in disguise claiming to have killed him. He deceived not only the usurper but the queen, Merope, as well; she was on the point of killing her son's supposed murderer with an axe while he slept, when he was saved, and reunited with his mother, by the intervention of the servant who had accompanied him into exile.

54a7 On Euripides' *Iphigeneia in Tauris*, in which Iphigeneia was to sacrifice her brother Orestes but recognised him in time, see on 52b6–8 and also 55b3–15, where Aristotle summarises the plot.

54a8 "the son" Phrixus, son of Athamas and brother of Helle. It is not known whose play is meant, and nothing more is known of how its plot illustrates the last-minute avoidance of catastrophe.

54a9–13 As at 53a17–22, Aristotle supports his theoretical conclusions by appealing to the development of tragedy. The need to produce the right effect has obliged poets to base their plays on a few families, whose situations make the best plots. Aristotle is not complaining that the poets were insufficiently inventive.

54a11 "this sort [of effect]" Aristotle still has in mind the arousal of pity and terror.

54a12 "not by art but by chance" The poets did not base their choice of stories on the principles of the art, as Aristotle now reveals them, but learned by trial and error which types of plot work best: compare 47a20.

54a13 This concludes the account of plot, begun at 50b21. But Aristotle will soon return to related topics.

54a16 Aristotle's account of CHARACTER may extend to 54b18, but this includes a digression on plot (54a37–b8). Plot and character are closely linked; as we saw (52b35–53a10), the characters of those involved in the reversal of fortune determine, to a large extent, the effectiveness of the plot in arousing the appropriate emotional response. Now Aristotle turns to a different aspect of character—what the people depicted in tragedies (and not just those who experience the reversal of fortune) should be like.

54a17–33 Aristotle states four requirements—that the characters be (1) GOOD, (2) APPROPRIATE, (3) LIKE and (4) consistent. Examples of poets who fail in each follow, except that there is none of (3).

(1) That the character be good is the primary requirement: Aristotle returns to it at b8–15. This depends on the principle, established at 48a16–18, that tragedy represents people better than the norm for whatever social class they may belong to. Tragic characters should not be *gratuitously* evil; otherwise they will lose our sympathy. Even a morally flawed character should be basically good (see b8–15).

(2) A character should receive an "appropriate" personality. It is not right to ascribe to one type of person, according to social standing, behaviour that is not normal for that type.

(3) The character should be "like", literally; but like what? This means either that the type should be recognisable to us as one we know, i.e. lifelike, or that it should be like us. As there is no explanation or example, Aristotle must have regarded the meaning as obvious. At 53b5 we were told that we feel pity for those "like", i.e. like ourselves. But 54b10, the discussion of lifelike portraiture, and *On Poets* frag. *5, support the former interpretation. Clearly a character who is not lifelike will also be unlike ourselves, so the first explanation brings the second with it.

(4) The character should be consistent; if someone who behaves inconsistently is to be portrayed, the poet must consistently portray such behaviour. Achilles' changeability was perhaps in Aristotle's mind: he calls his character at *Iliad* XXIV 569 "inconsistent" (*Homeric Questions* frag. 168R.)

54a17 A brief parenthesis recalls the definition of CHARACTER as that which reveals DECISION (50b9).

"[The tragedy] will have character" Not all tragedies possess character: see on 50a12. Others translate "[the speech or the action] will possess character", or (very freely) "there will be character".

54a20 "every class [of person]" Aristotle's opinions about women and slaves were standard for his time, and certainly not progressive: see *Politics* I 5.1254b13, 13.1260a20, 34–6, where women are said to be capable of a virtue less high than that of men, and slaves to need only as much virtue as will enable them to do their work.

54a22 "manly" I.e. brave; "manly brings out the implication of the Greek word *andreios*, which derives from *anēr*, "man, husband". I follow the MSS here. Kassel alters the text so it says "it is possible for a woman to be manly in character" (see Note on the Text). The meaning is the same; qualities less suited to particular types of person should be attributed to them to a lesser extent.

54a26 "the model for the representation" Literally "the person providing the representation", i.e. an actual person, whom the poet has in mind when he creates the character. Cf. *On Poets* frag. *5 (end).

54a29 In Euripides' *Orestes*, Menelaus, in refusing to help his nephew Orestes (lines 682ff.), is portrayed as baser than the needs of the plot demand. This violates the requirement that the characters should be good. Aristotle uses this example again at 61b21.

54a30 In the *Scylla*, a lost dithyramb by Timotheus (see on 48a15), Odysseus lamented the members of his crew who were devoured by the monster. This example gives the opposite of a manly woman—a man weeping in a womanly way, that may resemble a type we know, but *not* what we know of Odysseus. Aristotle brings up the *Scylla* again at 61b32, possibly at *Rhetoric* III 14.1415a10, and at *On Poets* frag. *5, where this same point is made more fully. The use of an example from lyric poetry shows that Aristotle is borrowing from his *On Poets* without worrying too much about the fact that he is supposed to be discussing tragedy; but he was conscious enough of the fact to add the example of Melanippe.

54a31 In the lost *Melanippe the Wise* of Euripides, the heroine displayed a cleverness in argument that many thought inappropriate. In her father's absence she secretly gave birth to twins (their father was the god Poseidon). She left them in a remote place to die, but when her father returned it was found that a cow was suckling them. It was falsely supposed that the cow had given them birth, and her father decided that these unnatural creatures should be burned. Melanippe attempted to save them by a rationalistic argument intended to prove that cows could not give birth to human children; but her speech failed, and she had to confess the truth, whereupon Poseidon intervened to save her and her babies.

54a32 "Iphigeneia at Aulis" In Euripides' play, Iphigeneia is at first horrified to learn that her father has reluctantly agreed to sacrifice her so that the Greek fleet can sail to Troy. But when her death seems inevitable, she willingly offers to die for the Greek cause. Her first reaction is revealed at lines 1211ff., where she begs her father to spare her, and her second at 1368ff.

54a33–b8 Like PLOT (52a18–21), CHARACTER should follow the principle of necessity or probability. Cf. 51b8–9, where this is implied. Aristotle digresses to stress that plots should not contain what is impossible or improbable, before he proceeds to bad traits of character. The first two ideas reappear at 60a26–b2, and all three at 61b9–24 (with similar examples) and *T.C.* 6(iii)-(vi), always in the same order. He is probably drawing on an account of error in poetry, and what makes a good poet, in his *On Poets* (see on 54a30, b18).

54a36 "and it is either . . . " It would have been clearer if Aristotle had written "just as" instead of "and".

54a37 "solutions of plots" Aristotle only explains this term ("unravelling" or "dénouement") at 55b24–32, where it is distinguished from the "knotting" or "complication".

54b1 "the plot itself" The Arabic reads "character itself" but this is clearly a mistake.

"contrivance" This originally denoted a kind of crane that was used to waft a god onto the stage at the end of the play, so he could pronounce on the fate of the characters (the so-called *deus ex machina*). Because of misuses of this device, it came to mean the bringing on of any character who was used arbitrarily to unravel a plot that had become excessively complicated.

"in the *Medea*" The reference is to Euripides' *Medea* (see on 53b27). Aristotle is probably criticising the very end of the play, where Medea is saved from her husband's vengeance by being unexpectedly whisked away to Athens in the supernatural chariot of her grandfather, the sun-god Helios (lines 1317ff.). This is supported by the reference to the gods that follows. At 61b20, in a parallel context, he criticises the play for another "improbability", the unexpected entry of King Aegeus of Athens, who offers Medea a safe refuge in Athens if she can once reach the city (lines 663–758). As this is another vital element in the drama's resolution, Aristotle may have it too in mind.

54b2 "sailing home" So the Arabic: the word is corrupt in the other sources. In Homer's *Iliad* (II 109–210), Agamemnon proposes to the troops that they should abandon the Trojan war and sail home. He intends to arouse their spirit for fighting, but his ruse has the opposite effect—they all rush to the ships. The goddess Athena, to save the Greeks from failure, inspires Odysseus to try to stop their flight, which he does. The "contrivance" is her intervention.

Aristotle discussed this in his *Homeric Questions* (frag. 142R.), as follows: "Why does Agamemnon make trial of the Greeks, and acts so that the exact opposite of what he wanted almost happened? It was prevented by a contrivance—Athena prevented it—but artifice is bad poetic practice, to resolve the situation otherwise than from the plot itself. But it is proper to poetry to represent probable events, and quite appropriate for poets to introduce crises". A long explanation follows of why it was probable that the Greeks would be in despair at this point, and of why Agamemnon's trial of his men was necessary, despite its consequences. "In fact the resolution does not result from a contrivance; when things happen in accord with probability, *this* is not a contrivance, but it is [so] when a god intervenes. In saying what was likely to happen among [the Greeks], [Homer] ascribed to a god the idea Odysseus had of doing what he would be likely to do." Thus, he implies, Athena's intervention was unnecessary. But he accepts the common use of a god in a prologue (as in Euripides), or at the end of a play, to tell us facts beyond human knowledge.

54b7 "outside the tragedy" I.e. outside the incidents depicted on stage. The same point is made at 60a29–32.

In *Oedipus the King*, there are several improbabilities in those parts of the story that are presupposed by the play. One, cited at 60a30, is why the new king, Oedipus, did not inquire into the death of his predecessor Laius.

54b8–15 The need to portray tragic characters as better than we are, and the comparison with painters who improve the looks of those they represent, was first stated at 48a1–18, cf. 61b12, *Politics* III 11.1281b10–15. Here there is a further point: even a person represented in a lifelike way, in that he has a fault of character, should also be good. The example is Homer's portrayal in the *Iliad* of Achilles as angry and stubborn but still admirable (contrast Plato's negative judgement of Achilles at *Republic* III 391A-C).

54b12 "other such traits" "Traits" is supplied. Aristotle still has in mind the idea that poets represent actual people, whom they have in mind as models when creating their characters (cf. 54a26).

54b14 We might expect the example to illustrate anger, but "stubbornness" is close enough. The words "an example of stubbornness" have been transposed by Lobel. Without the transposition, the text must be translated "an example of harshness is how even Homer [portrays] Achilles as good" (but why "*even* Homer"?), or (with the Latin and MS A) " . . . how Agathon and Homer [portray] Achilles". Agathon portrayed Achilles in his tragedy *Telephus*.

54b15 "[the poet] should guard against these things" I.e. errors in tragic character. This picks up 54a16, on what one should aim at and avoid in creating characters.

54b15–18 "reactions" A difficult sentence, which appears to mean that the poet should avoid provoking reactions or giving rise to perceptions contrary to those poetry should aim at, i.e. he should avoid causing displeasure. The "perceptions" are clearly those of the audience, as at 51a7 and 61b29, and most probably refer to effects that fail on stage, as at 55a22ff., and for which the poet can be held responsible.

54b18 "in my published work" I.e. the dialogue *On Poets*. This confirms that Aristotle is drawing on his account of error in poetry, and how to be a good poet, in that work (see on 54a33–b8). Compare *On Poets* frags. *4–7.

54b19–55a21 Aristotle now reverts to one of the main parts of plot, RECOGNITION; the topic remains plot, in various aspects, until 56a32. The explanation for this unannounced shift is the idea of error in poetry, which has just been mentioned and reappears at b35 below. The preceding reference to his *On Poets*, and lack of explicit structure, suggest that he is still borrowing material from his account of error in poetry in that work (perhaps in Book II); see the previous note.

Aristotle arranges the six kinds of recognition in ascending order, with the best last, according to how well the proof is integrated into the plot. The recognitions, and the proofs on which they depend, are divided into "artless" and "artful"; "artful" proofs and recognitions depend on the logic of the situation (which art constructs), but "artless" ones, e.g. scars or necklaces, do not. This classification of proofs is also found at *Rhetoric* I 2.1355b35 (see on *T.C.* 13).

54b22 "the spear-head that the earth-born bear" A quotation from tragedy, perhaps from Euripides' lost *Antigone*, in which Creon recognised the child of Antigone and Haemon by a birthmark of this shape, marking descent from the "Earthborn" men of Thebes, who were sprung from the dragon's teeth which Cadmus sowed.

"[birthmarks like] stars" When the gods brought Pelops back to life he was given an ivory shoulder in place of his own, which the goddess Demeter had eaten at the banquet where he was served as the entrée. His descendants, including Thyestes, inherited the marks of this.

54b23 "Carcinus" Of the two (related) tragedians of this name, the younger is almost certainly meant; he lived in the early fourth century. He is also mentioned at 55a26, *Rhetoric* II 23.1400b9, III 16.1417b18, *Ethics* VII 7.1150b10.

54b24 "necklaces" Recognition of a baby by the trinkets found with it was apparently common, and occurs in Euripides' *Ion*.

54b25 In Sophocles' *Tyro*, Tyro's sons were set adrift in a small boat, which was kept and eventually led to their being recognised by their mother.

54b26 In the *Odyssey* Homer twice uses the scar to bring about the recognition of Odysseus—when he is accidentally recognised by his old nurse as she bathes his feet (XIX 386–475, the "Bath-scene"), and when he deliberately reveals the scar to his loyal swineherd and cowherd, to convince them that he really is Odysseus (XXI 205–25). The first instance is superior, as it involves a reversal: Odysseus, by his own action in asking for a respectful older woman to wash his feet, and not one of the young women who keep company with his enemies (the suitors), himself brings about a recognition he is anxious to postpone.

In his lost *Homeric Questions* Aristotle criticised the use of such "signs", since "by such reasoning, according to the poet, everyone with a scar is Odysseus" (quoted by Eustathius 1873.28).

54b31 "recognitions" This is is supplied.

"not artful" Literally "inartistic"; such recognitions do not derive from the principles of the art of poetry, but are arbitrarily contrived by the poet, which is why they are not very good.

For this example, from Euripides' *Iphigeneia in Tauris*, see on 52b6 and below, 55b2–15. But Iphigeneia's recognition of her brother belongs to the best type of recognition (see 55a18).

"Orestes makes it known" MS B and the Arabic have "she recognises", perhaps rightly.

54b35 "the error we [just] mentioned" I.e. the first type of recognition, involving signs or tokens. Euripides could have made Orestes bring with him the piece of his sister's weaving which he describes. Aristotle's reference to "error" is an indication that his topic is still how to avoid error in poetry (see on 54a30).

54b36 "the shuttle's voice" This is probably a quotation from Sophocles' lost play. Tereus was married to Procne, but raped her sister Philomela. To keep Philomela silent about his crime, Tereus tore out her tongue, but she revealed the secret to her sister by weaving a picture on her loom.

55a1 Dicaeogenes was a minor tragedian and dithyrambic poet of ca 400 B.C. (see also *On Poets* frag. *3.18). Nothing is known of his play.

55a2 "the tale told to Alcinous" In the *Odyssey* (VIII 521ff.) Odysseus weeps to hear the bard Demodocus sing of the Wooden Horse: this leads to the disclosure of his identity to his host Alcinous and the Phaeacian court. He then tells Alcinous the tale of his adventures

(Books IX-XII). Aristotle says that his tale arouses pity and terror (*Rhetoric* III 16.1417a14).

55a4–6 In Aeschylus' *Libation Bearers* (lines 168ff., 205ff.) Electra finds a lock of hair dedicated at her father's tomb, and a footprint near it, that are like hers; she deduces from this that her brother Orestes has come.

55a6–8 Polyidus the SOPHIST is unknown, unless he is the same as Polyidus of Selymbria, an avant-garde dithyrambic poet, musician and critic of the early fourth century. Whether as poet or critic, he proposed a better way of bringing about the recognition of Orestes by Iphigeneia (cited again at b10 below). When Orestes was on the point of being sacrificed, it would be natural for him to say in Iphigeneia's hearing that his sister too had been a victim of human sacrifice (cf. the plot-summary at 55b2).

55a6 "**[proposed by]**" Literally "of".

55a7 "**he said**" This omitted in MS A and the Latin.

"**to infer**" I.e. to reason, evidently aloud so that Iphigeneia could hear him.

55a8 We know nothing more about the plot of the lost *Tydeus* by Theodectes (for whom see on 52a27). Tydeus was the father of Diomedes, but no known version of the story fits what we hear here; presumably Tydeus came looking for his son and was about to be killed by him, in ignorance of his identity, but was saved when he said he had come to find his son Diomedes.

55a10 "***Sons of Phineus***" Phineus blinded his sons (or let them be blinded) and left them to die in a remote place, because of the jealousy of their stepmother. They were rescued, and the guilty persons were punished with death at the scene of the crime. The recognition is one of fact rather than of identity. Whose play is meant is unknown (perhaps Sophocles' *Phineus*?), but Aristotle assumes that we know it well.

"**the women**" Literally "they" (feminine), i.e. the stepmother and perhaps the children's nurse, if she had a hand in the crime. The sharp changes of grammatical subject have rarely been understood, leading to the mistranslation *Daughters of Phineus* and the absurd idea that his daughters were the bird-like Harpies who tormented him.

55a12 "**combined recognition resulting from a false inference**" This is usually taken to mean "made up from a combination of true and false inference", but it is surely a false inference from the combination of two premises that yields the recognition. False inference is discussed again at 60a18–26 (see note), where it is the false reasoning that, if q follows from p, and q exists, p must exist too. E.g. "when it rains the ground is wet; the ground is wet; so it has rained." But there may be other reasons why the ground is wet, e.g. that someone poured a bucket of water on it. The example is Aristotle's (*Sophistical Refutations* 5.167b6).

55a13 The example, from a lost play by an unknown author, is obscure. The play's title shows that Odysseus returned in disguise with a false report of his own death. Apparently the playwright led the audience to expect that Odysseus would reveal his identity by stringing the great bow that nobody else could bend (as seen in *Odyssey* XXI), but in fact Odysseus did so as a result of claiming that he would be able to recognise the bow. How exactly this worked is not clear. Only MS B and the Arabic preserve the words "but nobody else . . . the bow".

55a16 That the best type of recognition comes directly from the plot, as already stated at 52a16–20; for that in the *Oedipus*, see on 52a32.

55a17 "astonishment" Cf. 52a1–6, where Aristotle says that AMAZEMENT accompanies pity and terror, and is best aroused by events that come to pass logically but not as we expect.

55a18 On the recognition of Iphigeneia by Orestes in Euripides' *Iphigeneia in Tauris* see on 52b6 and also 54b31, 55b2–15.

55a20 "made-up [incidents] and necklaces" Not only material signs, like necklaces, but also verbally contrived recognitions are inferior. After "made-up" all sources except the Arabic have "signs", which is probably an explanation added by a scribe (see Note on the Text).

55a21 "Recognitions as a result of inference" Both true and false inferences are presumably included.

55a22–56a32 Aristotle's discussion of avoiding error in tragedy continues with various remarks about how the work should be completed using other parts of tragedy too, e.g. diction, spectacle and song.

55a22 "using diction to bring them to completion" The priority of plot extends to the actual order of composition. The comedian Menander (ca 341–291 B.C.) is said to have planned his plots in detail before he wrote the verses, regarding this as the most important part of his task (Plutarch, *Moralia* 347F).

55a23 "before his eyes" The poet should visualise the events both as they happened and as they will appear, when represented, to the audience. "Before the eyes" is almost a technical term for "vivid" in the *Rhetoric*, where it is defined as "to indicate things in activity" (*energeia*, III 11.1411b25). If the poet sees the action vividly, then the audience will too. Compare 62a17.

55a24 "very vividly" So MS B (*enargestata*). MS A and the Latin have "very actively" (*energestata*). Although there is a connexion in the *Rhetoric* between vividness and *energeia*, the word order supports MS B's reading.

55a25 "what is suitable" This is usually thought to denote only movements and stage business, but more probably covers the far wider range of character, reasoning and diction (cf. *On Poets* frag. *5, "the good poet . . . is able to invent what Andromache would say . . . in diction, character and reasoning"). In the *Rhetoric*, the SUITABLE (*to prepon*) refers above all to suitable expression, and is vital to persuading us (III 12.1414a28, "what is believable arises from what is suitable"): the concept reappears in terms of diction at 58b14 and 59a4, and note the reference to believability below (a30).

55a26 "Carcinus" His play, evidently entitled *Amphiaraus*, is lost, but must have contained some statement that was ludicrously contradicted by what was actually happening on the stage. On Carcinus see on 54b23.

55a27 "as a spectator" Most editors delete this, believing that it is the poets' vision that is in question, but this is unnecessary (see Note on the Text). Compare 60a15, where we are told that the absurdity of the pursuit of Hector in the *Iliad* would be obvious on the stage, but passes unnoticed in the poem.

55a29 Aristotle's second recommendation is difficult. It is parallel in wording to the first: just as the poet should work out his composition by visualising it, so too he should do so with gestures. The context tells against the view that the *actors'* gestures are meant—why should this explain the *poets'* natures? The usual interpretation may seem odd but must be right. To represent faithfully his characters' emotions, the poet should try to feel them himself as he composes, using the gestures and facial expressions that go with such states. This is easier to understand if we remember that it was the invariable practice to read everything aloud; the poet should perform his drafts to see whether they evoke the right emotions. Such a theory is parodied by Aristophanes, who makes Euripides dress in rags and Agathon in women's clothes when they are writing the parts of impoverished heroes or of women (*Acharnians* 412, *Thesmophoriazusae* 148–52). The epic reciter Ion, when asked by Socrates whether he imagines in his mind that he is present at the events related in Homer, replies that he does, and his eyes water and his hair stands on end (Plato, *Ion* 535B-C). Ion experiences the physical signs of pity and terror as he performs: Aristotle suggests that a good tragedian should try to experience them as he composes. Elsewhere he says that orators who "bring their speeches to completion with gestures, voice, costume and delivery [i.e. acting] in general" arouse more pity, as they put things "before the eyes" (*Rhetoric* II 8.1386a32–5).

55a30 "Given the same nature" I.e. given the same natural talents as poets.

"who experience the emotions" (*pathē*) Literally "who are in the emotions".

55a32 "most truthfully" Truth to life (not in its particulars but in its universals), though little stressed in the *Poetics*, is in fact vital to Aristotle's theory of REPRESENTATION; see *On Poets*, Testimonium A(i).

55a32 The good poet can put himself into the minds of others because he is either gifted or mad. It is wrong to alter the text to make it say that poetry belongs to the genius *rather than* the madman: the important point is that both can go "outside themselves", although in different ways. Elsewhere, Aristotle postulates a link between genius and insanity (*Rhetoric* II 15.1390b27–9, cf. the pseudo-aristotelian *Problems* 30.954a32). Plato held that poets compose in a state of divinely inspired madness, thereby paying them a very back-handed compliment—they hardly understand what they are saying (e.g. *Apology* 22A-C). Aristotle's distinction between genius and insanity is a response to this. Compare *Problems* 30.954a38, "Maracus of Syracuse was *even* a better poet when he was beside himself".

55a34–b23 Aristotle next shows, with two detailed examples, how one should first sketch out a story in UNIVERSAL terms, and then fill in the details.

55a34 "stories" (*logoi*): this is not clearly distinct from PLOTS.

"those [already] made up" I.e. traditional stories (cf. 51b19–25), as opposed to those the poet makes up himself. This is better than the alternative translation "both those that are [already] composed [by others] and when he is himself composing", which produces a recommendation that a poet should practise analysing plays so as to learn the art of plot-construction.

55b1 "episodes" Aristotle uses EPISODE of a scene or act in a play, and by extension a scene or episode in an epic. All epics and plays have episodes, but these should not be irrelevant (see 51b34).

55b3 On Euripides' *Iphigeneia in Tauris*, see on 52b6, 54a7, b31. Aristotle evidently regarded this, along with Sophocles' *Oedipus the King*, as among the finest of Greek tragedies, which is why he summarises it here. Perhaps he considered that it stands to the *Oedipus* among tragedies as the *Odyssey* stands to the *Iliad* among epics, since, like the *Odyssey*, it eventually has a happy ending.

55b7 "that is not a universal" Literally "outside the universal". As the text stands, the *reason* for the gods' command to Orestes is said to be a PARTICULAR, not a UNIVERSAL (and so not essential to the outline); it is his need to escape from his madness, which is particular to him (see b13). The *fact* of the command, and Orestes' aim in visiting the Taurians, are both said to be "outside the plot", i.e. not represented in the drama (cf. 54b7, 60a29); both are mentioned in the prologue (lines 82ff.). What matters for the plot is that Orestes went thither. Editors usually delete "for some reason that is not a universal", and understand "outside the plot" as "not an integral part of the plot"; but there is no need to depart from the MSS (see Note on the Text).

55b10 "Polyidus" See on 55a6.

55b12 "supply the names" Compare 51b12.

55b13 "particular [to the story]" Orestes is captured because of a recurrence of his madness (*Iphigeneia in Tauris* lines 260–355), and he and his sister escape because of the supposed defilement of the goddess' statue by the presence of a murderer; the statue must be purified by washing it in the sea (lines 1031ff.). Both EPISODES follow from his murder of his mother, which drove him insane in the first place. Others think suitability to the characters is meant.

55b15 On the correct use of EPISODES to give epic its appropriate grandeur, in contrast to the practice of tragedy, see 59a35–b7 and b22–31.

55b17 "story" (*logos*): see on 55a34. On the "double plot" of the *Odyssey*, which ends well for the good and badly for the bad, see 53a30–3.

"not long" "Not" has fallen out, by an easy error, in all sources except the Arabic.

55b24–56a10 Aristotle now introduces another way of looking at PLOT, in terms of COMPLICATION (or DEVELOPMENT) and SOLUTION; he already mentioned this at 54a37. The solution is not quite the same as the dénouement, as it is more than the climactic scene of the drama. The basic idea is of tying and untying a knot, but SOLUTION also has the connotations of solving a problem. The practical reason why he makes these definitions is made clear at 56a9, after a digression.

55b25 "outside [the tragedy]" See 53b32, 54b3–7.

"often some of those inside it" The COMPLICATION can be entirely outside the drama. Aristotle expects that tragedy is predominantly a representation of the SOLUTION, which is the representation of the change of fortune.

55b26 "[tragedy]" We might have expected a word meaning "part" (and translators usually supply one), but there is none that is feminine, as the text demands; as often, Aristotle is equating tragedy and plot.

55b28 "the beginning" Not of the tragedy on the stage, but of the action and the prior incidents presupposed by the action.

55b29 For the lost *Lynceus* of Theodectes see on 52a27.

"its parents' explanation" Literally "their explanation". It seems that Lynceus escaped with Hypermnestra but not with their baby; the baby's capture somehow led to their own arrest by Danaus. "Explanation" and "is the solution" are preserved by the Arabic only (see Note on the Text).

"demand for the death penalty" So MS B (see Note on the Text): the other sources have "accusation of murder", which is hard to fit into what we know of the story. King Danaus demanded Lynceus' execution, but in the event was executed himself (52a27–9).

55b32–56a3 The abrupt introduction of four kinds of tragedy is generally regarded as one of the major puzzles of the *Poetics*. Each kind arises from the predominance in it of a single QUALITATIVE PART or subpart of tragedy. Thus CHARACTER is one of the six QUALITATIVE PARTS, but tragedies are also based on REVERSAL and RECOGNITION, and on SUFFERING (*pathos*), which are parts of PLOT (52b9–10). Aristotle lists four similar kinds of epic at 59b7. We may also compare his three-way classification of dance into representation of characters, sufferings or emotions (*pathos* means both), and actions (47a27), and the three similar kinds of MUSIC at *Politics* VIII 7.1342b32 (*On Poets* Testimonium A(ii)), i.e. those relating to character, action and ecstasy (an emotion). If we divide actions into simple and complex, we may obtain from this classification the four kinds of epic at 59b7. In his biological works he often applies to the same group of animals more than one system of classification, in order to bring out their full diversity and interconnexions. He may be doing something similar here, to bring out as many different yet important aspects of tragedy as possible.

"its parts too are of the same number" This has never been said; tragedy has six QUALITATIVE PARTS, not four. Many think SONG and SPECTACLE are the two disregarded here. But Aristotle is certainly putting the parts of PLOT on the same level as a PART of tragedy, CHARACTER. Moreover he uses such a procedure elsewhere (see on 59b10). The discussion of how tragedy can achieve its effect deals in particular with CHARACTER (52b28–53a17, 54a16–b15), SUFFERING (53b15–54a13), RECOGNITION (53b15–54a13, 54b19–55a20) and SPECTACLE (53b1–11, 55a22–9); perhaps Aristotle draws on this discussion to formulate his classification of tragedy here. This is preferable to the usual assumption that the *Poetics* incorporates divergent drafts and is imperfectly revised.

56a1 *"Ajax and Ixion"* The madness and violent deeds of Ajax, the great warrior before Troy, who claimed the armour of Achilles and went berserk when denied it, culminate in his suicide on stage in Sophocles' play *Ajax*. Other versions were by Carcinus, Theodectes and Astydamas. Ixion, the first murderer and also a would-be rapist of Hera, was punished by being bound to a revolving wheel; no plays about him survive. Aristotle puts the *Iliad* in the same category of poems about *pathos* (59b14), which shows that such plays need not necessarily represent suffering on the stage; it need only predominate in the action.

"tragedy of character" I.e. one in which character predominates. Tragedies differ in the degree to which they represent character (so

50a24–9). Epics other than Homer's represent people who lack character (cf. 60a11).

"**Women of Phthia** and **Peleus**" These were both perhaps by Sophocles, although Euripides too wrote a *Peleus*. The titles reveal that both plays concerned the family of Achilles, who was the son of Peleus and came from Phthia. An example from epic where character predominates is the *Odyssey* (59b15): in this case, Aristotle's judgment is confirmed by the work's survival.

56a2 "**spectacle**" The name of the fourth kind of tragedy has been miscopied, but Bywater's restoration of it as SPECTACLE convincingly explains the meaningless letters and the change in grammatical construction (see Note on the Text; the MSS contain an almost identical miscopying at 58a5). SPECTACLE matches the examples well. In the parallel classification of epic at 59b9 the *first* kind of epic is listed as "simple", and nothing corresponds to "spectacle" (the others are the same as the kinds of tragedy here). But spectacle is one part epic lacks (59b10). Aristotle recognises the existence of a class of plays that produce pity and terror by means of spectacle at 53b1–11, although he regards them as inferior to plays that do so by means of plot. It is reasonable he should mention them here, and no doubt they usually had "simple" plots without reversal or recognition (52a14).

"**Daughters of Phorcys**" The daughters of Phorcys were either the Graeae, three hideous old women who guarded the Gorgons, or the monstrous Gorgons themselves. They were outwitted by Perseus. Aeschylus wrote a play with this title.

"**Prometheus**" The Prometheus trilogy ascribed to Aeschylus consisted of three plays with this title, one of which, the *Prometheus Bound*, is extant, and contains a number of spectacular effects, for which Aeschylus was celebrated in later criticism ("he uses spectacular effects and plots more to produce monstrous astonishment than to deceive", *Life of Aeschylus*).

56a3 "**[dramas set] in Hades**" E.g. perhaps Aeschylus' lost *Sisyphus* and *Psychagogoi*. Aristophanes refers to such plays at *Acharnians* 388–92 and frag. 149K. They would be hospitable to spectacular and horrible effects, notably terrifying masks, as an ancient commentator on *Acharnians* 388 reports.

"**attempt to have all [the parts]**" Not every tragedy will contain all the QUALITATIVE PARTS (see on 50a12).

56a5–9 Aristotle disagrees with recent critics of tragedy who expected each poet to excel all his predecessors in every part. He implies that they are guilty of using false standards of comparison, in that only tragedies with the same plot are strictly comparable with one another.

56a9 "**development**" This is a synonym for COMPLICATION.

56a10 "harmonise both" I.e. complication and solution. The text is corrupt, and I translate a correction by Immisch. Another emendation gives the sense "always excel at both".

56a10 "what we have often said" The advice to avoid an "epic" plot-structure has not in fact been given before in this form, but is implied at 51a16–35, and less obviously at 49b12. Later Aristotle asserts that even epics should avoid such a plot-structure as far as possible (59a18ff., especially b1–7), and that even the *Iliad* and *Odyssey* are less unified than tragedy because of it (62b3–11).

56a12 "more than one plot" Or "more than one story" (see on 50a4, 53a37). "Plot" here must include the EPISODES that enlarge the basic story and give the epic its length (59b17–31), as in the case of the *Odyssey* (55b15–23). Aristotle's terminology is unclear, but his thought is not; compare 62b7–11.

56a13 The example is hypothetical—nobody composed such a tragedy.

56a14 Because of the sheer scale of the epic, its parts can harmonise with the size of the poem as a whole. A tragedy with an equivalent number of parts would seem too fragmented. What are mere episodes in epic are material for whole plots in tragedy.

56a15 "far from one's expectation" I.e. far worse than one would have supposed.

56a16 "Sack of Troy" This was the title of an epic sequel to the *Iliad*, by Arctinus of Miletus (ca 700 B.C.); a summary of its plot reveals that it was much more a chronicle than an artistic unity. Aristotle makes a similar point about other poems of the Epic Cycle at 59b1–7. Several lost tragedies had this title.

56a17 Euripides dramatised incidents from the *Sack of Troy* in his *Trojan Women* and *Hecuba*.

"or a Niobe" Niobe is an unexpected name here, as there were no epics about her, although Aeschylus certainly wrote a tragedy called *Niobe*. I suspect it is a mistake, connected perhaps with the loss of "or" in all the sources. If so, the correct title cannot be restored with certainty, although the *Thebaid* has been proposed from the Arabic. This epic related the story of the Argive attack on Thebes, and was ascribed to Homer; Aeschylus dramatised its climax in his extant *Seven against Thebes*.

56a18 "even Agathon" Aristotle had considerable regard for Agathon: see on 51b21.

56a19–25 This is one of the most obscure passages in the *Poetics*, because the sequence of thought is hard to establish, and the basic topic is not clear. As it stands in the MSS, the people in question are the inferior poets who compose "epic" plots, including even Agathon;

there is no need to change the text to make the paragraph a discussion of him alone.

56a19 "In reversals and in simple incidents" I.e. in the diverse episodes, simple and complex, that such poets' plots contain; or does it mean "in complex and simple plots"?.

56a20 "they aim to arouse the amazement they desire" Literally "they aim at the amazing things . . . " The MSS have "they aim at what they desire amazingly", which makes no sense, unless it means "they have amazing success in aiming at what they desire", i.e. the tragic effect. But the next sentence is then difficult. I translate a conjecture by Tyrwhitt, which changes only one letter (see Note on the Text). This provides the paragraph with a coherent and appropriate topic—how inferior poets aim to arouse pity and terror but moral satisfaction too, which Aristotle considers a less appropriate emotion for tragedy to aim at (53a30–6). There is no conflict with his recommendation for the best plot of tragedy.

56a21 "For this is tragic and morally satisfying" Amazement is tragic, i.e. it arouses pity and terror, the emotions required of a good tragedy (52b38). On the importance of surprise effects, provided they are in accord with probability, for arousing these emotions see on 52a1–11. Those who translate the previous sentence as it stands take this one as a statement of what the poets desire; but this strains the Greek.

"This is possible" "This" is ambiguous, but surely means the arousal of pity, terror and moral satisfaction caused by the downfall of someone like Sisyphus.

56a22 The defeat of a man who is clever but wicked, or brave but unjust (like Macbeth), can clearly amaze us; it provokes pity and terror because of the man's good quality, but moral satisfaction too because he receives what he deserves. The arousal of pity and terror is obviously desirable, that of moral satisfaction less so (see on 53a23–38); the ideal tragic hero should be better than the average, and definitely not like Sisyphus.

"Sisyphus" Renowned for his cunning, Sisyphus was the subject of a number of plays. He was punished for his misdeeds by perpetually rolling a boulder in Hades.

56a23 "This is even probable" "This" must mean the amazing defeat of a cunning man and similar plot-structures. "Even" is omitted by MS A and the Latin, but is favored by the argument. Aristotle ironically concedes that such plots can be claimed to accord with probability, but only because what is probable does not always happen! Agathon's verses about probability (frag. 9), which Aristotle quotes at *Rhetoric* II 24.1402a10, are mere special pleading, and do not excuse him from the requirement that the tragic incidents should be probable or necessary.

56a25–32 From inferior plots that lack coherence it is a small step to Aristotle's next requirement—that the chorus be properly integrated into the action: compare *On Poets* frag. *3.15. In his later dramas, Euripides' chorus makes a diminished contribution to the plot.

56a27 "in the rest" I.e. in poets after Euripides. So the Greek: the Arabic reads "in most [poets]". Agathon evidently took the final step of using prefabricated lyrics ("interludes") not necessarily written for a particular play; this was in ca 410 B.C. Clearly his innovation was often followed in fourth-century tragedy.

"no more" The negative survives only in the Arabic.

56a30–2 This passage may reflect contemporary complaints by poets about tragic actors' insertions of speeches taken from other dramas. Aristotle implies that the poets have no right to complain, as they set a bad example themselves.

56a33 After the long discussion of how to avoid error in tragedy, including PLOT, CHARACTER, and other parts of it as well, Aristotle resumes his systematic account of the remaining two main qualitative parts of tragedy, REASONING and DICTION. These are paired because the DICTION is intimately related to the REASONING, which is expressed in words.

56a34–b8 The treatment of REASONING is very cursory; Aristotle is content to refer his audience to his *Rhetoric*, Books I–II. Compare the summaries at *Rhetoric* I 2.1356a1–4, III 1.1403b6–14. He does not refer to the use of reasoning to represent CHARACTER, which is mentioned at e.g. 54a18.

56a37 "speech" (*logos*) This is equivalent to DICTION, and excludes only the sung portions.

"The types of these" Literally "parts"; this means the kinds of effects to be produced by speech. Again "part" (*meros*) is equivalent to "kind" or "element" (*eidos, idea*); cf. b3, b25, 58b12. The first part of REASONING is similar to the description of it at 50b11, except that here Aristotle omits universal statements.

56a38 Its second part is the arousal of EMOTIONS (*pathē*) in the audience. Examples are given, because until now *pathos* has been used to mean SUFFERING or violent deed. The inclusion of anger shows that the emotions that tragedy arouses are not restricted to pity and terror (see on 49b28). At *Ethics* II 5.1105b21 Aristotle also mentions appetite, confidence, envy, joy, love, hate, longing and jealousy; here only the painful emotions are exemplified, as is appropriate to tragedy.

56b2–7 Aristotle now returns to tragedy in particular. Many of the effects the REASONING produces can also be produced by the incidents: there is a rhetoric of action as well as of words.

56b5 "production" I.e. on stage.

56b7 "the element" Cf. b3 above. This depends on an emendation, which is supported by the Latin (see Note on the Text): the other MSS have "pleasant things". Another emendation produces the sense "if it were apparent as needed".

56b9 Before turning to the DICTION, Aristotle disposes of one aspect of it that might seem relevant—intonation, perhaps along with pronunciation and punctuation. He dismisses it likewise at the start of his account of DICTION in *Rhetoric* III (1.1403b20–36), noting that the subject had yet to be studied scientifically. It could be considered important, as ancient texts had no punctuation, italics, etc., and were always read aloud.

56b10 "the art of delivery" (*hupokritikē*) Literally "the art of acting". The term covers DELIVERY in rhetoric as well. Compare *Rhetoric* III 1.1403b31, where its parts are loudness, pitch and rhythm.

"mastery" Aristotle implies someone with a mastery of its principles, not just an outstanding practitioner.

56b11 "command . . . " Each of these requires a different intonation, and so a different delivery. Together with "narration" and "invocation", they represent the entire classification of Protagoras (see next note, and compare 57a21–3).

56b15 The sophist Protagoras of Abdera (ca. 485–415 B.C.) complained that the first line of Homer's *Iliad* confuses the first pair Aristotle listed, i.e. command and wish. As Protagoras was first to classify the forms of the sentence, his over-zealousness in applying his discovery is excusable.

56b20–59a16 Of the last of the four parts of tragedy, Aristotle deals with DICTION (*lexis*) in detail, starting from the first principles of grammar and syntax, which were not yet distinguished as separate subjects, but were taught along with literature. At 56b20–57a30 and 58a8–17 he discusses language in general, not poetry or tragedy in particular, and the relevance of 57a31–58a7 to tragedy and epic only becomes clear from his examples. But language in general is an essential part of poetry, and needed to be discussed somewhere. If Aristotle's account seems at times like a naive version of a modern grammar, this is a measure of its pioneering qualities; his work laid the foundation for the systematic study of language.

"the parts of diction" Aristotle begins at the smallest unit of diction and goes up to the largest. These are not the same as the later "parts of speech".

56b21 I follow the order of the parts given in the Arabic (see Note on the Text).

56b22 "element" The smallest unit of diction is for Aristotle the ELE-MENT or letter (*stoicheion*), not the phoneme. Since in ancient Greek almost every sound corresponds to a single letter, and every letter to a single sound, Aristotle had no need of the modern concept.

"sound" By SOUND ("voice", *phōnē*), Aristotle means sounds produced by the throats of animals including man, as distinct from mere "noise" (*psophos*). This is why he has to exclude the sounds animals make: man is distinct because he uses sounds to produce articulate speech (*dialektos*). See *Enquiry into Animals* IV 9.535a27, and *On Poets* frag. *3.12.

56b23 "composite" So the Arabic: the other sources have "intelligible", by an easy error. In the next line the Arabic has "none of which is a composite sound, none of which I mean . . . ", wrongly.

56b25–31 The types (literally "parts", see on a37) of ELEMENT are named according to how much sound ("voice") they have, and classified further by whether any contact between the different parts of the mouth is needed to produce them; this means mainly the tongue, but Aristotle knew that some elements are produced by contact between the lips (*On the Parts of Animals* II 16.660a6): so the Arabic is right to paraphrase "contact with the lips or teeth". Thus the vowel (literally "voiced [element]") has more sound than a "semi-vowel" ("half-voiced"), which in turn has more than a consonant ("voiceless"). By a SEMI-VOWEL Aristotle means what linguists call a "continuant", a sound that is not a vowel but which can continue and is not instantaneous, e.g. *n*, *r* or *s*. No doubt these were singled out as a class because, vowels excepted, only these sounds occur at the word-end in Greek (see 58a9). By CONSONANT he means what we call plosives or stops, e.g. *b*, *k*, *p* or *t*. Aristotle's triple division and terms are current in Plato's late works (*Philebus* 18B-C, *Cratylus* 424C).

56b31–4 The sophistication of this phonetic analysis, including questions of aspiration, vowel-length and pitch-accent, is explained by the advanced state of theory in the field of metrics (versification), which already had its own handbooks. Nowhere else in the *Poetics* does Aristotle refer his audience to experts outside his school; he refers to these same experts at *On the Parts of Animals* II 16.660a7.

56b36 "*gr* without an *a* is a syllable, and [it is also a syllable] with an *a*" So the Greek and the Latin; the Arabic has " . . . is not a syllable, but is [a syllable] only with an *a*". This could be right, but Aristotle has not said that a syllable must contain a vowel, only an element which has sound: this does not exclude the SEMI-VOWEL *r*. This was obviously a controversial question among the writers on metrics. Aristotle's definition of the syllable is imprecise, as there are also syllables consisting of a vowel only, e.g. *a*.

56b37 Writers on metrics were concerned with the different kinds of syllables because Greek verse depends on the principle that syllables are of two basic kinds, heavy and light (less correctly called long and short).

56b38–57a10 This is one of the most difficult passages in the *Poetics*, because the copyists found the repetitions of terms in the definitions very confusing. One passage was copied twice by mistake; there are also omissions, and the examples (when not omitted) do not match the text as it stands. Any restoration of the sense must be conjectural: I have largely followed that proposed by Bywater, with modifications suggested by the Arabic (see Note on the Text).

56b38 "particle" Literally "ligament", from anatomy. The PARTICLE receives two definitions, according to whether or not it is needed to produce a meaningful UTTERANCE, defined below at a23 as a significant combination of significant words, e.g. two or more nouns, or verbs, or noun plus verb. The first kind is the enclitic particle, a class of words in Greek which mainly indicates the tone of voice in which something is said; English uses intonation alone to produce the same nuances. Such enclitics cannot begin an UTTERANCE and cannot produce one. The second kind is what we call a preposition, yielding such UTTERANCES as "about Socrates".

"non-significant" Aristotle regards not only sounds but such small words as non-significant: SIGNIFICATION arises when something "stands for" or "is a symbol of" something else (cf. *On Interpretation* 1.16a3–4, 28). Particles only indicate relationships between other, significant, sounds.

57a6 A CONJUNCTION (literally "joint", again from anatomy) is also a non-significant word, but one that joins UTTERANCES together, e.g. "Socrates walks *and* Cleon walks".

57a10 "e.g. 'or', 'because', 'but' " This is preserved by the Arabic only.

57a10 "name" The NAME covers nouns, adjectives and probably adverbs, as well as names in our sense: such words "name" things, qualities, quantities etc. The similar definition at *On Interpretation* 1.16a19 adds that NAMES signify by convention, and gives a similar example of compound names.

57a14 "verb" Cf. the definition at *On Interpretation* 3.16b6, which makes the same distinction between NAMES and VERBS in terms of tense. Aristotle may have been the first to point this out, for Plato defines a verb as an action-word (*Sophist* 262A).

57a18 "inflection" INFLECTIONS are all formal or contextual modifications which affect the meaning, e.g. subject or object, singular or plural, including changes produced by intonation ("delivery") alone. Compare *On Interpretation* 1.16b1, 2.16b26. At *Categories* 1.1a4 even the alteration of "grammar" to "grammarian", which we would class under word-formation, is called an INFLECTION. Aristotle also uses the term in logic to describe the different forms of propositions.

57a21 "delivery" See 56b8–19.

57a23 "utterance" (*logos*) An UTTERANCE is a group of words, meaningful individually, which produces a collective meaning. It does not necessarily include a VERB, and is not necessarily a sentence or statement (predication): compare *On Interpetation* 4.16b27–17a8. Plato disagreed in both respects (*Sophist* 262A-C, a late work). The definition is formulated to distinguish the UTTERANCE from the NAME.

57a26 "definition of a human being" Aristotle gives several definitions, but most often "a two-footed animal": such phrases contain no verb, but are UTTERANCES. Only if we say *"a human being is* a two-footed animal" does the UTTERANCE turn into a proposition involving truth or falsity (so *On Interpretation* 5.17a11–14).

57a27 "a part that signifies something" I.e. a NAME or VERB, not a PARTICLE or CONJUNCTION.

57a28 The two kinds of unified UTTERANCE are distinguished likewise at *On Interpretation* 5.17a8–9, 16–17. The *Iliad* is of course an extreme example of the second type; two single UTTERANCES of the first type, e.g. "Cleon walks *and* Socrates walks", would suffice. Aristotle makes the same reference to the *Iliad* elsewhere (*Posterior Analytics* II 10.93b35, *Metaphysics* VII 4.1030b9).

57a31–58a17 Aristotle next examines those PARTS of the DICTION that have meaning in themselves, the NAMES and VERBS, which are here subsumed within NAMES. This section falls into three parts: (a) single and double NAMES, (b) their different usages and forms, and (c) their genders. (a) and (c) are limited to NAMES, but VERBS are clearly included in (b), as the examples prove (e.g. 57b10, 14). Compare *On Interpretation* 3.16b19: "verbs uttered alone of themselves are names". There are cross-references to this section of the *Poetics* in *Rhetoric* III (1.1404a39, 2.1404b7, 27).

57a32 "double" See above, a12–14. DOUBLE (compound) NAMES are more common in Greek than in English. Aristotle distinguishes (a) those made up from NAMES and "non-significant parts", e.g. prepositions and the like (e.g. "outdo" beside "do"), and (b) those made of two NAMES, e.g. "Theodore" (cf. a13 above), or "wedding-gift".

57a35 "Marseilles" The Greek colony of Massalia, in the south of France. The Arabic alone has the right reading here.

57a36 "Hermocaicoxanthus" This is a comical name compounded from three separate names of rivers in western Asia Minor, the area where the founders of Marseilles came from; the name scans in hexameter verse. "Who prays to Zeus" is in the Arabic only. It is unexplained: some consider it a trace of a quadruple name, but perhaps the whole quotation is from a hexameter poem like the burlesque *Margites*.

57b1 Each kind of NAME can be SINGLE or DOUBLE, so the eight kinds are introduced only after this initial division. The STANDARD NAME is in fact opposed in one way or another to all the rest. The first four kinds relate to usage, the second four to form.

57b3 "reduced" Elsewhere "shortened" (58a1); the Greek words differ by only one letter.

57b6 " 'exotic' name" (*glōtta*) The EXOTIC NAME includes foreign, dialectal and obsolete words, i.e. those current at other times or places, and is often rendered "gloss": but, since this term now means "interpretation", I have avoided it.

"*sigunon*" This was the word for "spear" in Cypriot dialect.

"and 'spear'. . . " This is preserved in the Arabic only (see Note on the Text).

57b7–32 "metaphor" METAPHOR is the "transference" (*metaphora*) of a STANDARD NAME from its proper object to another object. The term *metaphora* is used for both the process of transference and the name so transferred. Since only the fourth type of transference is equivalent to our "metaphor", retaining the literal rendering would have some advantages. The same classification of metaphor is assumed at *Rhetoric* III 2.1405a3ff., where there is a cross-reference to this passage, and at 10.1411a1. Much of *Rhetoric* III 2–4 and 10–12 is relevant here.

Like the exotic name, the metaphor is a standard name displaced; but the former is standard in another place or time, the latter is standard in another context. A metaphor cannot derive from any context at random, but requires there to be a relationship between both objects described. Aristotle arranges the kinds of metaphor in ascending order, according to how striking the transference is.

(a) There is hardly any transference between GENUS and SPECIES, as a species is by definition included in its genus, as the species "being moored" is included in the genus "being stationary".

(b) When the transference is in the opposite direction, it is more striking: Odysseus has done many fine deeds (where "many" is the genus), but not exactly ten thousand (a species of that genus).

(c) When the transference is from one species to another within the same genus, the process is still more striking. Compare *Rhetoric* III 10.1410b13–15: "metaphor [teaches us] most. For when [someone] called old age 'straw', he produced learning and knowledge from their genus: for both are [species of the genus of] things past their flowering". Cf. too 11.1411b26, 1413a16, where proverbs are said to be a transference of this type; and 4.1406b20, where similes are implied to be.

(d) The fourth kind is by an ANALOGY or proportion between four terms. See below on 57b16.

57b10 "here stands my ship" *Odyssey* I 185, XXIV 308.

"a [part of the genus]" Literally "a sort of". Similarly below at b12, 16.

"standing" I.e. being stationary, as opposed to moving.

57b11 "e.g." In the Arabic only.

"truly has Odysseus . . . " *Iliad* II 272.

57b13–14 Both quotations are from Empedocles (see on 47b18), whom Aristotle regarded as a genius at metaphor. The first (frag. 138D.) refers apparently to killing a man, the second (frag. 143D.) to drawing water.

57b16–33 "analogy" ANALOGY means that *a* is to *b* as *c* is to *d*. This is for Aristotle the most important type of metaphor, and is said to be the best kind (*Rhetoric* III 10.1410b36); hence it is listed last and treated most fully. It corresponds to "metaphor" in our sense, and depends on discerning likenesses between pairs of things (see 59a7). Aristotle gives numerous further examples in *Rhetoric* III (4.1406b31ff., 10.1411a1ff.).

57b22 "wine-bowl of Ares" The war-god, as opposed to the god of wine. The quotation is from Timotheus, frag. 21; for this lyric poet see on 48a15. The same pair of examples is cited at *Rhetoric* III 4.1407a17, cf. 11.1413a1.

57b24 "as Empedocles" (frag. 152D.). So the Arabic: the other sources have "or as Empedocles". The metaphors are commonplace.

57b25 "current" A synonym for STANDARD. Things that have no names are often given one by such analogical metaphor.

57b29 "sowing god-wrought radiance" The quotation, from lyric, is otherwise unknown (Page, *PMG* 1026).

57b30–3 Compare "lyreless song" for "trumpet-blast" quoted at *Rhetoric* III 6.1408a6.

57b33 An account of "ornament" (*kosmos*) is missing here in all sources, but should have been present once (cf. 58a33, 59a14). Its total disappearance is surprising. Luckily a passage in the *Rhetoric* (III 7.1408a10–16) makes clear that ORNAMENT means the ornamental epithet: "diction will be suitable, if . . . it is in proportion to the things in question. There will be no proportion if . . . there is an ornament applied to an ordinary word; otherwise, it seems like a comedy, e.g. the way Cleophon composed: he said some things just as if he were to say 'lady fig'." Here "lady" is not only an exotic term from epic, but also an ornamental epithet bathetically attached to a word with connotations of the everyday or worse. The "epithet" is paired with META-PHOR twice in *Rhetoric* III (1405a10, 1407b31), and at 1406a10–b5 it is discussed between the EXOTIC NAME and metaphor. This confirms that "ornament" and "epithet" are the same. It is a given term's *use* as an epithet, not any oddity in the word itself, that makes it an ornament: compare Aristotle's examples of epithets, e.g. "*white* milk", at *Rhetoric* III 3.1406a12–32. "Ornament" differs from the other kinds in being an addition to a STANDARD NAME, rather than a replacement of one.

57b33–58a7 The last four kinds of NAME were probably invented to deal with the peculiarities of Homeric Greek, which had a great influence on poetic diction in general. Since the Greeks had no understanding of historical linguistics, they regarded Homer's ancient words and forms as somehow modified from the standard ones, or as invented, unless they could prove that they were "exotic", i.e. found in other Greek dialects.

57b34 "the poet" Homer is probably meant, as at 58b7, 60b2. It is unknown which of the lost poems ascribed to him contained the word *ernux* "brancher" (it seems to derive from *ernos*, "branch"). *arēter* "prayerman", from *arasthai* "pray", is found thrice in the *Iliad*. Whether either word is in fact a new coinage is doubtful, and Aristotle's note of caution about such words is well-founded.

57b35–58a7 The remaining three kinds differ from the STANDARD NAME only in form, and are called "paronyms" ("modified names") in the parallel list at *T.C.* 5(iv). The first two differ by vowel-length or by an entire syllable, and the altered name is partly standard, but partly made up. Exactly how to tell the difference between the first and the third is not made clear by the examples, in which Homeric and therefore poetic forms are contrasted with those current in the Attic Greek of Aristotle's contemporaries.

58a5 "one seeing . . . " A quotation from Empedocles' hexameter poem *On Nature* (frag. 88D.); the line describes man's binocular vision. *Ops* is corrupted in the MSS as at 56a2, but is proved right by its occurrence in a longer version of the same list of examples in Strabo (VIII 364, probably derived from Aristotle's *Homeric Questions*).

58a6 "appellation" I.e. the STANDARD NAME.

58a7 "by her righter breast" *Iliad* V 393. The standard adjective "right", *dexios*, has the comparative ending added to it in the Homeric form *dexiteros*, with no change of meaning.

58a8–17 "among names [in] themselves . . . " Aristotle now returns to the classification of "names in themselves", i.e. nouns (and not verbs) in terms of gender, regardless of their composition or modifications. His triple classification goes back to Protagoras (see on 56b15). This paragraph has been thought superfluous, but there is no good reason to deny that Aristotle wrote it, and no explanation of why anyone else should have wanted to add it. At *Rhetoric* III 5.1407b6 Aristotle lists among the requirements for writing good Greek correctness in "the genders of names as Protagoras defined them". So such a discussion is in place here. It may be useful to tabulate the endings of each gender:

(i) masculine:	n, r, s (ps, x)
(ii) feminine:	ē, ō, a (ā)
(iii) neuter ("in between"):	a (shared with feminine);
	n, r, s (shared with masculine);
	i, u (shared with neither).

58a9 "in between" Protagoras had called neuters "objects" (see *Rhetoric* III 5.1407b8), but this is unsatisfactory: many objects are of masculine or feminine gender in Greek. Aristotle may have chosen this term because neuters share some endings with both masculines and feminines.

"n r s ... ps x" E.g. Platon, Crantor, Socrates, Cyclops, Hipponax. *ps* is a single Greek letter, *psi*. It is not in fact true that all nouns ending with such letters are masculine or neuter, e.g. *mētēr* "mother". "*s*" is lost in all sources except the Arabic.

58a10 "elements" This is supplied, as throughout the whole paragraph.

58a11 "ē and ō" E.g. Melanippē, Sapphō.

"a among the vowels that may be lengthened" Long and short *a*, *i* and *u* are written the same way in Greek, whereas long *e* and *o* are distinguished from short *e* and *o* by being written with the letters *ēta* and *ōmega*. Thus feminine nouns can end in both long and short *a*, e.g. Herā, Iphigeneia.

"equal in number" I.e. three. Unfortunately languages in general, Greek included, are less systematic in such matters than Aristotle would like.

58a14 "no name ends in a consonant" I.e. a stop or plosive, e.g. *g* or *p*. Names do end in the SEMI-VOWELS *n*, *r* and *s* (but not *l* or *m*). For Aristotle's definition of CONSONANT see 56b28.

"composite" So the Arabic: the other sources have "these" or "the same".

58a15 "short vowel [that is always short]" I.e. *e* and *o*, written with *epsilon* and *omicron*. The short vowels that can be lengthened are *a*, *i* and *u*.

58a16 The five neuter nouns ending in *u* survive only in the Arabic.

"end in these" "These" is usually interpreted as *i* and *u*. But there is a large class of neuters in *a*, and it is better to understand it as all the short vowels that can be lengthened.

58a17 "[r]" This is lost in all sources. After "*s*" the Arabic adds "like *arthron* (particle) in *n*, and *pathos* (emotion) in *s*", but this is probably a translator's addition.

58a18–59a14 After the classification of the parts of speech and the different types of NAMES, Aristotle lays down principles for how they may best be used. His principles are stated more fully in *Rhetoric* III, especially 2.1404b1–37.

58a18 "The virtue of diction is to be clear and not commonplace" For the VIRTUE of something, see Glossary; for that of diction, cf. *Rhetoric* III 2.1404b1–8: "let the virtue of diction be defined as to be clear—for speech is a sort of indication, and will not perform its function if it makes nothing clear—and neither commonplace nor above the dignity [of what is being described], but suitable [to it]. For poetic diction is probably not commonplace, but is not suitable for [prose] speech. Standard names and verbs produce clarity, but the other types of names discussed in the *Poetics* make the diction not commonplace but ornamented. For altering the diction makes it appear more grand."

58a20 On the poetry of Cleophon, see on 48a12 and 57b33. Obviously his diction was as commonplace as his characters. Sthenelus is perhaps a tragic poet whose style was mocked by Aristophanes (frag. 151K.).

58a21 "unfamiliar . . . everyday" There is an untranslatable antithesis here between the diction of the foreigner (*xenos*), which is UNFAMILIAR (*xenikon*), and that of the private citizen (*idiōtēs*), which is "everyday" (*idiōtikon*). This antithesis is explicit at *Rhetoric* III 2.1404b8–12: "just as people relate to foreigners and to citizens, so they stand towards diction too. For this reason [the orator] should make his speech foreign [i.e. 'unfamiliar']. For people are amazed at things from afar, and amazement is pleasant."

58a23–31 Aristotle digresses briefly to note that excessive use of UNFAMILIAR NAMES (all eight kinds listed at 57b1–3, except the STANDARD NAME) will deprive the diction of clarity: "all [the names]" is an exaggeration. The statement that metaphors and riddles are related, and the example of a riddle, reappear at *Rhetoric* III 2.1405a37–b5.

58a25 "gibberish" (*barbarismos*) This is the opposite of speaking good Greek (see *Rhetoric* III 5.1407a19–b25); it is when someone uses too many foreign words, or uses standard words too incorrectly, to be understood. At *Sophistical Refutations* 3.165b20 it is identified with the solecism (*soloikismos*).

58a28 "the other names" I.e. the NAMES other than metaphor; "other" is preserved by the Arabic only.

58a29 "with metaphor" So all the MSS. Editors often change one letter so the text reads "with [the combination of] metaphors"; this is thought superior because the riddle that follows depends on the juxtaposition of two metaphors. But the change is unnecessary, as metaphor is *in itself* riddling (*Rhetoric* III 2.1405b5). Thus when Homer asked some unsuccessful and lice-ridden fishermen what they had caught, they replied that they had left behind what they caught, but carried with them what they had not caught (i.e. the lice). The riddle is in the single verb "catch", metaphorically applied to (a) catching fish and (b) catching lice (see *On Poets* frag. 9).

"I saw a man glue bronze on a man with fire" A famous hexameter riddle, ascribed to Cleobulina (seventh century). It describes a doctor applying to a patient a bronze cupping-glass ("bronze"), in order to draw blood. This instrument was attached by heating it before application, which created a partial vacuum as it cooled, so that it stayed in place by suction. "Glue" is a metaphor from one species to another, as both gluing and making the cupping-glass stick are kinds of attachment (so *Rhetoric* III 2.1405b2); "bronze" is a metaphor from GENUS to SPECIES, as a cupping-class belongs to the genus of bronze objects.

58a31–4 Compare the parallels in *Rhetoric* III given above on 58a18. The mean of style is a mixture: compare *Rhetoric* III 12.1414a24–7, where it is said that a good mixture of common usage and the UNFAMILIAR will make the diction pleasant. The mean for comedy is likewise a mixture of the grand and the laughable, i.e. high and low (see *T.C.* 18).

58a31 "these [two kinds]" I.e. (a) UNFAMILIAR NAMES, and (b) STANDARD NAMES.

58a34–b5 Alterations of standard words, which seem so odd to us, are in fact a prominent feature of Greek poetic diction. They illustrate Aristotle's point perfectly, as they combine clarity with unfamiliarity.

57b34 "curtailments" (*apokopai*) A synonym for "shortenings".

58b5–59a4 After establishing his principles, Aristotle turns aside to rebut advocates of another view, just as at 53a24–38. He deals first with critics of Homer's diction, and then with Ariphrades who ridiculed the tragedians'.

58b7 "the poet" As often, this denotes Homer, the poet *par excellence*. See on 57b34.

"old Euclides" Unidentified; possibly a comic poet, or the Athenian archon or chief magistrate of 404–403 B.C., during whose administration the Athenian alphabet was reformed. The reforms included the introduction of separate letters for long and short *e* and *o*, and Euclides is making fun of the lack of such a distinction. His words will scan as epic hexameters if vowel-lengthening in the Homeric manner is admitted freely (Aristotle's definition of lengthening includes this, see 58a1). The parody is all the funnier, as the subject of this LAMPOON is prosaic and ludicrous: Epichares is the name of a politician despised for his deviousness in the events of 404 B.C., while hellebore was an herbal cure for madness. Why Euclides is called "old" (literally "ancient") is a puzzle; this cannot mean "the elder". If "old" (*archaios*) is not a nickname meaning "stick-in-the-mud", it could be a corruption either of "the archon" or of his father's name: was his father Archinus, the politician responsible for the reform, who wrote a pamphlet on the question?

"if [a poet] is allowed to" Literally "if someone allows that he may". The Arabic has "lengthen or shorten".

58b9 "in his words" Literally "in the diction itself", but this is an idiom for "to quote his actual words". The usual interpretations "in [Homer's] diction itself" and "in [Euclides'] diction itself" make no sense.

58b12 "due measure" This is *metron*, the same word as for "verse". Aristotle's point is that excessive use of any of these parts produces a ludicrous effect. He incidentally reveals how he thinks parody works.

"all the types" Literally "all the parts". As usual, "part", "kind" and "element" are interchangeable: see on 56a37.

58b16 "lengthened [names]" This is my emendation: the MSS have "epic verses", but there are no examples from epic until b25. The sentence should specify what kind of unfamiliar word is in question, before the parallel kinds in the next sentence.

"[standard] names" NAME is used to mean STANDARD NAME, as at b2.

58b21 "usual standard one" Although "eats" is a STANDARD NAME, its use in Aeschylus' line is a metaphor: so Aristotle cannot call it "standard" simply.

58b23–4 Both lines are from the lost *Philoctetes* of each playwright. This, and the two examples that follow, illustrate the effect of EXOTIC NAMES.

58b25 "now I am . . . " *Odyssey* IX 515.

58b29 "setting down . . . " *Odyssey* XX 259.

58b31 "the headlands . . . " *Iliad* XVII 265. Here the lengthened form *booōsin* "bellow" is replaced by a word without lengthening, *krazousin*.

"Ariphrades" The only Ariphrades we know of was a contemporary of Aristophanes notorious for his sexual habits; one source describes him as a singer to the lyre. But an unknown comic poet may be meant. The archaic forms and inversions of word-order that he mocks are all characteristic of Greek tragic diction; his remarks complement those of Euclides about epic.

58b34 "mine own" Literally "and I . . . him", with an EXOTIC word for "him".

59a4 "each of the [kinds]" Aristotle now reintroduces SINGLE and DOUBLE NAMES, as well as the eight kinds of NAME classed by form and usage.

59a5 "double names and exotic ones" These are picked out because they are particularly distinctive of poetic diction. At *Rhetoric* III 2.1404b28, Aristotle notes that in prose "exotic names, double ones and made-up ones must be used rarely and in few places".

59a6 "the metaphorical" For the importance of METAPHOR in poetry see *On Poets* frag. 10. In fact it is paramount in prose as well, as Aristotle says at *Rhetoric* III 2.1405a4, with a cross-reference to this passage: "metaphor most of all has clarity, pleasantness and unfamiliarity, and it cannot be acquired from another" (a8–10). Here he gives a clear indication of why it is so significant: one coins metaphors by observing *likenesses* (cf. too *Rhetoric* III 11.1412a11). Metaphor is, as it were, one NAME that *represents* another, just as NAMES are themselves REPRESENTATIONS (*Rhetoric* III 1.1404a21). Hence, no doubt, its importance in his theory.

59a7 "genius" Compare *Ethics* III 7.1114b8–12.

59a8 Different kinds of NAMES are best suited to different kinds of composition. This passage is expanded in *Rhetoric* III 3.1406b1–4, with reasons: "double diction [i.e. double names] is most useful to poets of dithyramb—for these are sonorous. Exotic names are most useful to epic poets—for this is grand and self-willed. Metaphor is most useful to iambic poets—for people actually use these." On DITHYRAMB see on 47a14, and on the types of NAME used in it see on *On Poets* frag. *13.

59a10 "heroic verses" I.e. the hexameter verses of epic (see on 48b33).

59a12 "iambic verses" The spoken verse of tragedy. See 49a20, where the same point is made about iambic verse being close to everyday speech. In Aristotle's view such verse in tragedy continually developed towards ordinary speech. Euripides made a significant contribution to this, by selecting from normal speech (*Rhetoric* III 2.1404b25). Cf. also 1.1404a31–5: "just as tragedians changed from tetrameters to iambic verse, because this verse among the others is the most like speech, so too they have given up those [kinds of] names that are contrary to everyday speech, which the first tragedians used as ornaments, and the composers of hexameters still do."

"[everyday] diction" The term *lexis* (DICTION) is used to mean *"everyday* speech", normally called *dialektos*.

59a14 Compare *Rhetoric* III 2.1404b31: "the standard i.e. current name, and metaphor, are the only ones useful for the diction of unadorned speech", i.e. prose speeches. These can in fact include ORNAMENT too, to a limited degree (*Rhetoric* III 3.1406a10ff.). Tragic iambics need ornament, however, as well as metaphor, to distinguish them from everyday speech, since metaphor mixed only with standard words produces the virtue of prose diction (see 58a18–23, 31–4).

59a15 **"representation by means of acting"** Aristotle loosely equates tragedy with representation by means of acting, which in fact includes comedy too. This is because he has in mind the contrast between acting and narration, i.e. epic, in the genres that represent serious actions and people, cf. 48a20–4. The division between the treatment of tragedy and that of epic is somewhat artificial, as Aristotle has already devoted considerable space to the diction of epic, its plots etc. This is why he treats it relatively briefly.

59a17 **"exposition"** (*diēgēmatikē*) A synonym for NARRATION.

"representation in verse" Aristotle's two criteria for poetry proper. The entire phrase means no more than "narrative poetry", as opposed to "dramatic poetry", i.e. tragedy; but it indicates the two important ways in which epic is distinct from tragedy, its MANNER of representation (i.e. narration) and its kind of verse (so too 49b11, *On Poets* frags. *3.8–9). Aristotle begins, however, by considering the similarities between epic and tragedy (59a17–b16).

59a18 **"dramatic"** I.e. like those of drama, "unified" plots, as he goes on to explain. Compare his warning at 56a10–13 that tragedies should not have a plot that is "epic", i.e. not unified.

59a19–21 Compare 50b21–51a6.

59a21–30 Compare 51a16–b7, where the order of topics is reversed. The major Greek victories Aristotle mentions, that of the allied Greek fleet over the Persians at Salamis near Athens, and that of the Sicilian Greeks over the Carthaginians at Himera in Sicily, were by coincidence both won in 480 B.C., according to some on the same day (Herodotus VII 166). Both are narrated by Herodotus, whom Aristotle perhaps has in mind here, as at 51b2. Some historians argued from the timing that there was collusion between the Greeks' enemies, but he evidently disagreed.

59a30 **"as we said"** Aristotle means 51a23, where he praises Homer for his superiority to other epic poets in plot-construction. Clearly none of the other early epics was at all like Homer's in the handling of plot.

59a31–4 "even the [Trojan] war . . . " Homer could have chosen a topic that (unlike the war) had no unity at all, but realised that even the Trojan war would be too big to be seen as a whole, if narrated at the length he uses (cf. 51a3–6, 10–11). If, to avoid excessive length, he had kept the narrative to a moderate length, as perhaps in a tragedy, the plot would have been too complex and its parts would not have the appropriate magnitude (cf. 56a13–17).

59a34 "or, if it were . . . " There is an unexpected shift in construction here, as if Aristotle were reporting Homer's own thoughts, but there is no need to alter the text.

59a35 "a single part" Forty days or so in the tenth year of the war.

"many of them" I.e. of the war's other parts or incidents. Thus the "Catalogue of Ships" in *Iliad* II is drawn from the assembly of the fleet at Aulis, before the Greeks had even sailed to Troy.

"diversifies his composition" On the relation between PLOT and EPISODES in epic see on 55b15. The episodes are used to divide up the PLOT and give it the proper magnitude and variety (see b28–30). Before "diversifies" MS A and the Latin have "twice", a scribal error.

59a37–b2 Compare 51a16–22, where Aristotle criticises epic poets who write about a single hero's various exploits. The two epics named here are parts of the Trojan Cycle, into which Homer's successors incorporated the *Iliad* and *Odyssey* to produce a version of the entire tale of Troy. The lost *Cypria* told the story of the origins of the Trojan War, up to the arrival of the Greeks at Troy; it was sometimes ascribed to Stasinus of Cyprus (ca 700 B.C.?). The lost *Little Iliad* deals with events after the *Iliad* ends, from the death of Achilles up to the Greeks' sack of Troy; it was usually ascribed to Lesches of Lesbos (ca 700?), but Aristotle's wording may imply that he ascribed both epics to the same author. Surviving summaries of their plots make it clear that they were so episodic that they can scarcely be said to deal with "a single action".

59b1 "or a single action" Literally "and . . . " The Arabic omits "and a single", probably in error. Although it seems unlikely that Aristotle would even hint at the unity of an action such as the whole Trojan war in this context, he probably does so; cf. a32 above, and next note.

59b2–7 The plots of the *Iliad* and *Odyssey* provide material for one or at most two tragedies each, but the other epics provide it for many. At 62b4, Aristotle says that any epic provides material for more than one tragedy; but this must include its episodes, e.g. *Iliad* X forms the basis of the tragedy *Rhesus*. For the same reason there is no real contradiction with 56a12, where even the plot of the *Iliad* is implied to contain "more than one story".

59b5 "more than eight" This list of dramas based on the *Little Iliad* is often rejected by editors, in whole or in part, as a learned later insertion, and the arithmetic is criticised as over-precise. But "more than eight" is in all MSS, and the list of ten titles proves the point. The *Judgement of Arms* was first play in Aeschylus' trilogy about Ajax, and told how Odysseus was adjudged the armour of Achilles after the latter's death. Philoctetes played a major part in the capture of Troy: Sophocles' tragedy about his being fetched from Lemnos by Achilles' son Neoptolemus is extant. Neoptolemus also killed Eurypylus, a Trojan ally. Thus *Neoptolemus* and *Eurypylus* could be alternative titles of the same play (the Arabic omits *Eurypylus*). The same is true of *Vagabondage* and the *Laconian Women* (the Arabic omits the latter): both deal with the story of how Odysseus penetrated Troy's defences disguised as a beggar, and reached the household of Helen with her Laconian servant-women (we know that Sophocles wrote plays with the latter titles).

The last four titles also fall into pairs: the *Sack of Troy* that was brought about by the traitor Sinon (title character of a lost play by Sophocles), and the embarkation of the Greeks with their prisoners, the Trojan women. Euripides' extant play with this latter title ends with the sailing of the fleet. It matters little exactly how many plays are listed; the point is simply that they are numerous.

59b7 The four kinds of epic resemble those of tragedy enumerated at 55b32–56a3 (see note). Each depends on the predominance of a particular QUALITATIVE PART. The tragic equivalent of "simple" epic appears to be plays based on spectacle (see on 56a2). Is it inherent in the nature of epic that it has these kinds, or is Aristotle recommending that poets strive after them? That both interpretations are in some degree correct is surely supported by the juxtaposition of 55b32, where a link between the four kinds of tragedy and its parts is asserted, and 56a3, where the poet is advised to try to excel in all of them if possible. By so doing, presumably, he will be realising the full potential offered by the nature of epic, and will bring it nearer to its most perfect form.

59b10 The "parts" meant here must be PLOT and its *sub*-divisions, i.e. REVERSAL, RECOGNITION and SUFFERING, plus its other qualitative parts, i.e. character, diction and reasoning. Yet it is odd that DICTION and REASONING are mentioned separately below. See on 55b32–56a3, where two parts of tragedy, CHARACTER and SPECTACLE, and two parts of plot, recognitions and suffering, are put on the same level, as it seems; perhaps a similar procedure is being used here.

59b12 Literally "Homer has used all these both first and adequately". The tone, however, is one of very strong, if understated, approval, with "first" used of Homer's rank, not only his chronological sequence.

59b14 "in each of the two ways" The text here is based on a corrupt word in MS B (see Note on the Text). The other sources' text must be translated awkwardly either "he has constructed each of his poems— the *Iliad* as simple . . . " or "each of his poems is constructed—the *Iliad* as simple . . . ". Evidently there is no reason why tragedies too should not belong to more than one kind, if more than one of the parts is very prominent in them. Aristotle describes the *Iliad* as SIMPLE on the ground that the change of FORTUNE in it takes place without REVERSALS and RECOGNITIONS (see 52a14–16).

59b15 "recognition right through" Telemachus is recognised by Nestor, Helen, and Menelaus; Odysseus by the Phaeacians, Polyphemus, Telemachus, Eurycleia, Eumaeus and the cowherd, the suitors, Penelope, Laertes etc.

59b16 "he has surpassed all [others]" So MS B. The other sources require the translation "[these poems] have surpassed all [other epic poems]". See Note on the Text.

59b17 Aristotle mentioned these divergences between epic and tragedy above (49b11–12).

"the definition that we stated" I.e. the limit of its length according to its nature (see 51a9–15).

59b21 "structures" I.e. "plots", used here as equivalent to the compositions themselves, no doubt because of the paramount importance of plot. See on 53a20, 60a3.

"smaller than the ancient ones" I.e. the *Iliad* and *Odyssey*. Aristotle implies that he prefers the length of the three tragedies per day that were performed in sequence at the Great Dionysia, amounting to four or five thousand lines. The *Iliad* and the *Odyssey* are about three times longer, so only portions could be presented in a single day. Yet he at once concedes that epic does have the potential for being very long without losing its interest.

59b22–8 Compare 55b15–23, where Aristotle summarises the *Odyssey* to show how much more epic admits episodes than does tragedy.

59b28 "provided they are particular [to it]" Compare 55b13.

"weight . . . splendour" Both terms are unusual, and correspond to "magnitude" (*megethos*) and "grandeur" (*semnotēs*) elsewhere.

"diverting the listener . . . " "Divert" is literally "change", with the implication of changing his emotional reactions, as well as of keeping him entertained; this will be accomplished by variety in the episodes (cf. 59a36).

59b30 "introducing episodes" There is a nuance of "divide it up with episodes", as at 59a36. In quantitative terms, episodes seem to fulfil the function in epic that is fulfilled by choral songs in tragedy: they divide up the action and diversify it. But Aristotle is by no means endorsing a plot that contains irrelevant episodes, or that consists of nothing but disconnected episodes. The apparent contradiction is caused by the two senses of EPISODE.

59b32 "from experience" Aristotle knew of no early attempts to compose narrative poetry in any other metre; he must be referring to more recent efforts, like Chaeremon's. Contrast the case of tragic poetry (49a21–4). For him, verse-forms, like genres, exist by nature, as he says at 49a24, but it takes trial and error to reveal their potential. Thus "experience" is equivalent to the "teaching of nature" below (60a4).

59b33 "or in many" I.e. as Chaeremon did (60a2); see on 47b21.

59b34 "stateliest" The opposite of "fast-moving" below. The adjective is the same as that applied to the "stationary" songs (*stasima*) of tragedy (52b23).

59b35–7 "for this reason . . . in this too" This is not an argument, which would be circular, but a restatement. At 59a8–11, Aristotle said that EXOTIC NAMES are most appropriate for hexameters, metaphors to iambics. Here he must mean that epic admits all the UNFAMILIAR NAMES (cf. 59a11, *Rhetoric* III 1.1404a35).

59b36 "and lengthenings" This is based on "and all lengthenings" in the Arabic. The phrase is omitted in the other sources (see Note on the Text).

"in this too" "In this", absent in all MSS, is added by Twining, but is needed for the sense (see Note on the Text).

60a1 Compare the discussion of these metres at 49a22–25, with notes.

"related to action" I.e. to the representation of action, by actors.

"still more odd" I.e. compared with producing a narrative poem in a single verse-form other than the hexameter (59b32).

60a2 "Chaeremon" See on 47b21. His *Centaur*, perhaps intended for recital like an epic poem, contained a mixture of metres.

60a3 "long structure" I.e. epic poem, as at 59b21.

60a4 "as we said" At 59b32 (see note).

"choose" So the Latin and Arabic; the Greek has "divide", which is clearly wrong.

60a5 "appropriate to it" I.e. to a long structure (a3).

60a5–b5 The third section of Aristotle's treatment of epic consists of remarks about what makes a good epic poem, combined with the continued theme of the relationship between epic and tragedy. The unannounced shift to an account of excellence and error in epic is parallel to that in the discussion of tragedy (see on 50a33–b8, 54b19–55a21, 55a22–56a32). Homer showed what to do in other ways as well as in his choice of metre, and his excellence forms a transition as at 59a29.

The topics are treated elsewhere in similar sequence. Thus the use of metre relates to the MEDIA of the representation, and the next topic, the use of characters speaking, to its MANNER (narrative or dramatic); these are treated together at the opening of the *Poetics*, except that they are separated by an account of the objects of the representation (omitted here because as the people represented are the same in epic as in tragedy). The topic of characters leads into that of improbability, and the related questions of false inference and impossibility, by the same curious progression as at 54a33–b8. The last topic, the use of diction in passages full of character and reasoning, brings in the remaining parts of epic; so we almost find the usual sequence of plot, character, reasoning and diction.

60a5–11 Homer's unique creation of "dramatic representations", by letting his characters speak for themselves far more than did other epic poets, was mentioned as his outstanding quality at 48b35.

60a8 "[a poet] represents" Literally "he is a representer" (*mimētēs*). Aristotle is playing on a Platonic meaning of *mimēsis*, impersonation; Plato had criticised poets as mere impersonators of others (*Republic* III 394D), but Aristotle's theory denies that this is basic to poetic REPRESENTATION (see Introduction, Section 4). Compare 48a21, where he describes the poet of narrative as "becoming another [character], . . . or remaining the same person and not changing", and 61b29.

60a11 "some other [person]" E.g. a deity like Athena, or a boy like Telemachus. The MSS have "some other character", but "character" should be deleted as a copyist's explanation, since it is contrary to Aristotle's use of the term, and impossible before the correct use of *ēthos* later in the sentence.

"with character" So MS B and the Arabic; A and the Latin have "with characters", an easy mistake in the context.

60a11–18 The AMAZING, and the ASTONISHMENT it produces, is an important part of the effect of tragedy (cf. 52a1–7), and evidently of epic too. Epic can use an IMPROBABILITY to produce it more easily. This passage shows that the emotions aroused by epic are very close to those aroused by tragedy (so too *Rhetoric* III 16.1417a13, where the tale Odysseus tells Alcinous in *Odyssey* IX-XII is said to arouse pity and terror).

Improbability is a fault unless it is used for such a purpose (compare 60b24–6). If overdone, or too visibly done on stage, it ceases to be amazing and becomes absurd; compare 55a22–8, and T.C. 6(iv). Violations of necessity and probability in the sequence of incidents need to be handled carefully.

60a15 "the pursuit of Hector" At *Iliad* XXII 131ff. Hector loses his courage as he sees Achilles approach him. He flees, pursued by Achilles, who motions to the rest of the Greek army not to intervene. It may seem improbable that they would obey him, and it would certainly look odd on stage. See also 60b26, where it is called an impossibility.

60a17 "what is amazing is pleasant" So also *Rhetoric* III 2.1404b11. Aristotle explains why elsewhere: "being amazed is pleasant for the most part: for the desire to learn is part of being amazed, and so what is amazing is desired" (*Rhetoric* I 11.1371a31). It follows from this passage that amazement, and the emotions that go with it, are pleasant, and so epic too aims at pleasure. On the relation of this to catharsis, see Introduction, Section 5.

60a18–26 The false inference is itself an improbability or illogicality (*alogon*), as it is contrary to logic (*para-logismos*). Aristotle uses the same term for the argument that leads to the false inference. His example, *Odyssey* XIX 220ff., shows the disguised Odysseus leading Penelope to believe that he had seen Odysseus. It is wrong to complain that Aristotle should have chosen an example in which the audience is misled; his point is that Homer showed other poets how to mislead.

Aristotle's praise of Homer for telling lies is intentionally paradoxical, since we do not usually praise liars: Plato's *Republic* (III 377D) had condemned Homer for precisely this reason.

60a20–25 The mistake depends on our readiness to assume that, if the consequence exists, so must the cause. E.g. "if it rains (p), the ground is wet (q). The ground is wet (q); therefore it has rained (p)". The inference need not be true, as there may be other reasons for q, e.g. that someone spilt a bucket of water (see on 55a12).

60a24 "should add it" Just as the amazing is truth with an *addition* of falsehood (a18), so the believable lie is a falsehood with an addition of truth.

60a25 "soul" The SOUL is for Aristotle the seat of the intelligence as well as of the emotions.

60a26 At *Odyssey* XIX 220ff. (the "Bath-scene"), Penelope's false inference is as follows: "if you see someone (p), you can describe him correctly (q). This stranger describes Odysseus correctly (q); therefore he saw Odysseus (p)". But the stranger *is* Odysseus. Aristotle is not referring to the recognition of him by the nurse, which results from a true inference, not a false one (see on 54b26).

60a27–b1 "impossible [incidents] that are probable" Aristotle's criterion for whether something can be believed is whether it seems likely or probable. His preference for a believable impossibility over an unbelievable possibility is another paradox, which he repeats at 61b11. It is better that a poet make us believe something that cannot happen, than that he fail to make us believe something that can.

60a27 "stories" (*logoi*) I.e. plots (cf. a34) of tragedy or epic.

60a28 "plot-structure" (*mutheuma*) This is a tentative rendering of a term found only here; it looks like a synonym for plot (*muthos*), but this presents a problem. How can Aristotle say that the improbability should be outside the plot, when he gives an example where it is outside the *drama*, i.e. within those antecedent events which are part of the plot, but not actually within the play (cf. 55b24–9)? The parallel "outside the drama" at 54b7 suggests that *mutheuma* means the plot as performed, in parallel to *drama*, i.e. the tragic performance. The examples that follow, from both tragedy and epic, show that the term applies to both genres. Alternatively, if it means exactly the same as "plot", Aristotle may simply be equating the plot with the tragedy or epic as performed, as he does elsewhere (see on 53a30, 59b21).

60a30 This aspect of Sophocles' *Oedipus the King* may also be mentioned at 54b7, and in a different context at 53b32 (see notes there).

"Oedipus' not knowing . . . " Oedipus reveals his ignorance of how the previous king, his father Laius, died at lines 112–23. The improbability is that he ought to have heard about it when he succeeded to the throne, years before; but his lack of curiosity at that time is safely "outside the play".

60a32 In Sophocles' *Electra* (lines 680–763), Orestes' tutor, helping the disguised Orestes himself in his plot to deceive Aegisthus and regain the throne, gives a vivid but fictitious account of how Orestes was killed in a chariot crash at the Pythian games. The impossibility is that the games were founded centuries after the time of the Trojan War when the play is set. This anachronism "within the drama" was noticed by the ancient commentators on it.

60a32 Plays entitled the *Mysians* were written by Aeschylus, Sophocles and others, but none survives. Telephus, after killing his uncle at Tegea in the Peloponnese, travelled all the way to Mysia in N.W. Asia Minor without speaking to anyone, since his unpurged blood-guilt made him an outcast. Comic poets of Aristotle's time made fun of this (Amphis frag. 30, Alexis frag. 178).

60a34 "if one is set up . . . " Even something quite outrageous can be put into the poem, if it is sufficiently well handled, as Aristotle goes on to remark. This sentence is difficult. As it stands in MSS A and B, two renderings are possible : (i) "if [the poet] sets up [such a plot], and it appears fairly reasonable, even an oddity [must] be admitted [into the poem]". (ii) "If [the poet] sets up [such a plot] and it is clear that he could have done so more logically, it is absurd as well". (i) is simpler and better, but would flow still more easily if the Latin preserves the original reading, which makes the improbable plot the subject of the sentence. This solution is adopted here (see Note on the Text).

60a36 There are several improbabilities (or indeed impossibilities) in this part of *Odyssey* XIII. Odysseus is conveyed to Ithaca sound asleep in a supernaturally swift Phaeacian ship; he is put ashore without being awakened, and the Phaeacian ship is turned to stone upon its return home (lines 86–184).

60b2 "good [qualities]" Literally "good things", i.e. above all virtues of diction, which Aristotle deals with next.

"embellishment" Literally "seasoning", to improve the taste, with the same metaphor from cooking as at 49b25 and 50b16.

60b3 "slack parts" Overelaborate diction detracts from the portrayal of character and the presentation of clear arguments.

60b6–61b25 "questions that are raised [about epic]" Aristotle's examination of the frequent use of improbability in epic leads easily into poetic "problems" in general (*problēmata*, literally "things put forward for discussion"), among which improbability bulks large. Since Homer was central to classical Greek education, but his poems were very archaic, discussion of their historical, linguistic, religious, social and moral difficulties began early (see Introduction, Section 2); by Aristotle's time there was a large body of writing on this topic. Many of Homer's earlier critics were very tendentious, and it was to refute them that Aristotle compiled his *Homeric Questions* in six books, from which this section of the *Poetics* is evidently drawn.

The organisation of this section is hard to follow, since there are five headings for the criticisms, and twelve for the solutions (61b22–5); moreover the same criticism may be answered now with one solution, now with another, as the particular passage requires; and not all criticisms can be answered, since poets do sometimes make mistakes. See on 61b22–5.

60b6–22 The discussion opens with three assumptions about the nature of a poet's work, from which the different types of "problems" and their solutions can be deduced. (i) Critics attack the objects of the poet's representation; but the poet may depict things as they are or were, are said to be or should be (cf. 60b33–61a4). (ii) Critics may perceive a problem when the poet is only using unfamiliar diction, which they do not understand (cf. 61a9–b1). (iii) The poet may commit an error, not against his own art, but against another art, e.g. from ignorance of medicine or zoology. In such cases critics are entitled to call him a bad doctor or zoologist, but not a bad poet (cf. 60b29–33). The next section takes these up in the order (iii), (i), (ii). Compare the sequence of five types of problem at 61b22–4.

60b6 Note the characteristic way of beginning a new subject, as at the start of the *Poetics*.

"solution" (*lusis*) The word is the same as the "solution" of the tragic plot at 55b24.

60b9 As at 48a5, when discussing the objects represented Aristotle uses an analogy from the visual arts, principally painting.

"three things" Literally "things three in number". MS A has "three items", as at 61b25.

60b12 "modifications" (*pathē*) I.e. the lengthening, shortening or alteration of names discussed at 58a1–7. Literally "things undergone"; the same word is used for SUFFERING and EMOTION.

60b14 "the art of civic life" (*politikē*) "Politics" gives the wrong sense, as the term means "the art of living in society", which for Aristotle amounts to life among other human beings. Homer and the other poets were considered the great teachers of this, and were therefore criticised for any bad behaviour their poetry depicts or seems to recommend (especially, of course, by Plato in *Republic* III, cf. *Laws* II 655B): see Introduction, Section 2. *politikē* and *poiētikē* resemble our antithesis between "life" and "art".

60b16 "by coincidence" The distinction is between errors in the poet's use of the poetic art itself, and those *accidental* to it, but essential to some other art. Cf. b30. By making this distinction Aristotle answers Plato's criticisms of poets' mistakes about various other arts, e.g. the art of war in Homer or of farming in Hesiod.

60b17 "[a horse . . . of his]" A few words are lost in the text here, but the supplement proposed must be more or less right (see Note on the Text). For the painter's failure at the representation of an animal cf. b30.

60b18 "thrown forward" Editors add "together", needlessly.

60b19–20 "an error . . . another art of whatever sort" The MSS read "whether an error . . . another art, or impossibilities have been produced, of whatever sort". The Latin version omits "or impossibilities", and the words "or impossibilities have been produced" are rightly deleted by editors, since they are clearly misplaced from b23. I have deleted "whether" too (see Note on the Text).

60b21 "the criticisms that are among the questions raised" Not all the "problems" imply a criticism of the poets, but many of them do. I translate a small emendation of Bywater's: see Note on the Text.

60b22 The category of problems to be solved with reference to the art itself surely extends to 61a9, where the solutions from diction begin, rather than only to 60b32, as is often thought. The first solution is that an impossibility serves the end of the poem. Failing that, it is wrong—unless it falls within another art.

60b23 "[If]" This is lost in the MSS (see Note on the Text).

60b25 "the end has been stated" By END Aristotle means the FUNC-
TION of poetry, the arousal of emotion, with which large parts of the
Poetics have been concerned. Here, astonishment is what is sought:
this is closely related to pity and terror (cf. 52a1–5).

60b26 "the pursuit of Hector" See a15 above, where this is specified
as an improbability.

60b27 "better or no worse" "No" is lost in the MSS; without it, the
sense is "more or less".

60b28 "the art concerned with these matters" I.e. technical matters
of some kind. Aristotle is already thinking of errors *not* in the poetic
art, which are to be avoided.

"the error is not correct" Aristotle plays on the paradox that "errors"
are not usually correct, but in poetry they sometimes are. Editors, not
understanding this, delete "the error is" (see Note on the Text).

60b29–32 The second defence—or at least plea in mitigation—for an
impossibility is that the error is only incidental to poetry, but falls
within some other art—e.g. the poet's knowledge of zoology is defec-
tive. The common idea that female deer have horns was disproved by
Aristotle in his biological works. Sophocles and Euripides both made
this mistake (Aelian, *On Animals* VII 39).

60b30 "[to those in it] by coincidence" Literally "according to another coincident", i.e. an accidental, something not essential to the nature of poetry, but inherent in some other art (see on b16).

60b33–61a9 The next four solutions are that the poet is representing
things as they should be, as people say they are, as things were, or as
they would be done given the circumstances. These respond to
charges of impossibility, improbability or (in the second and fourth
cases) gratuitously nasty characterisation

60b33 "[as] they should be" "As" has dropped out in the MSS.

60b34 Whether Sophocles really made this remark or not, it is very
apt. Compare 54b8–13 and 61b11–13.

60b35–61a1 Unworthy tales about the anthropomorphic gods like
Cronus' castration of his father Uranus or the adultery of Ares and
Aphrodite were often seen as morally harmful, notably by the early
thinker Xenophanes of Colophon (ca 570–470 B.C.), who denounced
them in his poems, and by Plato (*Republic* III 377D-383C and elsewhere). Aristotle's answer would hardly satisfy Plato, but accords with
the *Poetics'* tacit insistence that such questions are not integral to the art
of poetry as such (questions about the gods would for Aristotle belong
within theology or metaphysics). Such disreputable tales fall under the
criticism "what is harmful" in the list at 61b23.

61a1 "people say [it is] so" This is Spengel's emendation for "people
do not say" in the MSS (see Note on the Text).

61a3 The quotation is *Iliad* X 152, a well-known difficulty which Aristotle also dealt with in his *Homeric Questions* (frag. 160R.). Critics had suggested that sticking spears upright in the ground to keep them handy was a bad arrangement, as they might fall down in the night and wake up the whole camp. Aristotle refutes such nonsense by a comparison with the identical practice of another society (the Illyrians, in what is now Yugoslavia) in his own time. This proves that it could also have been the practice of the Homeric heroes.

61a4–9 Critics offended at the morality of a character's words or actions should take account of the full circumstances. The same principles for mitigating harsh moral judgments are spelt out at *Ethics* III 1.1111a3. This accords with Aristotle's statement that poetry has standards of correctness different from those of the other arts (60b14). If the words or actions are gratuitously nasty, i.e. not required by the characterisation and the plot, they are to be condemned as contrary to the art of poetry (see 61b19–21). Otherwise, criticism of the characters or their actions falls within ethics, not poetry.

61a10–31 The remaining six solutions are based on the DICTION. They strongly resemble the six methods of fallacious argument based on diction at *Sophistical Refutations* 4.

61a10–15 The three examples are lines from the *Iliad* where an objection disappears if there is an EXOTIC NAME, i.e. one used in an unusual sense.

(i) *Iliad* I 50. When Apollo punishes the Greeks by sending a plague, he first kills the "mules and dogs". Zoilus, a contemporary of Aristotle famous for his severe criticisms of Homer, ridiculed this as inappropriate. Aristotle's explanation is wrong; the word means "mules", but resembles "sentinels".

(ii) *Iliad* X 316. The supposed contradiction is that "ugly in form" might mean that Dolon was a cripple, but he is also described as "swift of foot". Aristotle is right this time.

(iii) *Iliad* IX 203. Achilles, welcoming the Greek envoys to his hut, tells Patroclus to "mix the wine purer". Zoilus objected that this was more appropriate to a drunken revel than a serious discussion. The objection is misguided, but Aristotle is wrong; the word does mean "purer", even though it resembles a word meaning "lively".

61a16 "Some things" So the Arabic: the other sources have "something" (see Note on the Text).

61a17 At *Iliad* X 11ff. Agamemnon "alone" lies awake at night, but hears sounds of celebration coming from the camp of the victorious Trojans. Not "all" men can be asleep if the Trojans are not. Aristotle's answer is that "all" is said by transference (METAPHOR) from the SPECIES "all" to the GENUS "much" or "many". At 57b11–13 the similar example of "ten thousand" for "many" works in the opposite direction.

"all gods" The MSS have "the other gods", but Aristotle must have had "all" in his quotation. At some stage a copyist altered the text to make it conform to the standard text of Homer, which has "the other". The Arabic and Latin read "men with war-crests" for the same reason.

61a20 The quotation is from *Iliad* XVIII 489 or *Odyssey* V 275. Homer's statement that the Bear is the only constellation which never dips below the horizon upset those critics who expected him to be an expert astronomer. The charge is one of not representing things as they are. Rather than admit that Homer made an incidental mistake, an impossibility according to the art of astronomy, Aristotle suggests that he called it the "only" constellation because it is by far the most important.

61a21 "pronunciation" (*prosōdia*) By "pronunciation" Aristotle means the pitch-accent, aspiration and vowel-length, which frequently distinguished the meanings of words that were written identically in his time. See on 56b31–4.

The examples are again from the *Iliad*, and are also discussed at *Sophistical Refutations* 4.166b1–9. (i) Aristotle's discussion there makes it clear that the first example was in his text of Homer at II 15 (though it is not in ours). Zeus tells the deceitful dream to say to Agamemnon that "we grant that he gain his prayer" for victory: this is of course not true. It was thought offensive that Zeus deceives Agamemnon, e.g. by Plato (*Republic* II 383A). By altering the accent on "grant", Hippias tried to shift the blame for the deceit away from Zeus, but the dream is Zeus' messenger, and the explanation is inadequate. (ii) *Iliad* XXIII 328, where a stump of wood is described in one of two ways, depending on the accentuation of a word written as *ou*. "Not rotted" is the right interpretation.

Hippias of Thasos, who must be distinguished from the famous sophist Hippias of Elis, is unknown, unless he is the same as a Hippias of Thasos who died in Athens in 404 B.C.

61a23 "punctuation" Literally "division". In Aristotle's time, texts were written without punctuation or indeed spaces between words, and "division" includes both: compare *Sophistical Refutations* 4.166a35. In the example, from Empedocles (frag. 35D.), the correct interpretation is "things were mixed [that were] pure before", which could be misunderstood as "things that were pure had been mixed before".

61a25 "ambiguity" Cf. *Sophistical Refutations* 4.166a6–21. The example, *Iliad* X 252–3, was very controversial: "more than two thirds of the night has gone, but a third is still left". Critics objected that this is arithmetically impossible. Aristotle gave his answer in the *Homeric*

Questions (frag. 161R.): Homer meant "the greater part has gone, i.e. two thirds", so that a third can be left.

61a27 "a habit of diction" Solutions based on verbal usage can reply to charges of impossibility or contradiction. Aristotle uses colloquial parallels to explain two related Homeric passages.

(i) Just as people call a mixture of wine and water "wine", so Homer at *Iliad* XXI 592 calls a mixture of copper and tin "tin", instead of bronze. Critics had objected to tin as impossible, because no soldier would wear armour made of so soft a metal.

(ii) Even though iron had long since replaced bronze as the hardest metal in use, the Greeks still called smiths "bronze-smiths". Similarly Homer calls Ganymede a "wine-pourer" (*Iliad* XX 234), though gods drink only nectar. Aristotle suggests another explanation for this apparent contradiction, which we may think superior: "wine-pourer" is a metaphor by ANALOGY, since wine is to men as nectar is to the gods (see 57b16–25). He discussed a similar problem about mixing nectar in his *Homeric Questions* (frag. 170R., on *Odyssey* V 93).

"mixed [wine] 'wine' " I add "[wine]", which is lost in all sources (see Note on the Text).

61a29 "[gods]" Literally "they . . . ".

61a31 "also" This is in the Arabic only.

61a31–b9 It is usually thought that a new topic begins here (contradictions) and still more solutions are proposed, making their number more than twelve. But several examples of contradiction have already been discussed among the solutions dependent on diction (e.g. a16–20, 31); moreover, there is a marked change in construction from "the solution may be by . . . " to "one should . . . ". Aristotle is generalising about how carefully one should seek a solution, whether linguistic (a31–b1) or non-linguistic (b1–9), before accepting a criticism as valid. Critics jump to conclusions too quickly (cf. b15–18).

The example is *Iliad* XX 267–72, where Aeneas' spear passes through two of the inner bronze layers of Achilles' shield, but is stopped by its layer of gold, which was on the outside! Aristotle implies that if "was held" is taken to mean "was checked", the problem somehow does not exist.

61b1 "Glaucon" This may be an interpreter of Homer mentioned by Plato (*Ion* 530D). He is probably not the same as Glaucus of Rhegium, author of an early treatise on poetry. We do not know what he said about this passage, or about method in general.

61b1–9 "Again, some people illogically . . . " Apparent contradictions may exist only in the mind of the critic. The example is Icarius, father of Penelope and grandfather of Telemachus in the *Odyssey*. Homer's critics assume that Icarius is a Spartan (Lacedaemonian), as the

Spartans claimed, and then complain that Telemachus does not meet him there during his visit to Sparta. Aristotle inclines to accept the Cephallenians' claims that he was called Icadius and was of local (Cephallenian) origins all along; but this is, to all appearances, a story cooked up by the Cephallenians to enhance their poor standing in the poem.

61b1 "Again" So the Arabic; a new paragraph begins here with "again", as at 60b29. The Greek and Latin have "something", which has been altered to "that" by all editors, causing utter confusion, as it falsely suggests that the sentence continues without a break as a quotation from Glaucon. See Note on the Text.

61b8 "It is probable . . . " The text is corrupt here but the sense is clear. One small change would produce "So it is probable . . . ", but something corresponding to "has arisen" is still missing.

61b9–25 Aristotle now sums up, basing his discussion on four of the five main kinds of problem—impossibility, improbability, contradiction and wickedness—which he lists at the end in the order impossibility, improbability, the harmful, contradiction and something incorrect in terms of another art. If "contradictions" correspond mainly to "solutions from the diction", this broadly follows the order of non-linguistic and linguistic solutions given above.

61b9 The impossible overlaps several kinds of solution. Its three solutions here correspond (a) to 60b24–6 and 11–12 below (attaining the end of the art); (b) to 60b33–4, and 13–14 below (making the characters better); (c) to 60b33–61a1 and 61b14 below, where "what people say" is equivalent to "opinion" here. This division leaves out impossibilities that belong to some art other than poetry.

61b11 See on 60a27–b1 and 60b22. A believable impossibility is better, because using it the poet can better attain the end of his art, as Zeuxis does.

61b12 "For it may be impossible" These words are preserved in the Arabic only (see Note on the Text). For the thought compare 54b8–13, although Zeuxis is not named there. On Zeuxis see on 50a27.

"model" The colloquial sense of *paradeigma*, which means "example" elsewhere in Aristotle.

61b14 "for one must solve them" This too is only in the Arabic; the other sources have "and" (see Note on the Text).

"an improbability" Again from the Arabic (see Note on the Text). The other sources say "there is no improbability".

61b15 "for it is probable . . . " This again paraphrases Agathon's saying that even an unlikely event is likely to happen sometime (cf. 56a24); it is a weak defence. Compare 61a1–4 on the spear-butts, which Aristotle considers an unlikely but attested arrangement.

61b16–18 Contradictions should be solved according to diction, it seems, based on the poet's own words or on sensible assumptions, which, Aristotle implies, many of Homer's critics do not make. False arguments often depend on words that are not used in the same sense (i.e. they do not stand for "the same thing"), with a different reference, or in a different way.

"Sayings that are contradictory" So the Arabic; the Greek has "contradictions as said" by a simple error.

61b17 "refutations in arguments" This is an implicit cross-reference to the *Sophistical Refutations*; refutations often depend on finding contradictions (*Sophistical Refutations* 5.167a26), and the "solutions from the diction" correspond closely to the types of fallacious argument from diction discussed in *Sophistical Refutations* 4.

61a18 "must be solved" This is an emendation for "and himself" in the Greek. To keep "himself" editors are obliged to supply "[one must compare what the poet] himself [says]", or "[one must see that the poet has contradicted] himself", which seem very far-fetched.

61b19–21 Criticisms can be right, when there is no need for either improbability or a gratuitously bad character. In fact impossibility, improbability and wickedness of character are all sources of humour in comedy at *T.C.* 6(iii)-(vi), and appear there in the same sequence as at b23 below. What is bad in tragedy or epic is funny in comedy.

61b20 "Aegeus" The reference is to Euripides' *Medea*, already mentioned at 54b1. The improbability is the poorly motivated arrival at Corinth of Aegeus, King of Athens, at line 663, which happens at just the right moment for Medea, to whom he promises the political asylum she needs.

61b21 "Menelaus" "Villainy" is fully synonymous with "wickedness", and corresponds to the criticism that something is "harmful" below. The characterisation of Menelaus in Euripides' *Orestes* was already criticised for unnecessary nastiness at 54a29. Unnecessarily nasty characterisation or action is one of the things Plato objected to in poetry as morally harmful (*Republic* III 391D-E), and Aristotle does not defend it as long as it is not in the service of the proper end of poetry. It is the violation of necessity or probability in the plot that makes Aristotle approve both criticisms. Although the problem of morally offensive characterisation has not been mentioned specifically before, it belongs with the solutions "things that are said" (60b35) and "things not done finely" (61a4–9).

Aristotle's omission of incidental errors like depicting a doe with horns suggests that he does not regard these as strictly relevant, though such things are better avoided (60b29).

61b22–5 This passage sums up the whole account of "problems" and solutions. The five criticisms are clear enough, provided that we accept the identification of "harmful" things suggested in the previous note. The last type, "incorrect in terms of [another] art", must be errors in other arts which are "incidental" to poetry. Others supplement "incorrect in terms of [the] art [of poetry]", but such errors surely constitute the first four criticisms.

There has been no agreement about how to find exactly twelve solutions in 60b23–61b9; many conclude that it is impossible, and suggest that Aristotle's count is based on his analysis in the lost *Homeric Questions*, not on that in the *Poetics*. The alternative first proposed here is that the last two "solutions" recognised by previous editors at 61a31–b9 are not solutions at all, but general remarks about how to avoid seeing contradictions where there are none (see on 61a31–b9).

61b26–62b15 The account of the serious genres, epic and tragedy, concludes with a comparison between them, which picks up many points made when they were first introduced at 49b9–20; compare also *On Poets* frag. *3.8–10. The topic was evidently controversial; in his late work the *Laws* (II 658D) Plato argued that epic is superior, because it is to the taste of old men, whereas educated women, youths and most people prefer tragedy, and children prefer comedy.

61b27–29 The contention of such opponents of tragedy is that it is vulgar, catering to the lowest elements in the audience. By "vulgar" (*phortikos*) Aristotle means distasteful to the superior type of person who constitutes the more educated part of the audience. The opposite of VULGAR is "free-born" (*eleutheros*), implying a cultured citizen not dependent on others for his living. Aristotle divides theatre audiences into these same categories at *Politics* VIII 7.1342a19, and Plato thought no differently.

The argument of this passage is very condensed. We expect *either* (i) the less vulgar art is better: the less vulgar art is that addressed to the better spectators: so the art addressed to all of them is vulgar, *or* (ii) the less vulgar art is better: the less vulgar art represents to a lesser degree: so the art that represents in all respects is vulgar. But as the text stands we find the premises of argument (i), but the conclusion of (ii). Editors have altered the text to obtain conclusion (i). But Aristotle's example shows that this should not be done; bad oboe-players are criticised for representing everything with gestures, but they do so precisely because they aim to please the whole audience, including its less cultured members. So the two arguments are related, and both have to be refuted.

61b29 "represents in all respects" I.e. tragedy is dramatic throughout, not narrative: compare the note on 60a8. If the sense is "represents everything", as is possible, compare Plato, *Republic* III 397A, on the folly of representing or mimicking all sorts of noises.

"react" Literally "perceive", and usually taken to mean "understand", but see on 54b15–18.

61b30 "They use a lot of movement" Literally "they move much movement". So the Arabic; for "they move" the Greek has "him moving", an easy error.

61b30–2 These examples are from another type of performance, DITH-YRAMB, where bad oboe-players evidently mimed as they played. The context where they would mime a rolling discus is unknown. They probably dragged the chorus-leader in the *Scylla* to mime the way the monster Scylla grabbed her victims; the work is that of Timotheus mentioned above (54a30).

61b32–5 A further example is overacting in tragedy. Aristotle remarks elsewhere that the actors had become more important than the poets (*Rhetoric* III 1.1403b33). No doubt he is referring to virtuoso performers. Mynniscus of Chalcis acted for Aeschylus; his career lasted from ca. 460–420 B.C. He probably criticised a youthful performance by the famous actor Callippides, who trod the boards ca 427–400. By calling him a monkey Mynniscus probably meant that he won his prizes by using cheap tricks, not that he was too imitative (as the other possible translation, "ape", would have suggested). Pindarus is unknown, but presumably of the same period.

62a1 "the whole art" I.e. tragedy is inferior not just when overacted, but by virtue of the fact that it is acted at all.

62a2–4 This recapitulates 61b27–9. Gestures and vulgar spectators go together.

62a3 "who" This is preserved in the Arabic only.

"gestures" (*schēmata*) This word is used as at 55a29; at 56b9 it refers to the different forms a sentence can take, e.g. a statement, question etc.

62a4 "So let us discuss these matters" This is in the Arabic only.

62a5–7 Though associated with the art of tragic composition, the art of acting or DELIVERY (*hupokritikē*) is for Aristotle quite distinct, as he made clear at 56b8–19: it belongs as much to rhetoric as to poetics (*Rhetoric* III 1.1403b24), just as SPECTACLE is least germane to poetry (50b17). Moreover—and even more to the point—overacting can apply just as much to performances in other branches of poetry, whether recited by a rhapsode (like epic), or sung. The epic reciter Sosistratus, and singer Mnasitheus, are otherwise unknown.

62a6 "[visual] signs" A synonym for "gestures".

"reciting an epic" Epics too were performed competitively by reciters at great public festivals, notably the Panathenaea at Athens; see Plato's dialogue *Ion*.

62a9–10 Not all movement should be banned from tragedy, because nobody would wish to ban the chorus from dancing. Callippides (see on 61b33–5) and others were evidently criticised for representing tragic heroines in an undignified way, i.e. with alluring movements like a prostitute's. As all the speaking parts were played by male actors, there was nothing new in his representing female characters in general.

62a11–13 Even when read, a tragedy can achieve its FUNCTION or END (the two are equivalent in Aristotle's teleological system), which is to arouse the emotions: cf. 53b4–7. Spectacle is useful for this, but not indispensable. Cf. 50b18–20.

62a12 "what sort [of tragedy] it is" The quality of the particular tragedy, in terms perhaps of the four kinds of it at 55b32. Others render "what sort [of thing] tragedy is", as at 50a8.

62a13 Aristotle anticipates his final conclusion that tragedy is superior in other respects (cf. 62b12). If the objection that tragedy is vulgar can be overcome, there will be nothing else against it.

"this" "This" has been interpreted (i) "this [objection]", (ii) "excessive movement" or (iii) "this [element]", i.e. spectacle. The parallel at 50b17, where spectacle is said to be least particular to the art of poetry, supports (iii).

62a14 Aristotle's positive arguments in favour of tragedy are introduced only by "furthermore", corresponding to "first" at 62a5. There is no need to suppose a gap in the text here.

62a14–15 "it has everything that epic has" This point that tragedy has all four parts epic has was made above at 49b16–20, but here turns into an argument in favour of tragedy. The same argument was used in the *On Poets*, frag. *3.10. Aristotle turns next to the parts tragedy has in addition, i.e. SONG and SPECTACLE.

62a15 That tragedy, unlike epic, uses a variety of metres was implied at 49b11. Aristotle's further point that it can even use the epic's own hexameter verse is based on a few short passages in tragedy where hexameters are used for semi-oracular pronouncements. At least in theory, tragedy can use the grandest metre, if it wishes. The same argument appears in the *On Poets*, frag. *3.9.

62a15–17 Aristotle now counter-attacks regarding music and spectacle, both of which appear in the arguments against tragedy. Had he written more fully, he probably would have said that, even though spectacle is not an intrinsic part of tragedy, and tragedy is spoilt when it is misused, its proper use can produce effects greatly superior to those of epic which lacks it. Whether he would have conceded that music is not fully a part of tragedy is doubtful; he discussed this in the *On Poets* (see frags. *3.11–18).

62a16 "and spectacles" I.e. spectacular effects. This is often deleted, despite its presence in all the sources, since (i) music corresponds to one PART of tragedy, which Aristotle calls "song" elsewhere, and spectacle to another; (ii) in "by means of which" the Greek indicates that only one item preceded; (iii) Aristotle is thought to contradict himself over spectacle. But "part" may be employed loosely here. Spectacle and song are paired at 50b16, and the logic of the argument supports a mention of both here. Moreover the Arabic suggests that "by means of which" originally indicated that more than one item preceded. Otherwise music is to be regarded as the main contributor to tragedy's pleasures, at least in this context of a defence against the charge that tragedy is vulgar (a charge to which Aristotle was sensitive). Compare 50b16, where song is called "most important of the embellishments", literally "pleasure-giving things", just as it gives pleasure here. But spectacle too is "enthralling".

62a17 "constructed very vividly" For Aristotle's concept of vividness see on 55a23. Vividness inheres in a text that the poet has composed by putting the incidents before his eyes (55a23), whether or not it is meant for dramatic performance; but since drama certainly is intended for such performance, it is likely to be more vividly conceived than epic, and this shows even in reading it (this is probably why Aristotle says "constructed"). Thus this point goes further than that made about reading at a12.

62a18 "in performance" Literally "in practice", but this is equivalent to "on the stage".

62a18–b3 Aristotle's argument from the concentration of tragedy in terms of length is clearly related to his next one, from its greater unity. He means that tragedy achieves its FUNCTION and END (*telos*) in a shorter compass, i.e. in a shorter work, than does epic. If the content of Sophocles' *Oedipus the King* were dragged out to fill a poem the length of the *Iliad* (the longest epic the Greeks knew), it would have much less effect. Compare 59b18–22, where he criticises the ancient epics as being too long, and especially 59a32–4. His opening discussion of tragedy and epic talks of "length" in the different sense of the length of time represented in the plot (see on 49b12); the two kinds of length are clearly related.

62b1 "more pleasurable" All sources are variously corrupt here, but this emendation must be right.

"diluted" The metaphor is from mixing wine with water, and continues at b7 below.

62b2 "the *Iliad"* So the Arabic. The Greek has an obvious corruption.

62b3–11 This no doubt is for Aristotle the clinching argument, which not only reverses the previous one but adds another point. At 59a30–b7 he uses these same arguments to prove Homer's superiority to the other epic poets. Even Homer, however, is obliged to use episodes to fill out his plot (55b16), and even the *Iliad* and *Odyssey*, which are constructed as well as epics can be, are still, because of the very nature of epic, less unified than is tragedy. Compare 56a10, where tragedians are warned not to compose an "epic structure . . . with more than one story", and the *Iliad* is at once mentioned. To be long, epic needs episodes, and they are part of its nature, giving it variety and grandeur (59b26–30); but they necessarily detract from its unity.

62b4 "unified" Literally "single, one", which is misplaced in the MSS to read "the single representation".

62b5 Compare 59b2–7 with notes: there is no real contradiction with that passage, as Aristotle goes on to explain. Episodes even of the *Iliad* were turned into tragedies (e.g. *Iliad* X).

62b6 If an epic had full unity in the tragic sense, it would be either too short (if it were only as long as a tragedy) or too padded out (if it were of the normal length). Note the usual equation of the plot with the composition as a whole. A very similar point is made at 59a32–4, about the difficulty of representing the whole Trojan War in a short epic or a long one.

"docked" Literally, "mouse-tailed" (so MS A), i.e. tapering off, cut off short, all tail. MS B has "curtailed", a metrical term with the same meaning. The hearer of an epic expects something long.

62b7 "the length [appropriate to] the verse-form" Literally " . . . of the verse-form". The hexameter is in terms of syllables the longest line the Greeks used regularly. But Aristotle must mean that it is the proper metre for a long poem (60a3), as well as the weightiest (59b35).

62b8 "several [complete] actions" I have supplied "complete" to make clear that Aristotle is using *praxis* in its strongest sense of "an action which, when represented, forms a whole plot". Aristotle's example is the most shocking he could choose, the Homeric epics themselves; even they are not completely representations of a single action, although they are as far as they can be. Given the full knowledge of other early epics he had (and we largely lack), his view of Greek epic was bound to be less positive than ours, which depends almost entirely on the Homeric poems. By their "parts" he means their episodes, which is why even these are not fully unified compositions.

62b9 "which have magnitude" "Which", lost in the MSS, is restored by the editors.

62b10 Compare 51a23, 59a30 for Homer's superiority in plot-construction.

62b12–15 In concluding, Aristotle adds one further point: tragedy achieves its FUNCTION, i.e. its END, better than epic. This is not an assertion that can go unsupported, unless Aristotle is assuming (as he must be) that the END of the two types of poetry is the same—the arousal of pity and terror, the pleasure he has stated at 52b32, 53b11. Thus at *Rhetoric* III 16.1417a12–15 he affirms that these are the emotions aroused by Books IX-XII of the *Odyssey*. The wording here makes this clear. Why is epic deficient in these? The answer must be because it is longer and more diffuse, so that the emotional impact is less.

62b12 "the art" I.e. of serious poetic composition. Epic and tragedy are regarded as one here.

62b15 "its end" The same as the FUNCTION, as for Aristotle these are synonymous (see Glossary).

62b16–19 Such concluding paragraphs as this signal the end of a major section, which began at 49b9 and covered the two serious genres. Since Aristotle promised to continue by discussing comedy (49b21), and the opening sections of the *Poetics* must logically determine the place of comedy in his theory, they are not included among the topics now dismissed. The sequence of these topics corresponds well to what we have seen: first the parts of tragedy and epic, both qualitative and quantitative, their number and which is better (for "their differences" may also imply this, in which case the arguments for the superiority of plot are meant); next, how best to use them; and lastly, criticisms and their solutions.

62b19–20 "Regarding lampoons and comedy" These doubtful and damaged words are in MS B only, and are followed by two more illegible words. They are evidently the start of Book II. The Latin translation concludes "here ends the first Book of Aristotle's *Poetics*".

Notes to the *Tractatus Coislinianus*

(including the fragments of *Poetics* II)

It is beyond doubt that Aristotle fulfilled his promise to speak later of comedy (*Poetics* 49b21, frag. I in Kassel). That the *Poetics* had two books originally is attested by three ancient lists of Aristotle's works. Book II, which contained his account of comedy, probably disappeared in around the sixth century A.D. The numbering of the fragments of it is Kassel's.

Aristotle refers to the lost part of the *Poetics* several times. In the *Rhetoric* he twice mentions its analysis of the laughable (frag. II; see notes on 5–6, 7–8 below), and also its discussion of synonyms. The *Poetics* is quoted by a later philosopher for a definition of these (frag. III; see on 5(i)–(ii) below). Aristotle also cited comedy there (frag. IV; see on 5(iv) below). At *Politics* VIII 7.1341b39 he promises to discuss catharsis in the *Poetics* (frag. V; see on 3 and 9 below). But the echoes of his account of it in later philosophers probably derive from the *On Poets* (see *On Poets* Testimonia A–D and frag. *4). Frag. VI of the *Poetics* is a mere mistake—a later philosopher erroneously wrote *Poetics* instead of *Physics*; it is omitted here.

If these fragments are all we have left of the second book, we can say little more about it. But I have argued elsewhere that we do in fact still have an outline of the work as a whole, into which its fragments can be fitted, and actually fit very well. I have used this summary, the so-called *Tractatus Coislinianus*, as a basis for reconstructing *Poetics* II itself.

The *Tractatus Coislinianus* (T.C.) is in a Greek manuscript now in Paris, written in ca 920 A.D., a little before the oldest surviving MS of the *Poetics*. The summary is found in the middle of a series of abstracts of Aristotle's logical works, apparently made in the sixth century A.D. It bears no name or title, but is composed in skeleton form like a student's lecture-notes, with headings broken down into sub-headings in a "family-tree" pattern. Even more difficult and corrupt than the *Poetics* itself, it summarises a more extensive text, which partly survives

among introductory material in the medieval MSS of Aristophanes (see
on 5–6 below). In my view, its language, contents and structure all
suggest that its ultimate source is the lost *Poetics* II.

1 The classification of poetry according to the criterion of REPRESEN-
TATION recapitulates the opening of *Poetics* I, but this time it is so arranged that the focus will turn out to be comedy, not tragedy and epic.
Thus the distinction between non-representational and representational versification is dealt with first (cf. *Poetics* 47a28–b24), then that
between narrative and dramatic (cf. 48a19–24), and lastly that between
serious and non-serious (cf. 48a1–18).

"non-representational poetry" Popular usage distinguished "poetry" because it is in verse, Aristotle because it represents people and
actions on a universal level (cf. 51b1–11). Thus at 59a17 he restricts the
discussion of hexameter poetry to poetry which is both REPRESENTA-
TIONAL and in verse. But he uses "poetry" in the popular sense elsewhere, e.g. when talking about Solon, the sixth-century Athenian
lawgiver who cast his political program into verse, or Empedocles (e.g.
Rhetoric III 5.1407a35). The division of x into x and y is paralleled in
Aristotle e.g. *Ethics* VI 8, where "politics" is divided into "politics"
and "law-giving", or V 8.1135b11ff., where "error" is divided into "error" and "accident". Compare too how he puts QUALITATIVE PARTS of
tragedy, like character and spectacle, on the same level as parts of plot
(itself one of the qualitative parts) in his classification of the four types
of tragedy at 55b32–56a3. See also on "pleasure and laughter" in 4.

"historical poetry" E.g. the *Persica* of Choerilus, who set in verse
the Persian Wars narrated by Herodotus. See on 51b2, where Aristotle
says that Herodotus' *Histories* would not become poetry simply by being put into verse.

"educational poetry" Examples here are Hesiod's *Works and Days*
(ca 700 B.C.) for instructional (didactic) poetry, and Empedocles' *On Nature* for theoretical poetry. Aristotle notes that versified treatises about
medicine or natural science are regarded as poems by most people, but
are not poems according to REPRESENTATION (*Poetics* 47b13–20).

2 "dramatic, i.e. enacted" The same pair of terms is used in reverse order at 48a27, "in action and doing"; compare too *On Poets* frag.
*3.8(a).

"mimes" See on 47b10.

"satyr-plays" See on 49a20, where it is implied that this is a less
significant and less serious genre than tragedy. Mimes and satyr-plays
are presumably appended because they are lesser types of poetry that
correspond to comedy and tragedy.

3 Just as the definition of poetry and its main divisions in *Poetics* 47a13–48a27 is followed by an account of its origins, so here it is followed by an account of its END, the catharsis of pity and terror in tragedy.

"the soul's emotions of [pity and] terror" The text omits "pity and". These emotions are reduced homeopathically, by being stimulated by a representation (not by a reality), and the process of catharsis results in a "due proportion" of the emotion, which is felt to the right degree, on the right occasion, towards the right person, etc. Catharsis brings us closer to moderation in our emotions. See on 9 below, the Introduction, Section 5; compare also *On Poets* Testimonia A–D and frag. *4.

"compassion and dread" These are synonyms for PITY and TERROR: see on 53b15.

"It wishes to have" I.e. "tragedy aims to produce". The MS says literally "and [he says] that it wishes to have", a trace of the process of summarisation.

"pain as its mother" This striking metaphor is peculiar and untypical of Aristotle, but compare plot as the "soul" of tragedy (*Poetics* 50a38). It probably means that, even though tragedy produces the pleasure particular to it, the cause of the pleasure is the arousal of our emotions of pain, principally pity and terror.

4 The definition of comedy is closely parallel to that of tragedy at 49b24–8, where most of its terms are explained.

"lacking in magnitude" In one sense of the term, that explained at *Poetics* 51a9–15, comic action cannot be lacking in MAGNITUDE, for it must have magnitude to be represented. The comic action must be complete, i.e. possess a beginning, middle and end. So the sense here is probably that at 49a19, where it is implied that early tragedy, which was less serious, lacked "magnitude". Aristotle's use of this term in the *Poetics* is inconsistent (see Glossary).

"[in embellished speech]" This is supplied from the definition of tragedy.

"parts . . . elements" These terms are reversed in the definition of tragedy, but are virtually synonymous in the *Poetics* (see on 56a37).

"[not] by narration" "Not" is lost in the MS, and restored from the definition of tragedy.

"pleasure and laughter" These are both emotions (see below on 9), but LAUGHTER evidently covers less wide a range than pleasure. Here PLEASURE must stand for pleasurable feelings in general, as PAIN stands for painful feelings in general at *Ethics* II 5.1105b21 (at b25 pain is put on the same level as anger and pity: compare above on 1). Aristotle divided the emotions into two broad categories, pleasurable and painful; from this passage it seems that the emotions which are the object of catharsis in tragedy and comedy are the painful and pleasurable emotions in general, not only pity and terror or laughter in particular. See on 49b28.

"laughter as its mother"   Compare the equally peculiar description of tragedy in 3. Comedy results in the comic pleasure, but that pleasure is caused by laughter, and perhaps by the pleasant emotions in general (compare 3). The emphasis on laughter leads into the analysis of what we laugh at.

5–6   In sections 5–6(ii) I translate not the *Tractatus Coislinianus*, which omits all the examples, but the fuller version of the same text preserved in the "Prolegomena to Aristophanes", no. VI, using the *Tractatus* to supplement it in a few places. The division of the causes of laughter into DICTION and INCIDENTS ("things done") should be compared with Aristotle's remarks in *Poetics* frag. II, which consists of two passages from his *Rhetoric*. The first reads "things laughable are pleasant, both people, words and deeds; a separate division of laughable things has been made in the *Poetics*" (I 11.1371b35). The second runs "how many kinds of laughable things there are has been stated in the *Poetics*" (III 18.1419b3). Both passages imply that these kinds were enumerated there, as they are in the *Tractatus*. Those from "words" correspond with 5, from "deeds" with 6, and from "people" with 7–8. The main division into "diction" and "incidents" recurs in *On Poets* *frag. *6.2, and in the classification of sophistical arguments into "those from diction" and "those outside diction" at *Sophistical Refutations* 4–6, where the list of six "from diction" begins and ends with the same two kinds as in 5, "homonymy" and "the form of the diction".

5 "The laughter of comedy . . . seven ways"   The expression is awkward and probably condensed. The *Tractatus* has only "laughter arises from diction and from actions".

"from diction"   So the *Tractatus*; the *Prolegomenon* has "from dictions", i.e. the different types of diction.

5(i)–(ii)   One of the few facts known for certain about *Poetics* II is that it discussed HOMONYMS and SYNONYMS: cf. *Rhetoric* III 2.1404b37, "among names homonyms are useful to the sophist (he uses these to do harm), and synonyms to the poet. I mean [names that are] standard and synonymous like "going" and "walking"—these are both standard and synonymous with each other. What each of these is . . . has been stated in the *Poetics*" (= frag. III). This is confirmed by Porphyry (ca 234–304 A.D.), who shows that Aristotle actually defined synonyms there: "Aristotle in the *Poetics* said that 'synonyms are things of which there is more than one name but the sense is the same', like polyonyms, 'cloak', 'wrap' and 'mantle' '" (quoted by Simplicius, *Commen-*

tary on Aristotle's Categories 36.13). The definition of homonyms must have run "homonyms are things of which the name is the same, but there is more than one sense". Neither definition is preserved in the MSS, but compare that of verbosity below.

The series homonyms - synonyms - paronyms recurs at the opening of Aristotle's *Categories*, 1.1a1–15. The examples show that homonyms are equivalent to puns.

"paying" I.e. paying out money or earning it, as in "a paying proposition". Alternatively there could be a pun on "being torn apart". Its source is unknown.

"metre" The reference is probably to Aristophanes, *Clouds* 638ff., where Socrates talks of poetic metres, and the ignorant Strepsiades misunderstands him to mean "measures" of corn.

5(ii) "I'm here and am arrived" The example is from Aristophanes' *Frogs* 1153ff., where Euripides criticises this line, quoted from the prologue of Aeschylus' *Libation Bearers*, for saying the same thing twice. In fact Orestes' words can mean "I am here and am back from exile", so they are not exactly synonymous.

5(iii) "verbosity" VERBOSITY (*adoleschia*) has no exact English equivalent, as Aristotle uses it in the technical sense of repeating a term in a definition, as well as of being garrulous in general. No example is preserved, but exact repetition must be meant: compare *Sophistical Refutations* 3.165b16, where verbosity is defined as "saying the same thing more than once". Otherwise it is hard to see how this would differ from synonymy.

"twice" This is a conjectural insertion by a Byzantine scribe, but it supplies the necessary sense.

"name" NAME is used in the same sense as in the *Poetics* (see on 57a31–58a17), i.e. a noun, adjective or even verb.

5(iv) "Paronymy" PARONYMS are different forms of the same word. Three of paronymy's four subdivisions—addition, shortening and alterations—are found in the same sequence at *Poetics* 57b1 (see on 57b35–58a7), where the first type is called "lengthening".

"by addition ... by shortening" These are supplied from the *Tractatus*. The example of lengthening is lost; compare those at 58a4.

"I'm called Midas the joke" The source of the quotation is unknown, but Midas is a common name for slaves in comedy. The shortened word is *bōmax*, a comic form of *bōmolochos*, "buffoon" (originally someone who scrounges scraps at the altar by telling jokes). *Bōmax* is now attested in Aristophanes (frag. 801 Kassel-Austin).

"diminutive" Headings (c) and (d) are independent of paronymy in both sources; I have assigned them to it, on the ground that alteration is found next to lengthened and shortened words in the *Poetics* (57b3, 58a6).

The comic possibilities of diminutives or pet names are remarked on by Aristotle at *Rhetoric* III 2.1405b28ff.: "the diminutive is that which makes smaller both the bad and the good, just as Aristophanes jests in his *Babylonians*, [saying] instead of 'gold coin' 'gold coinlet', instead of 'cloak' 'cloaklet', instead of 'abuse' 'abuselet', and 'plaguelet'." The examples, diminutives of Socrates and Euripides, both occur in Aristophanes.

"alteration"　This is the same as the "altered name" of *Poetics* 58a6, defined as "when [the poet] leaves some of the appellation [unaltered], but makes up some of it, e.g. 'by her righter breast' instead of 'right' " (*dexiteron* for *dexion*). The example which I insert here is *Poetics* frag. IV, " 'the worstest of all' [instead of 'the worst']" (*kuntotaton* for *kuntaton*), a word-play making fun of an EXOTIC NAME from epic. This fragment is cited as from the *Poetics* by an anonymous writer (the "Antiatticist") of ca. 180 A.D., and is obviously from comedy. The example given in the MSS, " 'O Clod Almighty' instead of 'O God' ", is a letter-substitution instead of the insertion of a syllable; since Aristotle's examples of paronymy are limited to changes affecting whole syllables, but this is a substitution of a letter, I have hesitantly assigned it to the next, lost, heading.

5(v)–(vi)　Two types of verbal humour have fallen out of the list, and the two last sub-types of paronymy were promoted to keep the number up to seven. Although my restoration of parody is guesswork, there is good evidence that an account of metaphor once stood here.

5(v) "parody"　Aristotle never defines parody, and uses it to mean an epic burlesque at *Poetics* 48a12. But at *Rhetoric* III 11.1412a26–36, in a list of kinds of the laughable, he mentions first, seemingly, paronyms (*parapepoiēmena*) and plays on letters, and then a form of humour "in verses", by which I think he means parody; for his example is a parody of an epic hexameter, "he strode with chilblains on his feet", where we expect "sandals". Aristotle says that all these kinds work by deceiving our expectations. So does "O Clod Almighty", where we expect "O God".

"O Clod"　My translation does not capture the obscenity of the original (*Bdeu* for *Zdeu*, vocative case of "Zeus"). This is a parody of a well-known cliché, found in Aristophanes (*Lysistrata* 940) and parodied by him at *Birds* 835 and twice elsewhere. The source of this form of the joke is unknown.

5(vi)　Metaphor is needed in any Aristotelian analysis of humour, as is clear from his remark at *Rhetoric* III 3.1406b7, "comic poets too use metaphors". He even says "most jokes arise from metaphor and the accompanying deception [of expectations]" (11.1412a19), and gives many examples of humorous metaphor there. Metaphor's presence here is confirmed by the sentence "this happens . . . genus". This is put after "alteration" in the *Tractatus*, but after "the form of the diction" in the Prolegomena to Aristophanes; it can belong to neither entry, for "things of the same genus" can relate only to metaphor (see on 57b7–32). The summary has apparently coordinated two originally distinct statements, both paralleled in the *Rhetoric*: (i) "one should not make metaphors from things that are remote, but from those *of the same genus* or species" (*Rhetoric* III 2.1405a35, cf. 11.1412a11); (ii) "one should make comic metaphors from things that are ugly, whether *in sound* or . . . some other perception" (this transposes into comic terms *Rhetoric* III 2.1405b17ff.).

5(vii) **"The form of the diction"**   To judge from 56b8–19, this refers to pronunciation, punctuation and intonation, aspects of delivery; none of these was regularly indicated in the written Greek of Aristotle's time. But elsewhere the phrase refers to the rhetorical shape of a sentence, e.g. an antithesis, which can be used by sophists to make what looks like a sound argument, but in fact is not (*Rhetoric* II 24.1401a1ff., *Sophistical Refutations* 4.166b10–19).

6 **"Laughter arises from the incidents"**   "Incidents" here is a catch-all category, including all forms of humour that do not depend purely on diction. In fact types (i)–(v) correspond to PLOT, (v)–(viii) to CHARACTER, and (ix) to REASONING; I think the discussion of laughter was intended to serve as a basis for deducing the four main QUALITATIVE PARTS of comedy, including DICTION.

"in two ways"   So the Prolegomena to Aristophanes, which breaks off after 6(ii). The *Tractatus*, however, lists nine ways, including the first two in reverse order. The reversal is owed to a scribal error, and shows that the first two items were somehow distinct from the rest in the original. Compare *Rhetoric* III 11.1412a19, where Aristotle says that most witticisms arise from "metaphor and the deception of expectations": these are the *verbal* equivalents of the first two types of humour *on stage* here.

6(i) **"deception"**   The deception of characters on stage is meant, for the example is Aristophanes, *Clouds* 144ff., where Strepsiades takes seriously Socrates' story of how he measured the distance a flea could jump: he dipped its feet in wax, took off the bootees that formed, and used these to compute in "flea-feet" the distance between his pupil's eyebrow and his own head where it landed. "Flea" is an emendation of "soul" in the MSS, an easy error.

6(ii) **"making [something] like"**   Literally "assimilation". This means making someone like someone else on stage, i.e. disguise, since

the example is from Aristophanes' *Frogs* 495ff., where the god Dionysus frantically makes his human slave Xanthias exchange his Heracles-
disguise with him in order to avoid a flogging.

6(iii) "the impossible"   From now on the text depends on the
Tractatus alone, and there are therefore no examples. (iii), (iv) and (vi)
occur in the same sequence twice in the *Poetics*, at 54a37–b14 (although
the terms used here do not appear) and 61b11–21; errors in serious
poetry are good sources of laughter in comedy.

IMPOSSIBILITIES, like flying up to heaven on a giant dung-beetle or
building a city in the sky, are an important comic resource in
Aristophanes.

6(iv) "the possible and inconsequential"   This is the same as the
IMPROBABLE, which Aristotle discussed extensively in the *Poetics* (54b6,
60a26–b2, where he also terms an improbability an "oddity",
61b11–15). Again, an improbability in the plot, damaging to serious
poetry, is a source of humour. This does not contradict 51b13, where
Aristotle says that comic poets construct their plots "according to
probability": many of Aristophanes' plays are based on an improbability or impossibility, whose logical consequences are then set before us
(e.g. Dicaeopolis' idea of making a personal peace with the enemy in
the *Acharnians*).

6(v) "things contrary to expectation"   This does not appear in the
corresponding list of errors in serious poetry at 61b9–15, 23, since surprise is only a fault if it is mishandled, when it becomes an
improbability.

6(vi) "making the characters tend to be wicked"   Literally " . . . incline toward the wicked". Gratuitously debased characters are ascribed
to comedy from the start of the *Poetics* (e.g. 48a16–18). Many of Aristophanes' characters are caricatured in this way, e.g. Dionysus in the
Frogs. In tragedy and epic bad characters should be avoided unless
they are required by the plot (54a29, 61b21).

6(vii) "vulgar dancing"   This looks out of place in the list, but in
fact it forms and reflects CHARACTER, cf. *Politics* VIII 5.1340b8ff., where
this is said of "music" (*mousikē*), i.e. poetry and song: rhythms "have a
character . . . of motion, and some of these have more vulgar motions,
others more civilised. So from this it is obvious that music can make
the character of the soul a certain kind." Aristotle calls trochaic
rhythms more suited to the comic dance (the cordax) at *Rhetoric* III
8.1408b36.

6(viii)   Poor DECISION, like vulgar dancing, reveals CHARACTER, e.g.
Dionysus' plan to bring back Euripides from the dead, when he could
have Sophocles instead (Aristophanes, *Frogs* 76f.). Compare *Ethics* III
2.1112a1ff.: "it is by making good or bad decisions that we are people

of a certain kind". Conversely, CHARACTER reveals DECISION (*Poetics* 50b8). For us to decide, the possibilities must be real, as stressed here: cf. *Ethics* III 2.1111b20, "there can be no decision about impossibilities".

6(ix) "When the argument is disjointed" By "argument" (*logos*), the *Tractatus* must mean the REASONING, because incoherence in the PLOT has already been covered by (iv), IMPROBABILITY. Thus this item refers to the fourth among the main parts of comedy, DICTION, PLOT, CHARACTER and REASONING. The last two receive less attention in this list, which matches their lesser importance in the *Poetics*, both in Aristotle's theory (50a15–b15) and in the amount of discussion he allots to each.

7–8 This paragraph, on how people are the objects of laughter, corresponds to the third part of Aristotle's division of laughable things into words, deeds and people (*Rhetoric* I 11.1371b36). Both abuse and comedy with its jokes point out people's mental and bodily faults, but abuse does so directly, comedy indirectly. As Aristotle says at *Ethics* IV 8.1128a30ff., jokes shade into abuse if they go too far. His follower Theophrastus likewise defined a joke as concealed criticism of an error (in Plutarch, *Moralia* 631E); this is the missing link in thought between abuse, innuendo and jokes in the *Tractatus*.

For Aristotle, comedy developed from the lampoon or poem of abuse concerned with particular people's faults (*Poetics* 48b26); the transition from lampoon to comedy at Athens was brought about by Crates, who "was the first to relinquish the form of the lampoon and compose generalised stories and plots" (49b7–9). Comedy differs from the lampoon because it is concerned with what is UNIVERSAL, not with PARTICULAR individuals, and therefore it uses names picked out at random, not those of real people (51b11–15). Poetry itself is distinguished from history because it represents UNIVERSALS rather than PARTICULARS (see note on 51b5). In this way Aristotle is able to maintain Plato's opposition to abuse, while circumventing his banning of comedy from the ideal state of the *Republic* (cf. e.g. X 606C). A similar distinction is being made here—direct abuse of individuals belongs to lampoon, not to comedy. Another distinction Aristotle could have made is that lampoon is a representation of all kinds of evil, not only of those kinds that are not painful or destructive, as comedy is (see *Poetics* 49a32–7).

Since Aristotle believed that comedy evolved from the lampoon, he is not likely to have thought that it gave up "the form of the lampoon" all at once; we should rather expect a gradual development, such as he postulates in the case of tragedy (*Poetics* 49a13–15). This will explain an apparent contradiction between this passage and *Ethics* IV 8.1128a4, 20–4: "those who go to excess in the laughable seem buffoons and vulgar fellows . . . The wit of the free-born man differs from that of the slave, and that of the educated [differs from] that of the uneducated. One can see this from the comedies of the old and the recent [comedians]. Obscenity aroused laughter in the former, but innuendo rather in the latter." Here "old" comedies admit obscene abuse. Compare also *T.C.* 18, where "old" comedy *"goes to excess in the laughable"* (my italics). Clearly comedy gradually evolved towards its perfect form, just as tragedy did.

Ethics IV 8 also raises the problem of Aristotle's attitude to Aristophanes, whose comedies eventually came to be called "Old" when Menander had produced his "New" comedies. Did Aristotle despise the dramas of Aristophanes? His implicit praise of Aristophanes at *Poetics* 48a27 makes this most unlikely (see note there), and a case can be made that he thought of him as belonging to "middle" comedy (see on 18).

7 "Comedy differs from abuse"   This could instead be translated "comedy is superior to abuse".

"innuendo"   This word (*emphasis* in Greek) differs from Aristotle's term for innuendo at *Ethics* IV 8.1128a24 (*huponoia*), and its sense may not be exactly the same: Aristotle uses *emphasis* to mean "appearance" or "suggestion", particularly in his writings on dreams. The implication is of an image that is blurred or out of focus, as perhaps in Aristophanes' transformations of reality into fantasy.

8 "errors of soul and body"   Comedy, no less than tragedy, is concerned with error (*hamartia, hamartēma*), but the results of comic error are less far-reaching. Tragic error brings misfortune (*Poetics* 53a15), but "the laughable is a sort of error and ugliness that is not painful or destructive, just as, obviously, a laughable mask is something ugly and distorted without pain" (49a34–7). The example of the comic mask confirms that comedy criticises bodily faults, accidents for which we are not usually held responsible, as well as mental errors and misbehaviour, for which we are: so too Plato, *Laws* 816D. Although at *Ethics* V 8 Aristotle distinguished accident, error and injustice according to our degree of responsibility in each case, at 1135b12 he uses "error" generically for the whole class of accidents and mistakes. It is likely that comic error is even broader, since mental errors may include faulty moral principles, and these lead to vice. In the case of tragic error Aristotle probably focusses on genuine mistakes because these best inspire pity and terror in others. See further on 53a10. As usual, the SOUL is regarded as having intellectual as well as emotional functions.

9   Now that the sources of comedy's effect, laughter, have been explained, there follows a restatement of the aim or END of comedy, already given in the definition at 4, and a comparison of it with the aim of tragedy, already explained in 3 (see note). That aim is catharsis, but the term used here, as in 3 and in several later witnesses to Aristotle's theory, is "due proportion" (*summetria*): see *On Poets* Testimonia B–D.

It may seem strange that the text compares the laughable, i.e. the things we laugh at, with terror, the emotion we feel. But both Plato and Aristotle are prone to equate the physical effects of an emotion with that emotion. Thus Plato complains that tragedy and comedy cause too much weeping and laughter (*Republic* X 606A–C), and Aristotle talks of a tragedian making us "shudder and feel pity" instead of "feel terror and pity" (*Poetics* 53b5); he could equally well have said "shudder and weep". At *On the Soul* I 1.403a4ff. he makes it very clear that the emotions have a physical correlative within the body. He never defines laughter itself, but Plato certainly regarded laughter as an emotion: see *Philebus* 50A, "we agreed a while ago that envy is a pain of the soul, and laughter is a pleasure". Compare also pseudo-Longinus, *On the Sublime* 38.6, "laughter is an emotion within pleasure". Whether laughter is a physical or emotional phenomenon is particularly difficult to pin down, as it undoubtedly has both physical and emotional elements, and neither ordinary language nor psychology has yet succeeded in separating the two.

"There wishes to be a due proportion"   The MS has "Things in due proportion . . . wish to be"; "a due proportion" is an emendation based on 3. The translation "he wishes there to be" seems excluded by the parallel with 3.

10–16   This analysis of the six QUALITATIVE PARTS of comedy is paralleled by the account of four of the qualitative parts of tragedy at *Poetics* 52b28–59a13; they are in the standard order Aristotle uses.

10 "elements"   The MS has "subject-matter", by an easy confusion of the letters.

11 "Comic plot"   For this rather uninformative statement cf. the definition of comedy in 4. It would be interesting to know whether plot is as important to comedy as to tragedy. Comic plot is said to be constructed "according to probability" at *Poetics* 51b13, except presumably for the occasions when an impossibility or improbability is used to raise a laugh, and the presence of plot is a distinguishing mark of comedy as against lampoon (49b8, cf. 16 below). However, among the sources of humour in 5–6 plot takes up less space than diction does (but more than character and reasoning). This accords with the *Tractatus'* nature as an analysis of Aristophanic comedy, in which plot is less important as a comic resource than it was to become later, in the plays of Menander.

"is structured"   Literally "has its structure".

12 "Characters of comedy"   The three examples of comic character are subtly chosen. All are departures from the mean, and therefore in error (cf. 8), but not to a criminal degree, precisely as Aristotle described the characters of comedy at *Poetics* 49a32–5. These three types, buffoon (*bōmolochos*), ironist (*eirōn*) and boaster (*alazōn*), are fundamental to Aristophanic comedy. They are found together at *Ethics* II 7.1108a21ff.: "pretension in the direction of overstatement is boastfulness and the person who has it is a boaster, but in the direction of understatement it is irony and [the person who has it is] an ironist. Regarding what is pleasant in fun, . . . the excess is buffoonery and the person who has it is a buffoon, but the person who is lacking in it is a kind of boor." Aristotle contrasts irony with buffoonery for a different reason at *Rhetoric* III 18.1419b6ff., where he is discussing how to use jokes in the law- court: "how many kinds of laughable things there are has been stated in the *Poetics*. Some of these are suited to a free man and others are not . . . Irony is more respectable than buffoonery, for the former makes the joke for his own sake, but the buffoon for another's."

13 "general statement and proof"   The same basic division of REASONING into general statement and proof is found in the brief description of it in the *Poetics* (50a6, b11), although generalisations are not present in the fuller list of its parts at 56a37–b2. Presumably, as there, we are expected to go to the *Rhetoric* for a full account of the subject.

"five [kinds of artless proof]"   At *Rhetoric* I 2.1355b35, Aristotle divides proofs into two classes, "artless" proofs which can be used as they are, e.g. witnesses, ordeals and contracts, and those "artful" proofs which have to be invented by the orator, i.e. arguments based on the logic of the case: compare the similar classification of recognitions at *Poetics* 54b19–55a21. The five kinds listed here belong to the former class, as *Rhetoric* I 15.1375a24 confirms. The "artful" proofs based on logic were perhaps omitted because they are less germane to comedy than the "artless" ones.

14 "Comic diction"   In the *Poetics* Aristotle emphasises that the DICTION should be appropriate to the genre (59a8–14). At *Rhetoric* III 7.1408a12ff. he warns public speakers not to use a high style for a trivial topic or vice versa—otherwise, comedy results. Since comedy is a representation of inferior persons (*Poetics* 49a32), and its characters are buffoons, impostors and people who pretend to be stupid (*T.C.* 13), their speech is hardly likely to be elevated. The kinds of words that can be exploited for verbal humour have already been exemplified (5).

"The comic poet . . ."   Whereas all the characters in Greek tragedy speak the same Greek dialect (Attic), in comedy characters from different regions use different dialects, for comic effect. Comedy also diverged from tragedy in that its dialect is not fixed (the comedies of Epicharmus, for example, were in Sicilian Doric dialect).

"their ancestral dialect"   The MS has "his" by an easy error.

"himself the local one"   This apparently refers to the parabasis, the mid-point of most Old Comedies, in which the chorus abandon their supposed character and speak as the mouthpiece of the poet himself.

15 "Song . . ."   With the dismissal of song as part of music, compare the dismissal of reasoning as part of rhetoric at *Poetics* 56a34. The *Poetics* has very little to say about the lyrics of tragedy: see on 49b34.

"Spectacle supplies * * "   The MS says "spectacle supplies harmony" (*sumphōnia*), but this makes no sense, and the word must be corrupt. Perhaps it was originally "scene-painting" (cf. *Poetics* 49a18) or "enthralment" (cf. 50a33).

"to dramas"   Neither the account of SONG nor that of SPECTACLE refers specifically to comedy, and it is possible that this paragraph is intended to supply the account of these two parts of drama that is absent from the first book of the *Poetics*, particularly as the word *drama* applies especially to tragedy. Its omission there was natural enough, as the account of DICTION led naturally into the discussion of epic, which has neither SONG nor SPECTACLE.

16 "Plot, diction and song"   Not every actual play has all the QUALITATIVE PARTS (see on 50a12). PLOT, DICTION and SONG are the essentials for any comic or tragic representation. Aristotle implies that only these three parts were present in the primitive stages of both (see on 49a19–24, a37–b9); even now there are tragedies without character (50a25).

"reasonings"   I.e. instances of reasoning.

"[not] a few"   This is a stronger expression than "many" (see on 50a12). I have inserted "not", which is absent in the MS. "A few" would be surprising, and the parallel at 50a12 makes it still less likely.

17   With the analysis of the QUANTITATIVE PARTS of comedy, needed for a complete account of the genre, compare *Poetics* 52b14–27, which does the same for tragedy. Like that passage, this section has been criticised as excessively schematic, and indeed inapplicable to Aristophanic comedy, because it omits entirely the parabasis, a metrically distinctive chorus at the centre of many of his plays. But the parabasis disappeared in Aristophanes' latest plays, setting the pattern for fourth-century comedy, which by Menander's time late in the century had attained a five-act structure separated by choral songs. Compare the note on 52b14–27. The principle of classification is the same as that applied in the *Poetics*: see on 52b19–21.

17(a) "A prologue is a part of a comedy"   The parallel definition at 52b19 has "a whole part" (see note there). The phrase "part of a comedy" is absent from the three definitions that follow, and was presumably omitted when the summary was made.

17(b) "choral [part]"   There is no definition of this in the *Poetics*, perhaps because it is so obvious: Aristotle at once focusses on its subdivisions. He also lists it last among the four parts, instead of second: both positions are logical, as the prologue precedes the first choral song, but the prologue and episode also belong together as spoken parts.

"sufficient magnitude"   This excludes minor choral songs that do not serve to separate the episodes from each other. The same exclusion is implied at 52b20 by the phrase "between whole choral songs" (see note there).

17(c)   On the meaning of EPISODE see on 51b34.

17(d) "exit"   The definition at 52b21 is different; this one corresponds more closely to the original sense of the term "exit" (*exodos*). But in structural terms it belongs to the same series as prologue and episode, as a type of "last act".

"uttered"   Not "sung", because the *exodos* of many comedies consists of marching metres like anapaests, instead of sung lyrics. Compare the similar definition of the processional song (*parodos*) as "the first whole utterance of the chorus" at 52b22.

18 "[The kinds] of comedy"   Like the *Poetics*, the *Tractatus* ends on a note of comparison, not however between genres, but within the genre itself, according to the degree of its development away from abuse (lampoon) and excessive buffoonery. The definition of "old" comedy resembles Aristotle's definition of a buffoon as one who "goes to excess in the laughable" (*Ethics* IV 8.1128a4). To refine the distinction between the buffoon and the wit, he at once draws an analogy with "old" and "recent" comedies: in the former the humour is supplied by obscene abuse, in the latter by innuendo (see on 7–8). The development of comedy posited here is in the same direction, with the difference that there is a middle type (in the *Ethics*, the introduction of a middle type would have blurred Aristotle's analogy). Strangely enough, tragedy developed in the same direction, from the laughable to the grand: "[starting] from trivial plots and laughable diction, . . . [tragedy only] became grand late" (*Poetics* 49a19). Aristotle also contrasts these two terms at *Rhetoric* III 3.1406b5, where he has comedy in mind: "some metaphors are unsuitable because they are laughable (comic poets too use metaphors), others because they are too grand and tragic". "Grand" (*semnos*) also means "serious, stately, severe". Fourth century comedy certainly did incline in this direction, under the influence of tragedy in general and Euripides in particular. By Menander's time there is little of the verbal, fantastical and sexual exuberance so typical of Aristophanes.

The description of "old" comedy as going to excess in the laughable at first seems odd: how can a comedy have too much laughter? However, the excess lies in the buffoonish nature of the laughter—the buffoon is not afraid of obscenity and of harming himself or others with his insults, as long as it is funny (so *Ethics* IV 8.1128a4ff., 34ff.). Clearly "old" comedy is not the best kind. But it seems equally unlikely that "new" comedy is to be approved either, since comedy depends on laughter for its effect. Thus "middle" comedy, which seems to occupy a mid-point in time as well as in content, should be the best; the mean of style, i.e. the best style, is likewise a mixture (see on 51a31–4).

What periods, and what comic poets, are meant by these terms? The epitomator has left no clues, and it is usually assumed that the "old" comedy is that of Aristophanes and his contemporaries (ca. 430–390), the "new" comedy that of Menander (from ca 320 onwards), and the "middle" comedy that of the poets in between; this is the modern classification of Greek comedy. If this is right, then the *T.C.* must be by a writer later than Aristotle, who died before Menander's earliest play was produced. But it need not be right, since a number of sources suggest that the original division of comedy into "old", "middle" and "new" made Aristophanes "middle" comedy, and did not include Menander at all; he was inserted later. Consider the following, from the anonymous *Life of Aristophanes* 2: "Aristophanes seems to have been the first to lead comedy towards what is more useful and grander, as she was still astray in the ancient style . . . He was also the first to display the manner of the new comedy in his *Cocalus*." Compare Tzetzes, *Introduction to Theocritus* II 5: "comedy is divided into the first [comedy], which abused everyone openly; this was begun by Susarion. In the second the abuse was against everyone, but concealed; best in it were Cratinus, Eupolis, Aristophanes and Plato [the comic poet]. In the third the abuse was concealed, and [aimed] at slaves and foreigners alone, not citizens any longer; Menander and Philemon were notable in it." Lastly compare the anonymous Scholia to Dionysius Thrax, p. 19.17ff.: "There were many [poets] of old comedy, but Cratinus was noteworthy . . . Eupolis and Aristophanes participated in old comedy *for a time*" (my italics). This source cites Plato the comic poet as typical of "middle" comedy, and Menander as typical of "new" comedy.

The assignment of Aristophanes to "middle" comedy is usual in these and related sources, and the poets who came after him are simply omitted in favour of Menander. It looks as if Aristophanes originally represented "middle" comedy, and the poets after him, like

Anaxandrides whom Aristotle quotes, represented "new" comedy; but when Menander invented a yet newer kind of comedy, Aristophanes became "Old" Comedy, Menander became "New", and those in between became "Middle". It is not at present proven that the original classification is Aristotle's, but it looks to me decidedly probable. If Aristophanes is "middle" comedy, and "middle" comedy is best, this will explain why he is chosen to provide many of the examples of the laughable in *T.C.* 5–6. That Aristotle considered Aristophanes the best comic poet he knew is evident from his juxtaposition of him with Homer and Sophocles at *Poetics* 48a27.

Hypothetical Reconstruction of Poetics II

This reconstruction is based on a combination of the known fragments of *Poetics* II with the *Tractatus Coislinianus*. It is offered to show how I believe the lost *Poetics* II looked according to the best available evidence; but it is to be treated as hypothetical only. For commentary, see the notes on the equivalent sections of the *Tractatus Coislinianus*, which has the same section-numbers (given in the margin here).

Notes to the fragments of the
On Poets

The *On Poets*, sometimes called by the same title as the *Poetics* in antiquity, was one of Aristotle's 'exoteric' or published works. These were in dialogue form and addressed to the educated public at large; the 'esoteric' works, on the other hand (including the *Poetics*), seem to be Aristotle's own scripts for his lecture-courses. Thus the *On Poets* had a more flowing and polished style and somewhat less technical contents than the *Poetics*; it was also read and quoted more widely, at least until late antiquity, when the *Poetics* drove it out of circulation, perhaps because of a mistaken belief that the esoteric works contained Aristotle's "real" or "secret" teaching.

In modern times the *On Poets* has been imagined as no more than a series of brilliant literary anecdotes, but this view is almost certainly wrong, since there are clear signs that it contained an account of Aristotle's literary theory. Aristotle's dialogues were not, like many of Plato's, conversations in which one speaker is continually interacting with another; instead, the speakers tended to give long monologues from different points of view. When the Roman statesman Cicero adopted this style of writing for his own philosophical works, he explained in his letters that he was emulating Aristotle's manner.

We do not know who the speakers of the *On Poets* were. If Aristotle followed his usual practice, he will have addressed the reader in a preface, and may have included himself among the participants. This is supported by the remark of a later philosopher that Plato's attack on the emotional effects of poetry in the *Republic* "provided Aristotle and the defenders of these kinds of poetry with their starting-point" (see Testimonium C(ii)). See also the Introduction, section 3.

Some of the following fragments are assigned to the *On Poets* only by conjecture. I have marked these numbers with an asterisk. Fragment-numbers in the form 'frag. 72R.' are those of V. Rose, *Aristoteles Pseudepigraphus*, third edition, Leipzig 1885. I omit frag. 71R. (on the chronology of Empedocles' life), since it has recently been shown to derive from Aristotle's *Olympic Victors*.

175

1–3   Only frags. 1 and 2 definitely belong to Book I. They cover the same ground as *Poetics* 47a18–b13, the argument that poetry is REPRE-SENTATION. Frag. *3 is not explicitly assigned to Aristotle in its source, but its argument continues that of the opening sections of the *Poetics*. Thus frag. *3.1–7 largely corresponds to 48a1–18, on the kinds of AC-TIONS and CHARACTERS represented; *3.8–10 blends 48a19–28, on the MANNER of representation, with 49b9–20, on the difference between tragedy and epic; and this is further explored in *3.11–18. I therefore have some confidence in concluding that these also are from the *On Poets*.

1(a)   (= frag. 72R.) This fragment is quoted verbatim by the ency-clopedist Athenaeus (ca 200 A.D.), *Intellectuals at Dinner* XI 505C. It probably comes from an argument that poetry should be defined ac-cording to REPRESENTATION, in which Aristotle pointed out that prose works like mimes and Socratic dialogues are representations even though they are not in verse; he makes the same point at *Poetics* 47b10–11. The whole passage reads: Plato, who "in his *Republic* ex-pelled Homer and representational poetry, himself wrote dialogues in a representational way, but was not even the discoverer of their form himself. For before him Alexamenus of Teos discovered this kind of [prose] works, as Nicias of Nicaea reports, and Sotion. Aristotle in his *On Poets* writes as follows . . . " (frag. 1(a) begins). It is unlikely that Aristotle himself directly criticised Plato by name for denouncing po-etic representation in dialogues that are themselves representational in form; had he done so, we would surely have heard of it.

"even though they are"   This has been lost in the MSS, and is in-serted by editors.

"mimes of Sophron"   See note on *Poetics* 47b10.

"[prose] speeches and representations"   Aristotle had no adjective meaning "prose", and expresses the concept by saying "speeches" (*logoi*). The point is that they are REPRESENTATIONS, which matters more than whether they are in prose or verse. Compare 51b2, "the writings of Herodotus could be put into verse, but they would be no less a sort of history in verse than they are without verses".

"Alexamenus of Teos"   Otherwise unknown; he was presumably active soon after (or even before) Socrates' execution in 399 B.C. Aris-totle does not use Alexamenus' name explicitly to deprive Plato of the credit for inventing the genre, but this implication is certainly present.

1(b)   This is from an anonymous writer on Plato, preserved in a pa-pyrus from Oxyrhynchus in Egypt (no. 3219, second century A.D.), which reads in full: [Plato] " . . . meanwhile(?) emulating Sophron the writer of mimes regarding the dramatic element in his dialogues. For one must not believe Aristotle when, in his jealousy of Plato, he says in the first book of his *On Poetry* that . . . " (frag. 1(b) follows).

1(c) This citation is from Diogenes Laertius (later third century A.D.), *Lives of the Famous Philosophers* III 48 (= frag. 72R.), quoting a source of the second century A.D. "They say that Zeno of Elea was first to write dialogues; but Aristotle in the first book of his *On Poets* says that . . . " (frag. 1(c) follows).

2 (= frag. 73R.) This too is from Diogenes Laertius, III 37. It may not be a verbatim quotation, but a paraphrase of what Aristotle says more obliquely in frag. 1.

*3 These fragments occur in the *On Poems* IV of the philosopher Philodemus (ca 110–40 B.C.), in a polemic where he extensively quotes and paraphrases an unnamed opponent. Philodemus' works were found at Herculaneum near Naples in 1754, where they had been preserved by the eruption of Vesuvius in A.D. 79. This papyrus (no. 207) is badly damaged, and the opponent's name has not survived; but the close similarity between his language and doctrines and those of Aristotle make the latter's *On Poets* an obvious source (this was first seen by F. Sbordone in 1952). Philodemus seems to have quoted his opponent in more or less the right order, since the sequence of the fragments he quotes permits us to reconstruct an argument that closely follows the sequence of topics in the *Poetics*. (The fragments are given in the order in which they appear in the papyrus. Unless indicated in the notes, square brackets mean that the words are missing because of damage to the papyrus, not—as elsewhere in this translation—supplied by the translator to complete the sense. References in the form "i 9" mean that the fragment begins at column i line 9 of the papyrus.)

*3.1 (i 9) This is perhaps only paraphrase. It is apparently from an argument for the superiority of PLOT over CHARACTER—the poet represents actions above all, and represents the persons who act only secondarily. Compare *Poetics* 50a16–38.

*3.2 (i 16) This is an argument for the superiority of character over plot, but it is put forward only to provoke discussion, as the full context shows: "his statement 'all these things [are] with a view to those who are acting' is, it seems, particular to him arguing [and] giving a starting-point", i.e. he does not really believe it. "Arguing" can also be translated "conversing", which would indicate that the work of Philodemus' opponent is a dialogue; perhaps the speaker here was Aristotle himself. "[Are]" is supplied by the translator.

*3.3 (iii 10) This fragment follows a considerable gap, in which Philodemus or his opponent mentions depicting fine and ugly persons in painting (compare *Poetics* 48a5). Here Philodemus attacks his opponent's view that the people represented in tragedy should be idealised, even though some poets tried to "humanise" tragedy. This is presumably not acceptable, since in Aristotle's view tragedy should represent people "better than ourselves", whereas lampoon and comedy represent people "worse than ourselves" or "like us" (*Poetics* 48a17).

*3.4   (iii 17) This is not explicitly a quotation.

"diction and incidents"   The two kinds of laughable things at *T.C.* 5–6; compare also frag. *6.2.

*3.5   (iv 5) In the section preceding this fragment, Philodemus argues that someone or something was in fact "outside representation"—clearly a phrase used by his opponent. Archilochus and Aristophanes are cited as the most prominent poets of lampoon and comedy respectively; Philodemus tells us that his opponent mentioned them to prove something about epic and tragedy, presumably that these two genres represent "good" and "serious" people and actions. Both comedy and lampoon represent inferior people and actions according to *Poetics* 48a17 and b26. For Archilochus see on 48b33; for Aristophanes, see on 48a27.

*3.6   (iv 11) This phrase is quoted by Philodemus in his rebuttal of frag. *3.5; his opponent must have compared Aristophanes to the painter Pauson, who depicted "inferior" people, just as comedy does. Aristotle compares Pauson's depiction of "inferior" people with those represented in comedy at *Poetics* 48a5 (see notes there). Again the papyrus follows closely the order of topics in the *Poetics*.

*3.7   (iv 18) This is not explicitly a quotation, but the terms are those of Philodemus' opponent. Presumably Sophocles was named as an example of the grander manner, just as Pauson exemplified the laughable manner in art: compare *Poetics* 48a26. The contrast between "the grand" and "the laughable" recurs at *T.C.* 18 (see note there).

"sharing in the emotion"   Compare *Politics* VIII 5.1340a13, quoted below as Testimonium A(ii) to catharsis.

*3.8–18   As in the *Poetics*, discussion of the kinds of persons and actions represented precedes an account of the difference between NARRATIVE and DRAMATIC representation (see 48a19–28); here it leads into a comparison between epic and tragedy, to the advantage of the latter. This blends the two comparisons between epic and tragedy at *Poetics* 49b9–20 and 61b26–62b15. The text is sufficiently well-preserved that a hypothetical reconstruction can be attempted (words in brackets are supplied mainly to complete the sense; which of these correspond to holes in the papyrus can be ascertained from the translation):

"[Tragedy is superior to epic, because] in tragedy there is narrative in messenger-speeches only and what is enacted in its other parts, but in epics there is narrative only. [Again, it is superior because] epic has [only] the heroic line instead of those of tragedy; for tragedy is composed of all the verse-forms. [Further,] everything that is in epic is also in tragedy, but the opposite does not hold: [for] tragedy may reasonably be thought to have [a kind of] song of its own, as it represents songs to the oboe. [Some say that tragedy is inferior to epic because it includes song; but this is not so, for the following reasons. First], the composition of nomes, if they are not in articulated [speech], has its end in sound and noises [only]; but since [in tragedy] there are words set to melody, they will have the end of the representation in speech as well. [Moreover,] as we say that actors relate to the composers of tragedy and epic reciters to the composers of epics, [so] singers relate to the composers of songs: [they all perform the words of the poet. Indeed] tragedy produces its entire effect in speech alone: [for the good tragic poet] manages the [choral] parts and the song with a view to the action. [People say that the songs of tragedy are not a part of tragedy, but merely an inferior kind of song. But Sophocles composes] songs inferior to nobody's. [Moreover, song must be a part of tragedy, because] the parts that are shared [by one art with another] belong to the same art. Not even Dicaeogenes composed songs [in his tragedies] inferior [to those he composed outside tragedy.]"

*3.8(a) (v 7) This is possibly paraphrase by Philodemus, but compare *Poetics* 49b11. It is an argument for the superiority of tragedy, since Aristotle regards even the epics of Homer as aspiring to be "dramatic", i.e. with the characters speaking for themselves much of the time (60a7–11). The corollary, that tragedies subsume narrative because they contain messenger-speeches, is not found in the *Poetics*. But it suggests the objection that messenger-speeches could be regarded as an "epic" element in tragedy. "[Done]" is supplied.

"what is enacted" The same term (*to praktikon*) is used at *T.C. 2*.

*3.8(b) (vi 9) This is paraphrased and quoted out of sequence, as its context shows.

*3.9(a) (v 16) With this verbatim quotation compare *Poetics* 62a15: "[tragedy is superior] because it has everything that epic has; for it is even possible to use its verse [in tragedy]". Epic's divergence from tragedy in using a single verse-form is cited alongside its being narrative at 49b11. "[Tragedy is . . . epic only]" is supplied to complete the sense.

*3.9(b) (vii 14) This is paraphrased and quoted out of sequence. Philodemus refers to tragedy using the "trimeter and with this the dimeter and hexameter and 'every verse-form', in his words", but the list of types of verse may not come from his opponent's text. A mention of tetrameters just before suggests that Philodemus pointed out a contradiction between the view that tragedy used all the metres, and a statement made elsewhere by his opponent that tragedy did not use the tetrameter; Aristotle indeed states that tragedy gave up this verse-form (*Poetics* 49a20).

*3.10(a)   (vi 12) This resembles, even in wording, *Poetics* 49b18–20, and the same point is made at 62a14. Epic lacks song and spectacle, but only song is discussed here.

*3.10(b)   (v 6) This is Philodemus' paraphrase, quoted out of sequence: "[elements]" is supplied.

*3.11   (vii 16) Tragedy had a special type of choral song accompanied by the flute. The arguments that follow aim to show that this kind of song is a real part of tragedy, not an inferior kind of choral lyric. "A kind of" is supplied.

*3.12   (viii 1) Nome, a choral song resembling dithyramb, was listed among those representations that use rhythm, words and melody at *Poetics* 47b26, so how can it be said to be "not in articulated speech" here? This passage in fact employs Aristotle's triple classification of things heard into (a) mere meaningless noise (*psophos*), produced even by inanimate objects when struck; (b) sound or voice (*phōnē*), made by animals with their throats; and (c) speech (*logos, dialektos*), where sound is made intelligible by articulation (*diarthrōsis*): see *Inquiry into Animals* IV 9.535a27ff. These distinctions are used at *Poetics* 56b24, where sounds made by animals are said not to be elements, i.e. parts of articulate speech. Elsewhere Aristotle calls dithyrambs "full of noise" (*Rhetoric* III 3.1406b2; see also on frag. *13). He must mean that in such genres of choral song the influence of the music over the words was such that the latter could not be clearly distinguished, e.g. because there were many notes per syllable. The pseudo-Aristotelian *Problems* (19.15.918b13–29) confirm that in nomes the music predominates over the words. Plato warned that this must not be allowed to happen in tragic lyrics (*Republic* III 398D); Aristotle clearly agreed.

"articulated [speech]"   "Speech", "only" and "in tragedy" are supplied.

"the end of the representation"   I.e. the aim or END of the representation. The same phrase is at *Poetics* 62a18.

*3.13   (viii 14) This comparison is meant to prove that even in lyric poetry speech is what is performed.

"singers"   The papyrus has "epic reciters", but this must be a mistake.

*3.14   (ix 12) The paramount importance of speech (*logos*) in tragedy is not stated outright in the *Poetics*, but is often implied, e.g. at 49a17, where Aeschylus "made speech play the main role".

*3.15   (ix 19) The essential point is the same as at *Poetics* 56a25–9: the poet "should regard the chorus as one of the actors . . .". This could refer to Sophocles.

*3.16   (x 1) Sophocles could again be meant.

*3.17   (ix 9, x 4) Since tragedy's choral songs are *in* tragedies, they fall within the art of composing tragedies.

*3.18   (x 8) From Philodemus' rebuttal it is clear that this formed part of an argument that tragic choral songs could be just as good as those outside tragedy. Dicaeogenes (ca 400 B.C.) composed dithyrambs as well as tragedies: Aristotle mentions a tragedy of his at *Poetics* 55a1. Philodemus condemns him as a very unsuccessful tragedian who lacked the ability to compose even non-tragic choral lyrics.

Testimonia to Aristotelian catharsis

Catharsis was surely discussed in the lost part of the *Poetics*, since Aristotle states in the *Politics* that he will deal with it there (Testimonium A(ii) here): see on *T.C.* 3 and 9. But later evidence makes clear that the question also appeared in the *On Poets* (Testimonium C(ii) below), probably in either Book I or Book II. For a general account of catharsis see Introduction, Section 5.

Testimonium A   These passages are from Aristotle's discussion, in Book VIII of his *Politics*, of the role of *mousikē* in the education of children. It is very important to bear in mind that *mousikē* means not only what we now call music, but includes poetry and song as well. The text translated is that of W.D. Ross (Oxford, 1957), unless otherwise indicated in the notes.

A(i) 1339b42–1340a27   In this section Aristotle argues first, that music should be used in children's education because it affects character, in a way similar to the way cathartic music and tragedy affect it; secondly, he proceeds to show precisely how music does so, since the representations it contains habituate us to feel the correct emotional responses, and this habituation affects our responses to the corresponding realities.

1340a4 "a kind of natural pleasure"   This is Ross' emendation for "the natural pleasure" in the MSS.

1340a9 "the songs of Olympus"   Olympus was a semi-legendary musician (ca 700 B.C.?) associated with the introduction to Greece of wild Asiatic music. His songs, apparently solo pieces for the oboe, evidently have the same effect as those "relating to ecstasy" below.

1340a11 "ecstasy"   (*enthousiasmos*) Literally "possession by the divine", but with the sense of "hysteria". See below on 1342a10 for the Greeks' use of music for healing such emotional disorders.

"an emotion of the character"   This could also be rendered "an experience of character", i.e. something that affects character.

1340a12 "listening to representations" This sentence surely describes the effect of epic and drama on the audience, because epic always lacks music, and tragedy lacks it when read. Moreover Aristotle uses the effect of both types of performance, cathartic songs and tragedy, to illustrate catharsis and its relation to character and emotion below (Testimonium A(ii)). Note that the emotional effect of representations applies to "everyone", not only those who are emotionally imbalanced: compare 1342b14.

1340a14–28 This paragraph contains the essential account of why the emotional effect of poetry is potentially beneficial, since developing the correct emotional responses contributes to virtue. Compare frag. *4.6–7. We shall see that all three types of poetry that Aristotle distinguishes below—those relating to character, which are used in children's education, those relating to action, which are presented before adults in the theatre, and those relating to ecstasy, which are used for calming emotional disorders but are also performed in the theatre—work in a similar manner.

1340a15 "feeling delight correctly" Compare VIII 5.1339a15–24, quoted in the note on 1341b32–1342a18.

1340a17 "decent characters and fine actions" These are what tragedy and epic represent according to *Poetics* 48a1–18. This passage gives clear support to the view that Aristotle thought poetry, and not only music, was important in moulding character.

1340a18 "likenesses" These are surely very similar to, if not the same as, "representations".

1340a19 "anger and mildness" Mildness is the virtue of character relating to anger (*Ethics* IV 5.1125b26–1126b10), bravery is that relating to terror, etc. Compare the list of emotions subject to excess, and therefore to catharsis, in frag. *4.6.

"[traits of] character" Literally "characters".

1340a25 "if someone delights in looking at the image . . . " For a similar analogy between poetic representation and visual images see *Poetics* 48b10–19 with notes.

A(ii) 1341b32–1342a18 In this section Aristotle is considering what kinds of music and poetry are suitable for use in educating children. It is important to understand the sequence of topics.

(i) He first identifies three kinds of music, songs relating to character, to action and to ecstasy (for this classification see on 55b32–56a3), and three benefits that music can provide—education, catharsis and entertainment (1341b32–41). By education (*paideia*), Aristotle means strictly the education *of children*; there was no concept of adult education. Thus tragedy has educative value for adults too, by habituating the soul to feel the correct emotional and intellectual reactions, without being "education" in Aristotle's sense; this is why he draws a distinction between education and catharsis.

By entertainment (*diagōgē*), he means something somewhat more important than mere amusement, since entertainment contributes to intelligence; it is for adults what play or amusement (*paidia*) is for children (5.1339a30f.). Although, like amusement, it produces relaxation, it has greater value, just as the leisure pursuits of adults have greater value than do those of children. This is clear from 5.1339a15–24, where a similar triple division appears: Aristotle asks whether we should participate in music for amusement and relaxation, like people who sleep, get drunk or dance, "or rather should one think that music [makes us] tend towards virtue, since, just as exercise makes one's body of a certain sort, so music is able to make one's character of a certain sort, habituating one to be able to feel delight correctly; or does music contribute something to entertainment and intelligence?"

It has rarely been remarked that, in this parallel passage, the effect of amusement corresponds to that of the "cathartic" or "holy" songs. This is confirmed by the way Aristotle applies medical metaphors to it in two passages nearby: "one must introduce amusements at the moment proper for their use, as if applying them for the sake of medication. For such a motion of the soul is a recreation, and because of the pleasure [it gives] it is a [kind of] relaxation" (1.1337b40ff.); "amusement is for the sake of relaxation, and relaxation must necessarily be pleasant, for it is a sort of therapy for the pain of our labours" (5.1339b15–17).

(ii) Aristotle goes on to distinguish between those songs to be used in children's education (songs relating to character), which they should learn to perform for themselves, and those to be used for catharsis and entertainment (songs relating to action and to ecstasy), which they should not (1342a1–4).

(iii) He next argues that the songs relating to action (which include tragedy) provide catharsis in the same way as do those relating to ecstasy (1342a5–15), and mentions briefly that the latter type of songs provide "harmless delight" (relaxation?) as well as catharsis (1342a15–16). Since he omits to specify which songs provide entertainment and relaxation, we must assume that he regards it as obvious that both do. Thus his last two types of songs, those to be performed by adults, can both provide catharsis as well as entertainment, which both lead to pleasure. He concludes that both types should be permitted in the theatre.

1341b33 "some people engaged in philosophy" Aristotle may mean his pupil, the musical theorist Aristoxenus. This triple classification is presupposed in the pseudo-Aristotelian *Problems*, 19.48. "Division" is Plato's and Aristotle's term for their standard method of dividing up a GENUS into distinct SPECIES (see DEFINE).

1341b34 "songs relating to character" (*ēthika*) Aristotle probably means elegiac poetry, e.g. Theognis', which contained moral maxims (see on 47b14), as well as the Homeric epics; children were required to perform and memorise such verses as part of their education (see Introduction, Section 2). However, he would not include in education all poems relating to character, but only those that depict good character. Thus he argues vigorously elsewhere that the lawgiver should ban obscenity from the state except in certain adult religious contexts (perhaps he means the festivals of Dionysus in particular), but that young people above all should be shielded from it: they "should not be spectators of lampoons and comedy, until they have reached the age when they can participate in reclining [at dinner] and drinking wine, and their education has made them immune to the harm that arises from such [poems]" (*Politics* VII 17.1336b20–3). Likewise representations of morally inferior persons are potentially "harmful" (see on *Poetics* 61b21). He held similar views about the visual arts: "the young should not look at the works of Pauson, but at those of Polygnotus and of any other painters or sculptors who are good at [representing] character" (*Politics* VIII 5.1340a36–8, cf. VII 17.1336b14). The point is that Pauson represented persons inferior to ourselves, Polygnotus the opposite (see on *Poetics* 48a5).

"relating to action" (*praktika*) I.e. poetry that represents action (*praxis*). Tragedy is included, as the reference below to pity and terror proves; but epic and comedy must be meant too, since both have plot, the representation of an action.

"relating to ecstasy" (*enthousiastika*) These are the same as the "songs of Olympus" above, and are called "holy" and "cathartic" songs below.

1341b35 "the nature of the melodies . . . " Different musical modes (i.e. scales) were thought to produce different emotional effects, much as the major and minor modes are still considered to do. Only certain modes were considered appropriate for each kind of sung poetry.

1341b36 "according to the type [of song]" The emendation "song" (*melos*) for "type" (*meros*) is attractive but not essential.

1341b40 "entertainment" Entertainment (*diagōgē*) is for adults what amusement or play (*paidia*) is for children (5.1339a30f.). But this does not mean that Aristotle sees no point in it, for he associates it with acquiring intelligence: see above on 1341b32–1342b18.

1342a4 "listening to while others play them" If songs relating to character are used in education, it follows that we listen to the two other kinds of music for the other two purposes Aristotle has listed, catharsis and entertainment. He takes the latter for granted, but has to argue that we also obtain catharsis from doing so.

1342a5 "the emotion . . . differs in its degree" See e.g. *Ethics* III 7.115b13–16 and frag. *4.6 below for fuller statements of this same point.

1342a7 "pity and terror" This is an important proof that "songs relating to action" include tragedy, since tragedy represents actions that arouse pity and terror.

1342a10 "healing, i.e. catharsis" Literally "healing and catharsis". Aristotle's phrasing leaves it uncertain whether the metaphor in catharsis, "purgation" or "purification", is medical (as its link with healing suggests) or religious (as the context suggests); but this question is far less important than is usually thought, since the term was probably already current, and the force of the analogy is clear in either case. Ritual impurity after committing murder, and excesses of black bile that needed purgation (see below), were both considered causes of madness in different but intertwined strands of Greek thought.

The use of music to calm hysteria was generally accepted as effective. The followers of Pythagoras "used catharsis of the body by means of medicine, and of the soul by means of music" (Aristoxenus, frag. 26). In Aristophanes, a comic hero's maniacal obsession with serving on juries is combatted with Corybantic rites, which involved frenzied dancing with a tambourine (*Wasps* 119). A Greek verb for "to be mad" (*korubantiō*) means literally "to need Corybantic rites". These rites had the peculiarity that they operated homoeopathically, i.e. by arousing emotion so as to reduce it, as Plato remarked (*Laws* 790D–791A).

Aristotle was just as familiar with the ritual purification of the murderer Orestes (*Poetics* 55b15) as with medical theories about the need for a balance between the four "humours" or liquids supposedly in the body (blood, phlegm, yellow bile and black bile, this last being nonexistent). But his use of other medical terms in this passage ("settle down", "relief") suggests that he has a mainly medical analogy in mind. In the theory reflected in the pseudo-Aristotelian *Problems* (30.954a10–955a40), excessive emotion was associated with an excess of black bile (*melancholia*). If Aristotle believed this (it was rather widely held), he no doubt thought that even seeing a tragedy would bring about some reduction of this humour, since the emotions have a physiological component; but this was surely not an important part of Aristotelian catharsis, since it is ignored by the later writers who refer to his theory.

1342a11 "this very same thing happens . . . " This sentence clearly describes the effect of tragedy on the audience. Basing his argument on the extreme case of people prone to ecstasy or hysteria, whose emotions are calmed by being excited with music, Aristotle concludes that even the rest of us, however well-balanced we may seem, are all prone to emotional excess to some extent, i.e. we can all err with respect to the mean in our emotions (compare frag. *4.6). From this analogy it follows that (i) catharsis is homoeopathic: by being made to feel pity and terror, our emotions of pity and terror are reduced; (ii) catharsis is caused artificially: it is not achieved by feeling the emotions produced by real events, but by feeling those aroused by poetry and music, i.e. by representations of events that arouse those emotions; (iii) catharsis applies to everyone, not just to a minority of unbalanced neurotics.

1342a15 "Likewise cathartic songs too" Returning to the "holy songs", Aristotle indicates that they give pleasure to people in general, not only to those who are prone to hysteria. It is wrong to alter "cathartic" to "relating to action", as some scholars do.

Testimonium B This is from the Neoplatonic philosopher Iamblichus (ca 280–340 A.D.). Although he does not name Aristotle, the concepts and wording used are so similar that Iamblichus' dependence on him is generally accepted.

"potentialities . . . activity" This is the typically Aristotelian polarity of *dunamis* and *energeia*, POTENTIALITY and activity.

"due proportion" (*to summetron*) The same term is used at T.C. 3 and 9, and in Testimonium D(i).

"others' emotions" This clear echo of Plato, *Republic* X 606A–B, shows that this argument is intended to answer Plato's attack on poetry's emotional effect. The same term, *allotrios* ("belonging to someone else") reappears in frags. *4.1 and *4.3.

"both comedy and tragedy" Catharsis evidently applied to both, as T.C. 9 and Testimonium C confirm.

Testimonium C The Neoplatonic philosopher Proclus (412–485 A.D.), while hostile to the theory of catharsis, provides a clear statement that he is citing the *On Poets*, and that Aristotle and the characters in the dialogue are responding to Plato's challenge to the defenders of poetry at *Republic* X 607C–D. Augustine (354–430 A.D.) raises similar objections to the theory at *Confessions* III 1.2, but does not name Aristotle as its author.

C(i) "expiation" (*aphosiōsis*) Proclus' wording departs freely from the sort of phraseology that Aristotle seems to have used.

C(ii) "to keep them tractable for education" On the importance of this remark, which connects the catharsis of the emotions with education, see Introduction, Section 5.

C(ii) "Aristotle ... " Whether or not this implies that Aristotle wrote himself into his dialogue as one of its participants, the speakers clearly defended particular poetic genres; were some of them poets?

Testimonium D The late Neoplatonist Olympiodorus (ca 565 A.D.) was dependent on intermediaries for the material he (mis-)quotes.

D(i) This is from a list of five different concepts of catharsis.

"cures evil with evil" I.e. it cures the emotions by stimulating them. This humorous proverbial phrase confirms the homoeopathic nature of catharsis, comparable to curing a fever by piling on blankets.

"the conflict of opposites" This is apparently an error based on the Stoics' concept of catharsis, which Olympiodorus also discusses.

D(ii) "enflamed" The same image is used in a long defence of mime in his *Oration* XXXII by the orator Choricius (early sixth century A.D.), who depends on Aristotle's theory but nowhere cites his name.

*4 The tantalising scraps that constitute frag. *4, like frag. *3, come from a papyrus from the library found at Herculaneum, no. 1581 in this case; they are too important to be omitted, despite their damaged state and extreme difficulty. They are is perhaps from early in Book V of Philodemus' *On Poems*, in which he is quoting or summarising at length the opinions of an unnamed opponent. But there is no solid evidence that the text is by Philodemus, and the parallels with the other evidence for Aristotle's theory of catharsis, and with his language and ethical theory, are very striking. So it seems possible that this is a summary of, or an actual text of, the *On Poets* or a work very like it.

This papyrus was first published by M.L. Nardelli in 1978. I have reversed the sequence of the fragments, since it seems likely that the Italian artist who first numbered the pieces worked backwards from the end; this is confirmed by the fact that the piece numbered *4.7 below refers to the topics discussed in *4.1–3 and *4.4–6 in that order. The Roman numerals in brackets are the traditional fragment-numbers. Unless stated, square brackets indicate words lost in gaps in the papyrus, not words supplied to clarify the translation; groups of dots indicate that a word or two is lost. It seems that about 100–150 words are missing between each fragment. Some completely unintelligible scraps at the start are omitted.

*4.1–3 (V, IVa, IVb) These fragments somehow connected a complete drama with the tragic catharsis of terror (*4.1) and pity (*4.3), probably by means of the representation of pitiable and terrifying events happening to other people (*4.1, *4.3) in a complete drama (*4.3).

*4.1, *4.3 "relating to other people" If the pitiable and terrifying events happen to ourselves or those close to us, there is no catharsis;

we need to see them happen to others in a representation. For this idea, and the same term for "relating to other people" (*allotrios*), see on Testimonium B above, and Introduction, Section 5.

*4.4–5 (III bis, III) These fragments deal with error and its correction in poetry, not only in the sense of errors in the composition of poetry and their relation to being a good poet (see *On Poets* frag. *5), but also in the unexpected sense of correcting moral and intellectual errors as part of the process of catharsis (see on *4.6). These two senses of "error" are perhaps connected by the idea that, if the poet composes incorrectly, he will produce incorrect emotional and intellectual responses in his audience: see Testimonium E below.

*4.4 "story" Or "argument" (*logos*).

"the ca[tharsis] of errors" Since the papyrus still has the *ca-* of catharsis, this supplement is surely right. It is not clear whether it refers to (i) poetry's ability to produce the catharsis of intellectual errors in the audience, which seems to be implied by frag. *4.6 below, or (ii) the errors of the people represented, which are "purified" when they discover the truth (both tragedy and comedy are founded on errors: see on 49a34, 53a10), or to (iii) the poet purifying his composition of errors, which will lead to the wrong emotional reactions in the audience. With the last interpretation, which is surely the likeliest, compare pseudo-Longinus, *On the Sublime* 33.1, who speaks of poets being "pure" (*katharos*), i.e. free of error.

"errors of [poe]ts" This supplement seems very likely.

*4.6 (II) We are all subject to error in some degree, and therefore (presumably) all in need of catharsis. Compare Aristotle's remarks in Testimonium A(ii), 1342a5–7, 11–15, where he notes that we are all subject to emotion, from which it must follow that we are all liable to emotional excess to some degree and can all err with regard to the mean in our emotions. The virtues listed there are bravery, temperance and their opposites, as here. But this fragment also contains a real surprise, by implying that the catharsis of error also applies to one of what Aristotle called the intellectual virtues: see next note.

"Folly" (*aphrosunē*) This is the opposite of one of the intellectual virtues, practical intelligence (*phronēsis*), which is concerned with action (*Ethics* VI 7.1141b8ff.). The greatest scientific or artistic genius may still be a dunce at taking practical decisions in his or her own interest (1141a4–8). The incontinent person who cannot control his desires or appetites may even benefit from his folly, if he mistakes a good course of action for a bad one and therefore chooses it (VII 3.1146a27); folly is juxtaposed with cowardice, intemperance and irritability in a similar list of excesses at 6.1149a5, and is called a source of error at *Politics* III 11.1281b27. At *Ethics* I 13.1102b12–1103a2 Aristotle distinguishes between the rational and non-rational parts of the soul. The first relates to virtues of intellect, notably practical intelligence, understanding an art or craft, and scientific understanding, and the second to virtues of character, e.g. bravery.

That folly appears here is remarkable, since it suggests that catharsis affects one of the intellectual virtues as well as those of character. But this should be less startling than it is, for practical intelligence is concerned with action, which is what tragedy, comedy and epic represent. The catharsis of intellectual errors explains the relation between two of the benefits poetry confers, education and catharsis (see Testimonium A(ii)). The formation of a good character requires education in thinking and reasoning, to help us make correct decisions, and also training in our emotions, to help us feel the correct desires; poetry can contribute to both processes, by means of education in school when we are young, and by means of catharsis in the theatre when we are adults. We willingly go to the theatre because of the third benefit poetry confers, entertainment, which brings relaxation and pleasure.

"intemperance" This, and its opposite "moderation", belong to the virtues of the desiring part of the soul, i.e. virtues of character: compare *Ethics* III 10.1117b23ff., where bravery was discussed just before, and the virtues listed at Testimonium A (i) 1340a20. Bravery and magnanimity are likewise virtues of character: see *Ethics* III 6.1115a6–1117b22, IV 3.1123b34–1125a35.

"sleep . . . drunkenness . . . emotions" The point is probably that everyone is affected to some degree by states that impede our knowledge of the correct principles of action: sleep, drunkenness and feeling strong emotions all have this effect. Compare *Ethics* VII 13.1147b10ff., where Aristotle is discussing people who are incontinent, i.e. unable to resist their desires or appetites, even though their reason tells them to do so. He suggests that such people have their knowledge of these principles suspended, like people who are asleep, insane or drunk; people feeling strong emotions (literally "in the emotions"), such as indignation or sexual desire, are in the same state. This reinforces the argument that catharsis applies to everyone.

*4.7 (I) This fragment summarises the preceding arguments before going on to make a new point.

"[We have concluded]" This recapitulates frags. *4.1–3.

"represents" Literally "is a representer of"

"a complete action" Compare *Poetics* 49b25, the definition of tragedy. Presumably a representation of a complete action is needed for the attainment of catharsis, since we need to see an action's results in order to understand it completely and feel the correct emotional reaction towards it.

"as we said" This refers back to fragments *4.4–6.

"the [related] part . . . " "Related" and "of the soul" are supplied, not missing in the papyrus. It seems clear from *4.6 that catharsis affects both rational and non-rational parts of the soul, so the text does not specify which part of the soul is meant. Compare *Ethics* VI 12.1144a2, where Aristotle calls the rational part of the soul simply "the part". Both the theory and the phrasing reappear in an ancient anonymous note on *Iliad* I 1: Homer started with the wrath of Achilles "so that, as a result of the emotion [i.e. anger], he would purify the like part of the soul, . . . and habituate us to bear the emotions nobly".

"every art can become [the origin] of what is best . . . " Literally " . . . of the best things". Compare *Ethics* I 1.1094a1ff., where Aristotle makes the point that different arts aim at a particular END, i.e. that which is best within that art. Thus the END of medicine is health, and that of house-building is a house. The papyrus presumably went on to say that the END of poetry is to produce catharsis.

Testimonium E This cross-reference to the *On Poets* in the *Poetics* reveals how error in poetry includes the arousal of incorrect emotional reactions. The topic of error in poetry is mentioned in frag. *4.4–5, as we have seen. Frag. *5 discusses errors in characterisation, frag. *6 what makes the best poet, and frag. 7 deals with error in poetry by coincidence, i.e. because of the poet's ignorance of PARTICULARS. Since frag. 7 is definitely from Book II, the other fragments may come from Book II as well.

*5 This comes from a damaged papyrus of the third century B.C. found in Egypt and now in Vienna (nos. 26008 and 29329). The title and author's name are not preserved, but the Aristotelian terminology and thought throughout, and the extraordinary parallels between the best-preserved passage and the discussion of character at *Poetics* 54a28–31, suggest strongly that this too is from the *On Poets*, to which Aristotle refers just afterwards (*Poetics* 54b15–18, i.e. Testimonium E). Words in square brackets are lost in the papyrus.

"costume . . . " The supplements are those of the editor, H. Oellacher, and are doubtful in places. Aristotle was well aware of the part played by dress in the representation of character and arousal of the emotions: "those who use gestures, voice, costume and delivery in general to contribute to the effect [of their speech] will necessarily arouse more pity [than those who do not]" (*Rhetoric* II 8.1386a32).

"The appropriate" (*to harmotton*) This is Aristotle's second requirement for character in tragedy and epic (see on *Poetics* 54a17–33): he specifies that a person should not be portrayed as behaving too differently from what is expected of someone from that particular social class.

Scraps of 61 short lines Although up to half of each line is preserved, it is difficult to extract the exact sense. The topic is clearly how
to imagine and express what a given character would say. Oellacher
restores as follows (this is very doubtful indeed in places):
"The appropriate is pro[portionate(?) to a decision(?)] within our
power. Dividing up(?) the diction(?) [in] epic verses, they say [the sorts
of thing which] a self-willed woman might have [said according to her
quality] . . . [*gap of 9 lines*] . . . might say . . . [as seems] to me. A person
so different [from others] in every [speech and diction . . . , like the]
rhetoricians [and] politicians and [dialecticians], regards it according to
[this quality(?), so that . . .] even to invent what is suitable. E.g. [even
the person] who is able [to invent what is life-]like [needs] the art of
critical judgement, [by means of] which it is possible [to invent the
proper] character, e.g. [to invent] an Ino [who is] to be unfortunate [as
a result of] her [being] a [certain] sort of woman in relation to her [suf-
fering]. As for things that [arouse terror, e.g.] costume [and the rest of]
that, he is able [to invent] this in proportion [to] the quality [of the
character]. But representation [by means of] the . . . of the [diction . . .
gap of 16 lines] . . . as [it is. He] who is . . . " (continuous text resumes).
     "render it exactly" "It" must mean either the character the poet
wishes to depict, or (better) the speech the character would use.
     "diction, character and reasoning" The three QUALITATIVE PARTS of
epic, apart from plot.
     "Andromache" The reference is to Homer, *Iliad* XXII 462–5, where
she sees her husband Hector's body being dragged behind Achilles'
chariot, and especially to her moving lament at lines 477–514.
     "some poets do not represent . . . " I.e. they make the character
"like", that is life-like, but not appropriate. That the character is lifelike is clear from the statement that such poets do represent someone,
perhaps someone they know (see *Poetics* 54a26, with note, for the same
idea). This is confirmed by the example, the lament of Odysseus in
Timotheus' *Scylla*, which is also cited at 54a30, where Aristotle calls it
"unsuitable and inappropriate" (see note there).
     "in our own midst" Who is meant by this emphatic phrase is un-
known, for it is not Timotheus. Is the speaker making fun of one of the
poets present at the discussion?
     "what someone is like" Literally "what is like someone".
     *6 These two sentences are quoted anonymously or paraphrased
by Philodemus (*On Poems* V ix 10–19), but seem Aristotelian because of
the similarity of *6.1 to frag. *5, where diction, character and reasoning
are singled out, and of *6.2 to frag. *3.4 and *T.C.* 5–6. Compare *Poetics*
56a3–7, on how poets should try to succeed in all the parts of tragedy.

"other characters" I.e., perhaps, the characters other than the epic poet himself.

7 This is quoted by the Roman polymath Macrobius (ca 430 A.D.) as from *On Poets* Book II (*Saturnalia* V 18.16, = frag. 74R.). The lines discussed are from Euripides' *Meleager* (frag. 530N.). Euripides is criticised for ignorance of an ethnographic detail: the Aetolians did keep one foot bare, to keep them from slipping in the marshes, but Euripides gets the foot wrong. This is an instance of an error "not within the poetic art" but "in it by coincidence", like saying that female deer have horns (see on *Poetics* 60b16, b29–32). Clearly the *On Poets*'s discussion of error in poetry extended to factual inaccuracy. Aristotle displays extensive knowledge of local customs at *Poetics* 61a4 also.

8–9 The two definite fragments of Book III are both on literary history; it seems that this is where Aristotle surveyed the various genres and the lives of major poets within each genre.

8 This is quoted word for word by Diogenes Laertius, II 5.46 (= frag. 75R.). It mingles poets and philosophers as the instructors of Greece; they all had their critics. Socrates and Pythagoras are perhaps juxtaposed for their mystical beliefs, unorthodox lives, and lack of written teachings. Homer and Hesiod were criticised by Xenophanes for giving the Greeks a false view of the gods (see note on *Poetics* 60b35–61a1). The lyric poets Pindar of Thebes (ca 522–445 B.C.) and Simonides of Ceos (ca 557–468), who was hated by the lyric poet Timocreon of Rhodes (ca 475), sandwich between them three of the Seven Wise Men, Thales of Miletus (ca 585), Bias of Priene (ca 546) and Pittacus of Mytilene (ca 610, with his political enemies the poet Alcaeus and his brother Antimenidas), as well as Anaxagoras of Miletus, a speculative physicist and friend of Pericles (ca 498–28). Little is known of the other persons named.

9 This is from pseudo-Plutarch, *Life of Homer* 3–4 (frag. 76R.). That Aristotle said Homer was born on Ios in the southern Aegean is confirmed by Aulus Gellius, *Athenian Nights* III 11.7 (ca 150 A.D.), and by other *Lives of Homer*. Exactly how much of this passage is by Aristotle is not certain, for the *Life* may have changed sources without saying so; but I see no reason to deny that all of it is his. The legend of Homer's death was already mentioned by the philosopher Heraclitus (ca 500 B.C.) and narrated by the fourth-century rhetorician Alcidamas in his *Contest of Homer and Hesiod*. There were various stories about Homer's parentage, birth and naming; none of them is likely to have much basis in fact. This version accounts for most of them. Homer is taken to Smyrna, now Izmir in western Turkey, because of the strong tradition that he was born there; he is born by the river Meles to explain his

alleged alternative name Melesigenes (others said the river was his father); he is raised by Maeon to account for his nick-name Maeonides;
and the hostage-story accounts for the name Homer, which others said
means "blind". Here the story of his death implies that Homer was not
blind, yet the second oracle quoted alludes to the legend that he was
("dark with twin suns"); despite this contradiction, both oracles support Aristotle's major and controversial statement that Homer was
born on Ios. For an explanation of how the fishermen's riddle works
see on 58a29.

10   (frag. 70R.) This is from Diogenes Laertius VII 2.57–8. For Empedocles see on *Poetics* 47b18. Some think that this passage is from
Book I, and was intended to soften a denial that Empedocles was a
poet in the proper sense, like that at 47a18f. But it could equally well
come from a discussion in Book III of poets who wrote in hexameters.
Aristotle quotes Empedocles' verses, especially his metaphors, in his
account of poetic diction (57b13, 24, 58a5, cf. 61a24).

"Xerxes' Crossing"   The Persian king Xerxes bridged the Helles-
pont during his invasion of Greece (480 B.C.).

"tragedies"   Since there is a later report that Empedocles' grandson
of the same name was a tragedian, it seems likely that the latter's
works were ascribed to his grandfather by mistake.

*11–16   Several fragments in which Aristotle is given as the author-
ity for the origins of a particular literary genre probably come from the
On Poets, and from Book III in particular. Thus the sketch of the history
of tragedy and comedy in the *Poetics* may, like much else in that work,
have received a larger-scale treatment in the *On Poets*.

*11   (frag. 676R.) This is from the Scholia Bobiensia (of late antiquity) on Cicero, *Pro Archia* p.358. For the elegiac verse-form see on
Poetics 47b14. Callinus and Archilochus were both active around 650
B.C., Mimnermus and Solon of Athens over fifty years later, and Antimachus ca 400. The last sentence may not come from Aristotle.

*12   This is from an anonymous papyrus from Oxyrhynchus in
Egypt, no. 2389 (second century A.D.), which discusses the birthplace
of the Spartan poet Alcman (ca 600 B.C.). Because of a passage in his
work (frag. 16), it was widely thought that he was from not Sparta but
Sardis in Lydia (now Western Turkey).

*13   (frag. 677R.) This is from the *Chrestomathy* of a Proclus, perhaps
the same as the Neoplatonist (see Testimonium D). On Arion see on
Poetics 49a10; since Arion worked at Corinth, Aristotle may well have
cited Pindar as evidence. The following passage may share the same
source: "Arion is said to have been the discoverer of the tragic manner
and was first to set up a chorus, sing a dithyramb, name what is sung

by the chorus, and bring on satyrs speaking in verse" (the *Suda*, a Byzantine encyclopedia, under "Arion").

A papyrus of ca 200 A.D., now in Berlin (no. 9571 verso), is closely related to Aristotle's account of the history of both the dithyramb and tragedy. Unfortunately much of each line is lost, but the order of topics is as follows. (i) A quotation of Euripides' *Hypsipyle*, used to illustrate the relationship between Apollo and Dionysus at Delphi. (ii) A discussion of whether the prize for the dithyramb was a tripod or a bull, with a quotation of Pindar, *Olympian* XIII 18f., in favour of the latter; this is precisely the passage where Pindar says that the dithyramb was invented at Corinth, which Aristotle probably quoted in the *On Poets*. (iii) Discussion of a dithyramb by Pindar on the story of Orion's blinding; at the start of the poem, the poet said something about Dionysus. (iv) References to tragedy arising(?) "from the dithyramb", "he developed it into . . . " and satyr-play. This passage is very badly damaged, but it is a rare parallel for the connexions Aristotle draws between tragedy, dithyramb and satyr-play (*Poetics* 49a10, 20); the only other place where this connexion is made is a passage quoted in the Byzantine encyclopedia called the *Suda* (*omicron* 806), which explains the proverb "nothing to do with Dionysus". It runs as follows: "when Epigenes of Sicyon composed a tragedy to Dionysus some people made up this saying, whence comes the proverb. But [a] better [explanation is] as follows. Formerly, writing for Dionysus, they competed with these [types of plays], which are also called satyric; later, as they changed to the writing of tragedies, they gradually turned to stories (*muthoi*) and histories (*historiai*), no longer mentioning Dionysus; hence they made up this saying. Chamaeleon in his *On Thespis* says something similar." Chamaeleon was a pupil of Aristotle; for Epigenes of Sicyon see on 49a10. (v) An account of the nature of dithyrambic music and diction. Dithyramb is "full of noise", a point made by Aristotle at *Rhetoric* III 3.1406b2 (see on frag. *3.12 above). The papyrus quotes a dithyramb by Pindar to illustrate this, and mentions harmony, verse-form, singing and perhaps the effect of dithyramb on the soul, supported by an unidentified lyric quotation. It ends "some . . . will have no dithyrambic quality . . . dithyrambic names"; at *Poetics* 59a9 Aristotle remarks that double or compound NAMES are most suited to dithyramb, which is no doubt what is meant here.

Although this papyrus is too fragmentary for its authorship to be determined with any certainty, the inclusion of long poetic quotations does not mean that its author cannot be Aristotle, since he used such quotations in the *On Poets* (cf. frags. 7, 9). At present, we should not exclude the possibility that this piece is from Book III.

*14(a)   This is from the *Commentary on Hermogenes' "On how to be Forceful"* 33, by John the Deacon (sixth century A.D.). The *Poetics* does not reveal clearly where Aristotle thought tragedy and comedy arose and were developed, but it seems likely that he thought both had Dorian origins but were perfected at Athens (see note on 49a10). Only the first sentence need be from him. Solon's statement about Arion is otherwise unattested, but may be the ultimate source for the statement that Arion invented the "tragic manner" (see previous note).

*14(b)   This is from *Oration* XXVII 337B of Themistius (ca 317–388 A.D.), an enthusiastic follower of Aristotelian philosophy. Aristotle is not named here, but the statement about comedy is paralleled at *Poetics* 49b5 (see note there). For Sicyonian tragedy see the notes on 49a10 and on frag. *13 above; both Sicily and Sicyon were Dorian areas (see on 48a31).

*15(a)   This too is from Themistius, *Oration* XXVI 316D. The steps in the evolution of tragedy are essentially the same as those in the *Poetics*. It was originally a choral performance addressed "to the gods" (i.e. to Dionysus, like dithyramb?: see note on 49a10). The next step was the addition of an actor or poet-composer who performed a prologue and speeches; then a second actor, to make dialogue possible, and finally a third.

"Thespis"   Thespis is said to have been an Athenian from the village of Icaria, who produced the first tragedy at the Athenian Dionysia between 535 and 533 B.C.

"Aeschylus the third actor"   It is odd that the introduction of the second actor is omitted, and both the parallel passage 14(b) and *Poetics* 49a18 ascribe this major innovation to Aeschylus and the third actor to Sophocles. Thus this is probably an error for "the second actor". I have left it unchanged, because another ancient source credits Aeschylus with both the second and the third actor (*Life of Aeschylus*, last paragraph). The confusion perhaps arose because (as seems certain) this innovation took place between 468 and 458 B.C., when Aeschylus and Sophocles were both producing plays at Athens.

"high boots"   We hear nothing of these in the *Poetics*, but they are mentioned in the last paragraph of the *Life of Aeschylus*.

*15(b)   This is from Diogenes Laertius (III 56), who does not name his source.

*16   This is from the Scholia to Dionysius Thrax, p. 306 (from late antiquity), which say that Susarion founded *tragedy*, an obvious error for comedy. Some claimed that Susarion was from the Dorian city of Megara near Athens, others that he was from Athens itself, but what Aristotle thought is unknown (see on *Poetics* 48a31).

Glossary

Items occurring only once are discussed in the note on the relevant passage. Cross-references are indicated by words in capitals, e.g. ACT; this can also serve as a reminder when terms are being used in Aristotle's technical sense, especially in the case of NAME. For convenience I have also indicated where proper names and titles that occur several times are explained; those found only once or twice are explained in the notes.

be about to, *mellein*. The SUFFERING or deed of violence in a tragedy need only be present POTENTIALLY, i.e. it need only be about to happen and need not actually be carried through, for tragedy to have its emotional EFFECT; see on 53b15–22.

abuse, *loidoria* See COMEDY, LAMPOON, and on *T.C.* 7–8, 18.

accomplish, *perainein, apergazesthai* The first verb means to carry something through to its *peras*, i.e. END (e.g. in the definition of the END of tragedy as catharsis, 49b27); the second has connotations of "workmanship", *ergon*.

act See DO.

action, *praxis* In its most basic sense, *praxis*, its cognate verb *prattein* and its synonym *dran* (related to "drama"; both are translated "do" or sometimes "be in action") refers simply to any action aimed at an END, whether based on a rational DECISION or not; but, since the *Poetics* is dealing with human actions, Aristotle commonly uses it to mean a purposeful action based on a DECISION, for which its agent is responsible (see on 48a1). Whatever its immediate end, the ultimate end of action is HAPPINESS, whatever the agent considers that to be (it may of course be something others would not enjoy!): see on 50a16–23. The related adjective *praktikos* means both "related to action" (which is what epic and drama represent), and "enacted" as opposed to "narrated"; for the first usage see 60a1, *On Poets* Testimonium A(ii) 1340a14–28, and for the second see on 49b36–7 and *T.C.* 2. Another verb sometimes translated "do", *poiein*, really means "make", "compose" or "produce"; see further under COMPOSE. For the difference between action and production, see ART.

activity, be in activity, *energeia, energoun* Activity or actualisation is the realisation of something's POTENTIAL or potentiality: see on 47a9. At

196

48a23 it is conjoined with ACTION, since only in action is human potential realised: see on HAPPINESS.

actor, *hupokritēs* In Greek this means perhaps "answerer", excluding the chorus whom the actor "answers", so the relationship between the actors and acting or action is less obvious than in English; this is why Aristotle specifies that the chorus should be regarded as one of the actors (56a25). The Greeks focussed instead on acting as the DELIVERY of the verses, which was often overdone in Aristotle's view (see on 61b32–5, 62a9–10). Thus even good poets would insert irrelevant episodes so the actors could perform a *tour de force* (see on 51b37). Since they always wore masks, the actors were limited to three in number (see on 49a16, 49b4, *On Poets* frag. *15), and doubled up the different roles; they were always male.

adunaton IMPOSSIBLE

Aeschylus An Athenian tragic poet: see on 49a16.

Agathon An Athenian tragic poet: see on 51b21.

agathos GOOD

agnoia IGNORANCE

agōn COMPETITION

aim at, *stochazesthai* See END.

aischros UGLY

aisthēsis PERCEPTION

aitia, aitios CAUSE

alogia, alogos IMPROBABILITY, IMPROBABLE

alter, alteration, *exallattein, exallagē* A kind of NAME or PARONYM: see on 57b35–58a7, and *T.C.* 5(iv).

amazing, amazement, *thaumastos, to thaumaston*, astonishing, astonishment, *ekplēktikos, ekplēxis* These seem to be synonyms, although astonishment is a somewhat stronger term. This reaction is best aroused by events that come about in accord with PROBABILITY but contrary to EXPECTATION; it is strongly associated with events that arouse PITY and TERROR in tragedy (see on 52a1–11, 56a21, where "amazement" is the term used, and on 53b37–54a9, 55a17, where it is "astonishment"). The arousal of amazement (60a11–18) or astonishment (60b25) is easier but no less important in epic, of which it is the END; it contributes to LAUGHTER in comedy (see on *T.C.* 6, especially 6(v)), and to PLEASURE in general, since amazement includes the desire to learn (see on 60a17). It is also aroused by UNFAMILIAR diction (see on 58a21).

anankē, anankaios NECESSITY, NECESSARY

anagnōrizein, anagnōrisis RECOGNISE, RECOGNITION

analogy, *analogon* The basis of a major type of METAPHOR: see on 57b16–33.

anapaest A metrical pattern in Greek verse consisting of two light sylla-bles followed by one heavy one; it had associations with marching. See 52b22–3 with notes.

andreios BRAVE

anger, *orgē* An EMOTION (see on 47a27) among those related to PAIN rather than PLEASURE (see on 56a38); as such it is subject to catharsis in tragedy (see on 49b28) and epic (see on *On Poets* frag. *4.7).

animal, *zōon* The analogy between a FINE animal and a fine poem in terms of MAGNITUDE and UNITY is drawn at 50b21–51a6 (see notes there), and repeated at 59a20.

apangellein, apangelia NARRATE, NARRATION

aphairesis, aphēirēmenos SHORTENING, SHORTENED

aphōnon CONSONANT

apithanos, **unbelievable** See BELIEVABLE.

appear, *phainesthai* Greek uses two constructions with this verb—the participle, when it means that something is apparent and obvious (hence my translation "is obviously" or the like; compare the adjective *phaneros* "obvious"), and the more hesitant sense with the infinitive, translated "ap-pears to be" or similar. "Evidently" renders the idiomatic adverb *euthus*, and "clear" renders *dēlos*. I use "seem" for the tentative *eoika*, related to *eikos* (see PROBABLE), reserving "would seem" for *dokei* (cognate with *doxa* "opinion"), although they do not differ in meaning. See also CLEAR.

appropriate, *harmotton,* **suitable,** *prepon* These are clearly synony-mous (e.g. at 54a30, 58b14–15), and mean that which is in proportion to the thing in question, whether in verse (see on 48b31), diction (notes on 57b33, 58a18, 59a4–14, T.C. 18) or behaviour (thus appropriateness is Aristotle's second requirement for tragic CHARACTER: see on 54a17–33, *On Poets* frag. *5). For the SUITABLE in plot see 56a15, and note on 55a25.

archē BEGINNING, ORIGIN

Archilochus An Ionian composer of LAMPOONS: see on 48b33.

aretē VIRTUE

argument See REASON, SPEECH.

arise, happen, *ginesthai;* **come about, happen,** *sumbainein;* **occur,** *sumpiptein* *Ginesthai* is used of both events and emotions, whether these arise by accident or not, and its participle is sometimes translated "event" (e.g. 52a20, cf. 54b4; otherwise "event" is supplied). *sumbainein* is limited to events, and often has the connotation of "coincidence" (cf. 60b30, where this translates its participle, and 1340a1); it is translated "arise" at 60a12, 1340a5.

Aristophanes An Athenian comic poet: see on 48a27, T.C. 18.

art, *technē* In the *Poetics* this corresponds to art in the modern sense: painting, music, sculpture and poetry are all REPRESENTATIONAL "arts", and "poetry", *poiētikē*, is actually short for "the art of poetry". But within the wider thought of Plato and Aristotle, *technē* includes what we would call "crafts" or "skills" like shoe-making or house-building; Aristotle defines it as "a state involving reason concerned with production" (*Ethics* VI 5.1140a6ff.). By "production" or "making" (*poiēsis*, from *poiein* "do" or "make") he means a rational process which results in a product, whose ORIGIN is in its producer and not in itself, e.g. a shoe, a house or a poem (the same result can sometimes be achieved by chance or by nature: see on 47a20, 54a10, and 51a24, and on the relation of art to nature see NATURE). Thus the FUNCTION or END of an art is its product, e.g. a shoe or a poem, although of course that product may have a further end, e.g. protecting one's feet or catharsis, and an end beyond that, i.e. HAPPINESS. Poetry itself (*poiēsis*) means literally "production". But it is a very remarkable productive process, because it is a production that represents ACTION. In an action there is no product left when the action is complete, e.g. saving a child's life does not *make* anything. The word "poetry" itself gave Aristotle strong grounds for his assumption that poetry is a *technē*; this assumption is fundamental to the *Poetics*, since it follows that poetry is a rational process of production (not a matter of inspiration, as Plato thought), works in a rational way, and can be rationally analysed (see Introduction, Section 4).

artless, *atechnos* When Aristotle calls SPECTACLE artless, he does not mean that there is no ART involved in producing it, but that it is less closely related to the art of poetry (50b17, 53b1–11). Similarly he divides PROOFS into "artful" and "artless" (see on 54b19–55a21, *T.C.* 13).

astonishment See AMAZEMENT.

***atopia*, oddity** See IMPROBABILITY.

***atuchia*, misfortune** See FORTUNE.

aulos OBOE

bad, *kakos* See VIRTUE, WICKED.

beginning, *archē* This is related to *archein*, "begin" or "lead". Its sense is often non-technical; thus, with a middle and a conclusion, a beginning is an essential part of a WHOLE (see 50b26–8). In two passages where it has a technical sense, it means something like "first principle" and is translated "origin" (50a38, *On Poets* frag. *4.7); in fact it refers to both the formal and final causes, which Aristotle often calls "origins" in his other works (see CAUSE). For how the "origin" can be equivalent to the FUNCTION or END of something, see NATURE.

believable, *pithanos* This is related to PROOF (*pistis*). Making things believable is vital to the success of the poetic representation (55a30), as it is in RHETORIC. We usually believe what is POSSIBLE (51b17) or PROBABLE, but something IMPOSSIBLE may work better than something that is possible but IMPROBABLE (see on 60a27–b1).

blaberos HARMFUL

brave, bravery, *andreios, andreia* This is the VIRTUE of CHARACTER concerned with EMOTION of TERROR: see on *On Poets* frag. *4.6. It is translated "manly" at 54a22, to bring out the connection between *andreia* and *anēr*, an adult male (see HUMAN BEING).

catharsis, *katharsis* Literally this means "cleansing", "purification" or "purgation" (the term is originally from medicine or ritual: see on *On Poets* Testimonium A(ii) 1342a10); it leads to PLEASURE, unlike its opposite, what is shocking, literally "dirty" or "polluting" (*miaron*, 52b36). Along with EDUCATION and ENTERTAINMENT, catharsis is the FUNCTION or END of poetic representation in general (see *On Poets* Testimonium A(ii)), and arises through REPRESENTATION: see on 53b11, and *On Poets* Testimonium B, frag. *4.1–3, and Introduction, Section 5. It applies to both comedy and tragedy (see *T.C.* 9, *On Poets* Testimonia B and C). In tragedy it operates on the PAINFUL EMOTIONS, especially but not only PITY and TERROR (see on 49b28, *On Poets* frags. *4.1–3); this is also true of epic, which likewise arouses pity and terror (see on 55a2, 60a11–18), and can produce a catharsis of ANGER (see on *On Poets* frag. *4.7). Comedy brings about the catharsis of the PLEASURABLE EMOTIONS, notably LAUGHTER (see on *T.C.* 4, 9). Like education, catharsis works on the SOUL, by habituating us to feel the correct emotional responses: see *On Poets* Testimonium A(i) and C(ii). By this means we attain a DUE PROPORTION in them (see *T.C.* 3, 9 and *On Poets* Testimonia B, D); thus purified of ERROR (see *On Poets* frags. *4.4– 7), both intellectual and emotional (*On Poets* frags. *4.6–7), we are better placed to attain VIRTUE.

cause, *aitia, aition* Although Aristotle has a sophisticated classification of causes into four types (the material, formal, efficient and final causes), he does not use this system explicitly in the *Poetics*; but knowledge of it does help us to understand his theory of art. The material cause states what something is made of, e.g. "a painting is made of paint and canvas". Its formal cause is implied by its DEFINITION and ESSENCE, and is best expressed by giving its SPECIES, e.g. "this is a painting of Napoleon". Its efficient cause states who or what produced it, e.g. "this painting is by David". Its final cause states for what purpose it exists, i.e. its END, e.g. "it was painted to glorify Napoleon". It is worth briefly analysing Aristotle's theory of poetic REPRESENTATION in the light of this system. The material cause of a tragedy is paper and ink, or perhaps actors and their voices when it is performed (SPECTACLE). Its formal causes are stated by Aristotle at 49b24, in his definition of tragedy; it is the representation of an action, etc. Its efficient cause is the poet who composes it, or (regarded as an entity in performance) the actors who perform it. Its final cause is its END or FUNCTION, the catharsis of the tragic emotions of the audience (49b27). In two passages Aristotle refers to the formal and final causes as "origins" (see BEGINNING). "For which reason" renders expressions like "on account of which", *dio*; this is unconnected with REASONING, *dianoia*.

chairein, delight See PLEASURE.

change, *metaballein, metabolē*, transformation, *metabasis* The plot of tragedy must contain a change of FORTUNE (51a13); such changes are classified at 52b34–53a17. More sudden changes, which are parts of the PLOT, are REVERSAL (52a22) and RECOGNITION (a31). The purpose of such changes is to "change" the EMOTIONS of the audience (this use of the word is translated by "divert": see 59b29). There were also changes in the development of dramatic poetry (49a14 etc.).

character, *ēthos* Our character depends on our VIRTUES and vices, which are expressed in our DECISIONS; along with our REASONING and our ACTIONS, character defines us as a certain sort of person (48a1, 49b36–50a7). Hence, like REASONING and PLOT (the representation of ACTION), it is one of the six QUALITATIVE PARTS of tragedy (50a5), and indeed of comedy too (*T.C.* 6(vi)–(viii), 10, 12); tragedy differs from comedy because it represents SERIOUS, GOOD CHARACTERS rather than the opposite (48a16). By "character" Aristotle does not mean simply a person in a drama, since there can be a tragedy without character, i.e. one which gives no explanation in moral terms of why the person does what he does (see on 50a25). For Aristotle's discussion of character in relation to the PLOT of tragedy see 52b34–53a17, and for his general requirements see 54a16–33 and *On Poets* frag. *5. A whole class of tragedies and epics is based on character: see on 55b32–56a3 and 60b3. This may be related to the similar classification of dance at 47a27, and of MUSIC in *On Poets* Testimonium A(ii). On the relation between habituation and character, and the function of poetry in habituating one to feel the correct EMOTIONS, see EDUCATION.

chorus, choral [part], *choros, chorikon* The chorus performs the element in tragedy that Aristotle calls SONG (which includes the words sung); the choral part is one of the four QUANTITATIVE PARTS of tragedy (see on 52b22–4, where it is subdivided) and of comedy (see *T.C.* 17). It was present from the start in both tragedy (49a10, 49a16, *On Poets* frags. *13, *15) and comedy (see on 49a37–b9). Aristotle thought it should be integrated into the PLOT as far as possible (see on 56a25–32, *On Poets* frag. *3.15).

chrē See MUST.

civic life, *politikē* This has a wider sense than our "politics": see notes on 50b6, 60b14. Since in its educative aspect MUSIC (including poetry) falls within the province of the legislator, Aristotle discusses this aspect of it in his *Politics* (see *On Poets* Testimonium A).

clear, *saphēs* Clarity is the VIRTUE of DICTION (see on 58a18). In other contexts "clear" translates *dēlos* (see APPEAR).

class, *genos* See GENUS.

coincidence See ARISE.

comedy, *komōidia* This means LAUGHABLE DRAMATIC poetry (composed in a mixture of SONG and spoken VERSE). For the difference between comedy and tragedy in terms of the OBJECTS it represents, see 48a25, *On Poets* frag. *3.5. For its etymology and origins, see on 48a36, 49a11, *On Poets* frags. *14, *16; for its development and relation to LAMPOON, see on 49a32–7, 49b8, 51b11, *T.C.* 7, 18. For a complete definition and analysis into PARTS see *T.C.* 4–18. Like tragedy, it represents UNIVERSALS (see 51b11), but the PLEASURE derived from it is quite different (see on 53a37), since it accomplishes the CATHARSIS of PLEASANT EMOTIONS like LAUGHTER (*T.C.* 4, 9).

commonplace, *tapeinos*, ordinary, *euteles* The DICTION of tragedy and epic (as opposed to that of comedy) should avoid being commonplace or ordinary (see on 57b33, 58a18, b23, *T.C.* 14). It was more ordinary people who generated comic poetry (48b26). Its opposite is GRAND.

compassion, arousing compassion See PITY.

competition, compete, performance, perform, *agōn*, *agōnizesthai* Tragedy, comedy and epic were all performed in competitions for prizes at Athens (see on 51a7, 51b37, 62a6): hence "competition" was also the Greek word for "performance", and is thus translated at 50b18, 51a7 and elsewhere (at 62a18 this renders *ergon*).

complete, *teleios* This is related to *telos*, END; Aristotle explains what something complete is, i.e. a WHOLE, at 50b24. Poets represent complete ACTIONS (*On Poets* frag. *4.7); this applies to tragedy (49b25), comedy (*T.C.* 4) and epic (58a19).

complex, *peplegmenos* An complex ACTION, and therefore a PLOT representing such an action, is characterised by REVERSAL and RECOGNITION (52a11–21, 52b31); hence a complex tragedy or epic is one with such a plot (55b32–4, 59b7, and see on 56a19). Its opposite is a SIMPLE plot.

complication, *desis*, development, *plokē* A part of PLOT, contrasted with its SOLUTION: see on 55b24–56a10.

compose, *poiein*, composer, poet, *poiētēs*, composition, poem, *poiēsis*, poiēma A "poet" is literally a "maker", "composer" or "producer" in Greek: see on 47a10, and for "producer" see ACTION. Aristotle sometimes plays on this ambiguity (e.g. at 51b27). In popular usage, poetry was simply something composed in VERSE; Aristotle redefines it as a kind of REPRESENTATION (47b13–23), but uses the word in the popular sense elsewhere (see on *T.C.* 1).

conclusion, *teleutē* See WHOLE.

conjunction, *sundesmos* One of the parts of DICTION: see on 57a6.

consistent, *homalos* Consistency is one of the requirements for tragic CHARACTER: see on 54a17–33.

consonant, *aphōnon* See 56b26–31.

construct, *sunistasthai*, structure, *sustasis*, construction, *sunthesis* These terms are synonymous. Aristotle defines PLOT as the construction of the INCIDENTS (50a5), and repeatedly refers to the plot simply as the "structure" (see on 53a30, 59b21). Another synonym is *sustēma* at 56a12 (in a different context at 58a26, *sunthesis* is translated "combination").

contradiction, *to hupenantion*, *hupenantiōma* At 55a25 this is opposed to what is suitable or APPROPRIATE, and is an ERROR in tragedy: thus it reappears among the criticisms that are made against poetry (see on 60b6–22, 61a31–b9, 61b16).

correct, correctness, *orthos*, *orthotēs* This indicates the right way to achieve an END or indeed the right decision about what end to aim at it, as opposed to ERROR (*hamartia*); neither term has a specifically moral sense. Thus different kinds of correctness are required in different ARTS, e.g. painting (see on 60b6–22), and it can refer to Euripides' correct choice of tragic ending (53a26) or to the correctness or error of poets (60b6–61b25, *On Poets* *4.4–5). On the connection between correct emotional responses and catharsis, see CATHARSIS.

dance, *orchēsis* Dance is one of the REPRESENTATIONAL ARTS like MUSIC and poetry (47a27), and was prominent in early tragedy (48b23); the chorus still danced in Aristotle's time (62a7). For dance in comedy see on *T.C.* 6(vii).

decent, *epieikēs* This is a synonym for GOOD, and describes the sort of people tragedy (52b34) and epic (54b13) should represent: compare *On Poets* Testimonium A(i), 1340a17.

decision, *prohairesis* This means literally "choosing something over something else" (which is why I translate the related verb as "prefer" at 60a2). A DECISION is the outcome of a rational desire for an END, and of reasoning about how to attain that end; it results in ACTION. CHARACTER is that which reveals decision (see 50b9), just as correct decision is necessary for the VIRTUE of character. Incorrect decision can be tragic, amounting to tragic ERROR, or comical: see on *T.C.* 6(viii).

define, definition, *horizein*, *dihorizein*, *horos*, *horismos* These terms derive from *horos* "limit"; the ambiguity of *horos* is apparent at 51a6. Aristotle often uses "define" to mean "draw distinctions", i.e. show where the limits of something lie vis-à-vis something else (e.g. the different kinds of REPRESENTATIONS at 47a15–b24). The distinctions between them are their DIFFERENCES; by means of such differences we can classify them into the different SPECIES of a single GENUS. So a full definition, like that of tragedy at 49b25, gives the ESSENCE (*ousia*) of something by stating its GENUS (in the case of tragedy, REPRESENTATION) and its differences, e.g. that it is dramatic not narrative. But Aristotle wishes to include within such formal definitions a statement of something's FUNCTION and END, in this case that tragedy accomplishes catharsis.

dein See MUST.

deinos, deos, dreadful, dread See TERROR.

delight, chairein See PLEASURE.

delivery, hupokritikē Literally "the art of being an actor": see on 56b8, b10, and also ACTOR.

desis COMPLICATION

development, plokē See COMPLICATION.

dialektos, [everyday] speech See SPEECH.

dianoia REASONING

diaphora DIFFERENCE

diction, lexis In its widest sense this means spoken language in general (notably at 56b20–58a17). Specifically, diction is one of the QUALITATIVE PARTS of tragedy (49b34), epic, and comedy (*T.C.* 5, 10, 14). It is limited to spoken diction, as opposed to the words of songs, which are included within SONG (see 49b34, 50b13–15); when the chorus chants rather than sings, this is made clear by using *lexis* (translated "utterance" at 52b22, cf. *T.C.* 17). For a full account of diction, especially in tragedy, see 56b20–59a16; for solutions to poetic problems based on diction, see 61a10–31; for diction as a source of LAUGHTER, see *T.C.* 5; for the diction of early tragedy and of comedy, see on 49a19–24.

diēgēmatikos, diēgēsis, expository, exposition See NARRATE.

difference, point of difference, diaphora See on 47b29, and DEFINE.

Dionysus The god of wine, wild nature and inspiration, in whose honour DITHYRAMB, tragedy and comedy were performed at Athens; the Dionysia was his festival. See on 49a10, a11, a20, *On Poets* frags. *13–15.

discover See INVENT.

dithyramb A non-tragic choral song in honour of Dionysus: see on 47a14. For its role in the origins of tragedy see the notes on 49a10 and *On Poets* frag. *13. On its diction see 59a9 and the note on *On Poets* frag. *13.

do, dran, poiein, prattein See ACTION, ART, COMPOSE.

dokein, seem See APPEAR.

double See SINGLE.

drama, drama Derived from *dran* "do", this means literally "thing done" (see on 48b1), but came to denote drama in our sense, and is opposed to the NARRATIVE MANNER of REPRESENTATION; even the use in epic of direct speech and unified plots like those of drama is called "dramatic" (see on 48b35).

dran DO

dreadful, dread, deinos, deos See TERROR.

due proportion, summetria The mean between the extremes of feeling emotion, where VIRTUE lies, which can be attained by means of catharsis: see CATHARSIS.

dunamis POTENTIAL

dunatos possible See IMPOSSIBLE.

dustuchia, misfortune See FORTUNE.

ecstasy, enthousiasmos A violent EMOTION calmed by wild MUSIC, used by Aristotle to explain how CATHARSIS works. See *On Poets* Testimonium A, especially the notes on 1340a11, 1342a10.

education, paideia This means strictly the education of children (*paides*); Greek education was based on reading and writing, sports and MUSIC (i.e. poetry and music). Homer was prominent among the authors read (see Introduction, Section 2). Moral education accustoms one by habituation to feel the EMOTIONS in the right way, which is essential to the VIRTUE of CHARACTER; poetry can contribute to this, which is why Aristotle includes it in his discussion of the use of MUSIC in education, and implies that it affects children in the same way that CATHARSIS affects adults. See Introduction, Section 5; *On Poets* Testimonium A, C(ii), and frag. *4.7.

eidos ELEMENT

eikōn IMAGE

eikos PROBABLE

ekplēxis ASTONISHMENT

elegy, elegiac A kind of verse-form: see on 47b14.

element, stoicheion, element, kind, species, eidos, element, form, idea This has two distinct senses. (1) In the discussion of DICTION at 56b20–38, 58a8–17, an "element" means a letter of the alphabet, *stoicheion*; but since, in the Greek of the time, nearly every letter corresponded to a single SOUND and every sound to a single letter, it cannot simply be translated "letter" (see Aristotle's definition of it at 56b22). So I have retained "element", as in "elementary", which denotes the school where we learn the alphabet.

(2) Elsewhere "element" represents *eidos*, except that twice it renders *idea* (50b34, 56b3, where it is clearly an exact equivalent of *eidos*: see FORM). Both words originally meant "form", as in Plato's Theory of Forms (see Introduction, Section 2). In Aristotle *eidos* has two related senses, which have given this translator some difficulty. (a) A KIND or SPECIES of something, as opposed to its overall GENUS. In translating this usage I have preferred "kind" to "species", except for a single passage on METAPHOR where the contrast with GENUS is vital to the argument (57b7–16); "sort" renders the indefinite pronoun *tis, hoios, poios* or *toioutos*, or is supplied. (b) A PART of something. Since, for Aristotle, dividing something up into its KINDS or SPECIES is essential to the process of reaching its DEFINITION, and these kinds or species can be regarded as the PARTS of a single GENUS, it comes to mean the same as PART. In such cases I have translated it as "element". Thus the six QUALITATIVE PARTS of tragedy are actually called its "elements" (49b25 etc.); yet the four kinds of epic (59b7) and of tragedy

(55b32–56a3) are also literally its "elements", and Aristotle indicates that these are connected with what he now calls its "parts", meaning its qualitative parts or elements (55b32)! See on 47a8. Conversely, he sometimes uses PART where we would say KIND (I have translated such uses of PART with "type": see PART, and the note on 56a37).

eleos, eleeinos PITY, PITIABLE

embellished, embellishment, hēdusmenos, hēdusma See on 50b16.

emotion, pathos, pathēma These synonyms basically mean something one undergoes or experiences (from *paschein* "undergo", "suffer"); thus at 60b12 *pathos* even denotes the things that words undergo, their "modifications". But it has two related senses in the *Poetics*. (1) When applied to something physical it means a deed of violence which one does or undergoes, which I translate "suffering": see SUFFERING. (2) When applied to something non-physical it means an emotion one experiences, such as PITY, TERROR or ANGER (the PAINFUL emotions), and confidence, joy or LAUGHTER (the PLEASANT emotions): see on 49b28, 56a38. The emotions have a physical component, as when we weep from PITY, shudder from TERROR or laugh in amusement: see on 53b5. Feeling the emotions CORRECTLY is essential to the VIRTUE of CHARACTER. The CATHARSIS poetry accomplishes operates on the emotions so as to bring this about: see EDUCATION, and *On Poets* Testimonia A–D and frag. *4 with notes. Aristotle regards emotion as a "movement" (*kinēsis*) of the SOUL (see *On Poets* Testimonium A(ii) 1342a8, where it is translated "agitation").

Empedocles A speculative natural-scientist and poet: see on 47b18.

enact See ACTION.

enargēs VIVID

end, telos An end is the intended aim or goal of something, in more technical terms its final cause (see CAUSE), which is brought about by that something and benefits some being with a SOUL; the end's existence answers the question 'what is this thing for?' The end of something is identical with its FUNCTION. Thus the function or end of a shoe is to protect one's foot, and that of a knife is to cut. The highest end, that at which all human actions aim, is HAPPINESS (see 50a16–23). The fact that there are higher and lower ends explains how Aristotle can argue that PLOT is the end of tragedy (because it is through plot, above all, that tragedy functions), but also argue that the FUNCTION or END of poetry is to arouse the EMOTIONS (see on 60b25, 62a11–13, 62a18–b3, 62b12–15), and thereby to produce CATHARSIS (49b27). When he says that we use MUSIC for the sake of three benefits, education, catharsis and entertainment, he is stating its three ends (see *On Poets* Testimonium A(ii)). He also uses "end" in the non-technical sense of e.g. the end of a play; a synonym for this is "conclusion", which renders *teleutē* (the related verb *teleutan* is translated "end").

energeia ACTIVITY

enjoy See PLEASURE.

entertainment, *diagōgē* See *On Poets* Testimonium A(ii), with notes on 1341b32–1342a18 and 1341b40.

enthousiasmos ECSTASY

enthrall, enthralment, *psuchagōgein, psuchagōgia* See on 50a33.

***eoike* seem** See APPEAR.

epic, epic poem, *epikos, epos, epopoiia* Serious narrative poetry composed in HEXAMETER verse (*epos*), also called from its usual content "heroic" verse (48b33). Homer's *Iliad* and *Odyssey* were for Aristotle its finest examples. For its difference from tragedy in terms of MANNER see 48a19–28; most of what Aristotle says about tragedy, i.e. serious dramatic poetry, also applies to epic (see especially 49b9–20). For his treatment of epic specifically see 59a17–61b25; it is compared with tragedy at 61b26–62b15, *On Poets* frag. *3.8–10. For the catharsis epic produces, see CATHARSIS.

epieikēs DECENT

episode, *epeisodion* The original sense of this is a scene or act introduced by the entry of an additional character (*ep-eisodos*); as such, it is one of the QUANTITATIVE PARTS of tragedy (52b20) and comedy (*T.C.* 17). By analogy, it means a scene or episode in epic too (e.g. 55b1, b15, 59b22–31). Such scenes were sometimes of doubtful relevance to the PLOT, so that Aristotle calls tragic plots containing such irrelevant scenes "episodic" (51b33).

episodic See EPISODE.

ergon FUNCTION.

error, *hamartia, hamartēma* Like CORRECTNESS, this has no specifically moral sense; thus it can refer to errors in composing poetry (see 60b6–22, *On Poets* frags. *4.4–5, *5–7), which may produce the wrong effect and make the poem fail. But it also refers to error in feeling the EMOTIONS appropriately (see CATHARSIS). For error and its place in the PLOT of tragedy, where it is related to IGNORANCE, see the note on 53a10; for error in comedy see on 49a34, *T.C.* 8.

essence See DEFINE.

ethos HABIT

ēthos CHARACTER

eudaimonia HAPPINESS

***euphuia*, genius** See NATURE.

Euripides An Athenian tragic poet: see on 53a24.

***eutelēs*, ordinary** See COMMONPLACE.

***eutuchia*, good fortune** See FORTUNE.

everyday See UNFAMILIAR.

exallagē ALTERATION

excellent See GOOD.

exotic name, glōtta A kind of NAME, that which is STANDARD somewhere else: see on 57b6.

expectation At 52a4 this renders *doxa*, "opinion"; the deception of our opinions or expectations is vital to AMAZEMENT. But it is also vital to LAUGHTER (see on *T.C.* 6, especially 6(v), where the term is *prosdokia*).

exposition, diēgēsis See NARRATION.

false inference, paralogismos See INFERENCE.

fear See TERROR.

fine, kalos This is the opposite both of "bad" (*kakos*) in the moral sense, and of "ugly" (*aischros*) in the aesthetic sense. Similarly *spoudaios*, "serious" or "good", is opposed to both *phaulos* "inferior" and *geloios* "laughable". The ACTIONS and persons represented by tragedy and epic should be "fine" and "serious" (see 48b25, 49b24), whereas those represented by comedy and LAMPOON are "inferior" and "laughable" (48b25, *T.C.* 4). For the connection between fineness, COMPLETENESS and MAGNITUDE see on 50b37.

form, schēma, form, element, idea *Schēma* means basically a shape or form, e.g. in painting at 47a19 or in dance at 47a27; compare with this latter usage its meaning "gesture" at 55a29, 62a3. Thus at 48b36, 49a6 and 49b2 it refers to the form or outline of comedy, and is clearly equivalent to *idea* at 49b8; the "forms of DICTION" at 56b9 and *T.C.* 5(vii) are the different types of sentence. *Idea* is translated "form" at 49b8, 58a26, and 58b18: see ELEMENT. "Shape" translates *morphē*.

fortune Good fortune, *eutuchia*, and misfortune, *atuchia*, *dustuchia*, are both derived from *tuchē* "chance". They describe events which affect us but which we cannot control, although they may be the unforeseen results of our DECISIONS or indeed of our ERRORS. In the *Ethics*, Aristotle explains that our fortunes may affect our HAPPINESS but are not the same as our happiness; the happiness of a virtuous person depends mainly (but not solely) on his character (e.g. *Ethics* I 8.1099a32–1100a9). The plot of tragedy must contain a CHANGE of fortune (51a13), generally (or at least potentially) a change from good fortune to misfortune (see 52b34–53a17).

friend, philos, friendship, friendly relationship, philia This is much stronger than in English, denoting someone connected by blood, marriage or the sacred ties of hospitality: see on 52a31.

function, ergon This originally meant "work", and sometimes only means "undertaking" (49a31), "fact" (48b10) or "performance" (62a18). But usually it has a more technical sense; the function of something is the same as its END or aim. The function of a POET is to represent UNIVERSALS (51a35– 8). Tragedy best performs its function through PLOT (see on 50a29–33, 52b28–30); its function, the arousal of PITY and TERROR by means of REPRESENTATION, is the same as that of epic (see on 62b12–15). "Effect" (*ergasia*) is equivalent (*On Poets* frag. *3.14).

geloios, laughable See LAUGHTER.

generalised See UNIVERSAL.

genus, class, genos This originally meant "family", as it does at 53a11 and 54a10; but it came to mean the wider "class" or "genus" to which individual KINDS or SPECIES belong. I translate this sense of it as "class" except at 57b7–16, where the contrast between genus and species is vital to the argument. See DEFINE, ELEMENT.

gesture See FORM.

glōtta EXOTIC NAME

good, agathos, good, serious, spoudaios, good, chrēstos In the *Poetics* these words are used in three related contexts; English lacks suitable terms to distinguish completely between them in translation. (1) *Agathos* describes poets or painters who are "good" because they achieve the FUNCTION of their ART, and possess VIRTUE in it (see 50a28, 51b37, 54b9, 56a6, *On Poets* frags. *4.5, *5); the opposite of this is INFERIOR. Elsewhere it has the sense of a "good" or "advantage" (59b29, 61a8). (2) *Spoudaios* means both "good" and "serious", because it denotes someone or something we take seriously in social and moral terms; I have had to translate it in both ways, depending on whether the context opposes it to "inferior" or to "laughable". Thus the people and actions tragedy and epic represent are called *spoudaioi* (48a25–8) as well as FINE (48b25), whereas those in comedy are "inferior" (48b25–7) and "laughable" (49a32–7, T.C. 4). (3) One of Aristotle's requirements for tragic character is that the character be *chrēstos*, literally "useful" or "good" (54a16–25). He perhaps avoids *spoudaios* here because he wishes to include classes of people who were of lesser social status in antiquity, namely women and slaves. The opposite of "good" in this sense is WICKED.

grand, grandeur, semnos, semnotēs This is opposed to "ordinary", whether it refers to the people who started serious poetry (48b25) or to the DICTION of epic and tragedy (see on 58a18, 59a8, T.C. 18). It is opposed to "small" or "trivial" and to "laughable" at 49a20, and to "laughable" at T.C. 18 (compare *On Poets* frag. *3.7). At 59b28 the "weight" and "splendour" that epic has are probably synonyms for MAGNITUDE and grandeur.

habit, habituation, ethos, ethismos See CATHARSIS, EDUCATION.

hamartēma, hamartia ERROR

haplous SIMPLE, SINGLE

happiness, eudaimonia Aristotle regards the highest human END as happiness or "doing well"; this is the ultimate aim of human ACTION, whatever intermediate ends actions may have, and is therefore the COMPLETE end, i.e. one that is not sought for the sake of any further goal. It is not the same as PLEASURE or as FORTUNE, although good fortune contributes to it; thus tragedy, which represents human actions aiming at happiness, must contain a change of fortune. See on 50a16–23.

harmful, *blaberos* In the *Poetics* this refers to the harm that can come from seeing WICKED characters represented (see on 60b6–22, b35–61a1, 61b21). Aristotle makes clear in the *Politics* that children can be harmed by seeing LAMPOON and comedy when they are too young (see on *On Poets* Testimonium A(ii), 1341b23); this is presumably for the same reason.

harmonia MELODY

harmottein, to harmotton APPROPRIATE

hēdonē PLEASURE

hēdusmenos EMBELLISHED

heis SINGLE, UNIFIED

hēmiphōnon SEMI-VOWEL

hexameter The VERSE-FORM of EPIC, consisting of six "measures", each based on the alternation of one heavy with two light syllables; it was also called "heroic" verse, from its usual content (see 48b33).

holos WHOLE

homalos CONSISTENT

Homer The Ionian epic poet who composed the *Iliad* and *Odyssey*: see on 47b18.

homoios LIKE

homonymy, *homōnumia* See on T.C. 5–6, 5(i)–(ii).

horos, horismos DEFINITION

human being This renders *anthrōpos*, and may have the connotation "fallible", i.e. all too human, e.g. at *On Poets* frag. *3.3, *3.5. It is distinct from *anēr* "man", which means an adult male. "Person" and "people" are used to translate participial or adjectival expressions where neither noun appears.

to hupenantion CONTRADICTION

hupokritikē DELIVERY

iambic verse, *iambeion* This is the main VERSE-FORM of tragedy, comedy and LAMPOON; the iambic trimeter contains three "measures", each consisting of a heavy syllable followed by a light syllable followed by another heavy one with an extra syllable at the front. See on 48b31, 49a21, 59a12.

iambos LAMPOON

idea See ELEMENT, FORM.

idios PARTICULAR TO

idiōtikos See UNFAMILIAR.

ignorance, *agnoia* See on 52a30, a31; for the relation between ignorance and ERROR in tragedy, see on 53a10; for the importance of ignorance in the best kind of PLOT, see on 53b37–54a9.

Iliad See HOMER.

image, *eikōn,* **make an image,** *apeikazein, eikazein* This is related to PROBABLE (*eikos*) and "seem" (*eoikenai*); compare "likeness" and "likely" in

English. Visual images, like poems, are REPRESENTATIONS (47a18, 48a5); Aristotle uses analogies with them to explain how representation works (see on 48b10, 1340a25 and Introduction, Section 4). See also on 50a39–b3, and PAINTING.

impossible, impossibility, *adunatos, to adunaton* This means something contrary to what is NECESSARY or possible; it is closely related to the IMPROBABLE: see on 54a33–b8, T.C. 6(iii)–(iv). Yet even an impossibility can be made to seem PROBABLE or believable (see on 60a27–b1). See also PLOT, and the notes on 60b6–22, 60b22, 60b29–32.

improbability, improbable, *alogia, alogos* This means something that is contrary to reason (*logos*) and to what is reasonable or PROBABLE (*eikos*): see on 54a33–b8. This can arouse AMAZEMENT in epic and LAUGHTER in comedy (see on 60a11–18 and T.C. 6(iv)). See also 54b1, 60a30, 60b6–61b25, 61b15. "Oddity" (*atopia*) is synonymous (60a35, b2, 61b5, cf. 60a1). I translate the adverb *alogōs* "illogically" at 61b1.

incidents, *pragmata* This is literally the "things done", with more emphasis on ACTION than the English word has. It differs from *praxis*, however, since the latter means "action" viewed as a process, and not as an outcome. The PLOT is the CONSTRUCTION of the incidents (50a5); "incidents" is sometimes used as a synonym for PLOT (e.g. 50a22, 56a19). For "event" see ARISE.

indication, *sēmeion* Related to *sēmainein* "SIGNIFY", this usually means a sign of something that does not amount to a formal proof of it; when used of visible signs or gestures, it is translated "sign" (54b21, 55a20, 62a6).

inference, *sullogismos;* false inference, *paralogismos* Inference is the process of using REASONING to reach a conclusion by combining propositions (premises). For RECOGNITION depending on inference or on false inference see 55a4–16, and 60a18–26.

inferior, *phaulos* See FINE, GOOD.

inflection, *ptōsis* See on 57a18.

invective, *psogos* See LAMPOON.

invent, find, discover, *heuriskein* Alongside the standard meaning "find", this can mean "invent" plot, characters and diction (53b25, *On Poets* frag. *5); this accords with the idea of poetry as an ART or craft. In *On Poets* frags. *13–14 it is used of the poets who "invented" tragedy. It is translated "discover" at 54a11, 55a25.

investigation See OBSERVATION.

Iphigeneia The title-character of two plays by Euripides: see on 52b6, 54a32, and the plot-summary at 55b2–15.

***kakos*, bad, *kakia* vice** See WICKED, VIRTUE.

kalos FINE

katharsis CATHARSIS

kath' hekaston, hekasta PARTICULAR
katholou UNIVERSAL
kind, *eidos* See DEFINE, ELEMENT.
kosmos ORNAMENT
kōmōidia COMEDY
kurios STANDARD
lampoon, *iambos* This is a poem abusing PARTICULAR individuals (see
51b11), normally in IAMBIC verse: see on 48b27, b31. "Invective" (*psogos*)
and "abuse" (*loidoria*) are equivalent (48b27, b37; *T.C.* 7). Like comedy, it
represents "inferior" persons (see FINE, HARMFUL), but presumably aims to
arouse rightful anger (*nemesis*) at their ERRORS and VICES rather than
LAUGHTER. For its relation to comedy, see further under COMEDY.

laughter, laughable, *gelōs, geloios* Laughter is the EMOTION aroused
by COMEDY. For its association with comedy see on 49a32–7, a34, where the
laughable (i.e. that at which we laugh) is defined as a kind of ERROR and
UGLINESS that is not PAINFUL or destructive; for an analysis of its kinds
(laughter from DICTION, PLOT, CHARACTER and REASONING), and its relation
to LAMPOON and ERROR, see *T.C.* 5–8. For evidence that laughter is one of
the PLEASANT EMOTIONS see on *T.C.* 9; as such, it is the main emotion subject to comic CATHARSIS (see on *T.C.* 4, 9).

length, *mēkos* This is used in two main senses, for the duration of time
represented in the epic or tragedy, and for the time taken to perform it (see
49b12 with note, 51a6–15); the length of performance is of course indirectly
related to the length of time represented in it (see 59b17–31, 62a18–b3).
Epic is more easily "lengthened out" (*mēkunein*) with EPISODES (55b16), and
so acquires MAGNITUDE (56a14, cf. 62b4–10). At 56b32 "length" refers to
whether a vowel is long or short.

lengthened, lengthening, *epektetamenos, epektasis* This refers to a
kind of NAME: see 57b35, and for the uses to which it is put see 58a23, b2,
59b36. The same kind of alteration is called "addition" (*prosthesis*) at *T.C.*
5(iv). The related verb *epekteinein* is used of lengthening vowels at 58a12.

lexis DICTION, UTTERANCE
like, *homoios* Although being like something else is clearly basic to
REPRESENTATION, Aristotle does not express this directly, but implies it at
On Poets Testimonium A(i) 1340a17; similarly, METAPHOR is based on seeing what is like something else (59a8). In a number of places he refers to
poets or painters representing people as "like", which means "lifelike" or
"like ourselves" according to context (the two are related: see on 54a17–33
and *On Poets* frag. *5, where it is one of the requirements for tragic CHAR-
ACTER). "Making like" (*homoiōsis*) is also basic to LAUGHTER: see on *T.C.* 6,
and 6(ii).

logos SPEECH, STORY, WORDS
lupē pain See PLEASURE.

lusis SOLUTION

made-up, *pepoiēmenos* This refers to something rather artificial produced by the poet: stories that he invents completely for himself (55a34), RECOGNITIONS based on contrived SIGNS (54b30, 55a20), and a kind of NAME, i.e. a word invented by the poet (see on 57b34).

magnitude, *megethos* This is related to LENGTH (51a9–15), but in addition has positive connotations of seriousness and GRANDEUR (see on 49a19, 50b37, 59b28). Tragedy (50b26) and epic both have it, especially the latter (56a14, 59a34, b23, 62b10); comedy, and early tragedy, do not (*T.C.* 4, 49a19).

make, compose, produce The standard verb for "making" something is *poiein*, which is related to "poet" and "poem"; I translate it "compose" in the context of poetry and "produce" elsewhere: see ACTION, COMPOSE. In expressions like "produce pleasure", "produce" often translates *paraskeuazein* (e.g. 53b37, 54a11), but *poiein* is used in the same way.

manner This is one of the three DIFFERENCES between the kinds of REPRESENTATION, the way in which the representation is produced; the manner of epic is NARRATIVE, that of tragedy is DRAMATIC: see 48a19–28. The term translated is sometimes *tropos* "manner", sometimes only an adverb like "how" (see on 47a17).

media This is another of the DIFFERENCES between the kinds of representation, the means by which the representation is produced (in the case of drama, DICTION and SONG). Again Aristotle has no noun for this concept, but says simply "the things by means of which" (see on 47a17).

megethos MAGNITUDE

mēkos LENGTH

mellein be ABOUT to

melody, *harmonia* It is simplest to think of this as the musical tune, but more accurate to understand that it includes the musical "mode" or scale according to which the instrument was tuned, like the Dorian or Phrygian mode (see on *On Poets* Testimonium A(ii) 1341b35). SONG consists of RHYTHM, SPEECH and melody (47a22). At 49a28 the *harmonia* of speech means something like its "intonation".

melopoiia, melos SONG

meros PART

metabolē CHANGE

***metabasis*, transformation** See CHANGE.

metaphor, *metaphora* One of the kinds of NAME, so-called from the "transference" (*metaphora*) of the STANDARD NAME to something else, by a process of recognising a LIKENESS (see on 59a6). For the main account of metaphor see 57b7–32 with notes, and also 58a23–31 (metaphor and riddle), 59a6 (the importance of metaphor, its relation to GENIUS), a14,

59b35–7 (its value in prose and epic), 61a17–22 (SOLUTIONS based on it), *T.C.* 5(vi), 6, 18 (its use in comedy).

metron VERSE

miaros SHOCKING

middle, meson See WHOLE.

mime, mimos See on 47b10.

mimēsis REPRESENTATION

mochthēros WICKED

moral satisfaction, philanthrōpia, to philanthrōpon See on 52b36, 56a20–22.

morion PART

music, mousikē Aristotle's discussion of the function of music in EDU-CATION makes it clear that by "music" he understands, like most Greeks, primarily instrumental and vocal music (cf. 62a16, where it is equivalent to "SONG"), but also poetry as well, i.e. literature in general: for evidence of this see *On Poets* Testimonium A with notes, especially 1340a12. Thus his account of CATHARSIS in music is applicable to poetry in general.

must, ought, should I can discern no difference in meaning between these in the *Poetics*. For the sake of accuracy, "must" renders verbal adjectives in *-teon* (twice it renders *dei*, at 51b28 and 52b5, and twice *prosēkei*); "must necessarily" or "necessarily" renders *anankē* (see NECESSARY); "ought" renders *chrē*; and "should" renders *dei*, except when the verb is not impersonal, where it is translated "require" or "need" (as a noun, "need" translates *chreia*).

muthos PLOT

name, onoma The basic sense of *onoma* is "name", but in his discussion of DICTION Aristotle uses it in the extended sense of a noun or adjective (see his definition at 57a10): since English has no equivalent of this, I have translated it as "name" ("word" at 52a30). For the different kinds of name see 57a31–58a17, 59a8.

narrate, narration, apangellein, apangelia, expository, exposition, diēgēmatikē, diēgēsis These are synonyms for the MANNER of REPRESEN-TATION that is narrative (as in epic) rather than DRAMATIC (as in comedy and tragedy): see on 48a20–24, *T.C.* 2, *On Poets* frag. *3.8. Another synonym is "recount" (*aparithmein*) at 53a8.

nature, phusis Nature is that which has the origin of its movement or CHANGE in itself, as opposed to ART, which has the origin of its movement in something else (*Physics* II 1.192b21, *Metaphysics* 1070a7). Thus the fact that representation is natural to human beings (48b4) implies that they have a natural POTENTIAL for it which is actualised in the development of poetry; people with different natures bring this about in different ways (49a4) and to differing degrees. Similarly an ART has a natural potential to perform its FUNCTION and achieve its END (see *On Poets* *4.7); this potential is realised by the artists who develop it.

is realised by the artists who develop it. Thus the nature of something implies its FUNCTION and END, e.g. tragedy ceased to change because "it had attained its own nature" (49a15); not all its natural potentialities will be actualised, because of external factors (49a7–9, cf. 51a7–11). Nature reveals itself or "teaches" by experience (see on 59b32). The artists best able to develop the natural potential of their art and achieve its end possess genius (*euphuia*), i.e. natural talent: see 55a32, 59a7 (cf. 51a24). I translate the verb *pephukenai* as "be by nature" or the like.

necessity, ananke, necessary, anankaios If something is necessary it cannot be otherwise, e.g. in the conclusion of a logical argument, where adverbial *anankē* is rendered "necessarily". In the *Poetics* Aristotle specifies that INCIDENTS should follow one another according to necessity or PROBABILITY, i.e. they should follow from the preceding actions according to rules that are true either always (by necessity) or most of the time (by probability): see 50b30, and especially 51a11–52a20. The opposite of the necessary is the IMPOSSIBLE (something otherwise than it must be); see also IMPROBABLE.

need See MUST.

nome, *nomos* A type of non-tragic choral lyric: see on 47b26.

object This is one of the three DIFFERENCES between the kinds of REPRESENTATION, the objects which are represented (see 48a1–18); in the case of tragedy and epic, the objects are FINE, SERIOUS persons and actions. Aristotle has no abstract term for "objects", but uses simply "the things which" or the like (see on 47a17).

oboe, *aulos* See on 47a24.

observation, investigation, *theōria, theōrēma* This is related to *thea* "sight", and means to look at something closely, and so to study or investigate it.

Odyssey See HOMER.

Oedipus The title character of Sophocles' tragedy *Oedipus the King*: see on 52a24, 53b32.

oikeios PARTICULAR TO

oiktos See PITY.

onoma NAME

opsis SPECTACLE

orchēsis DANCE

ordinary See COMMONPLACE.

Orestes See on 52b6, 53a20, a36.

orgē ANGER

origin, *archē* See BEGINNING, CAUSE.

ornament, *kosmos* A type of NAME, in fact the ornamental epithet: see on 57b33.

orthos CORRECT

ousia   ESSENCE

pain, *lupē, odunē*   See PLEASURE.

painting   Like poetry (to which Aristotle often compares it), painting is a form of REPRESENTATION (47a18, 48b10– 19, 50b1, 60b8, *On Poets* Testimonium A(i) 1340a25), and can represent different OBJECTS (48a5, *On Poets* frag. *3.6) and CHARACTERS (50a26–9, 54b8–15).

***paralogismos*, false inference**   See INFERENCE.

paraskeuazein   MAKE

parody, *parōidia*   See 48a12, *T.C.* 5(v).

paronymy, *parōnumia*   The modification of NAMES: see on 57b35–58a7, *T.C.* 5(iv).

part, type, *meros*, part, *morion*   This is simply a constituent of a WHOLE, but of course a whole can have several different sets of parts: thus tragedy has QUANTITATIVE PARTS like episodes and prologues, but also QUALITATIVE PARTS (ELEMENTS) like PLOT and CHARACTER. Aristotle tends to regard the parts of something as equivalent to its kinds or species (see DEFINE, ELEMENT); hence a species (*eidos*) of something can be equated with its parts, and in such cases *eidos* is translated "element". Conversely, he may speak of the "parts" of something where we would speak of its "kinds"; in such cases *meros* is translated "type" (see on 56a37).

particle, *arthron*   See on 56b38.

particular, a particular, *kath' hekaston*   This means literally something "according to each one", i.e. considered individually. A particular is an individual object, person, experience or action (e.g. this book, Socrates, today's game), as opposed to a UNIVERSAL on a higher level of generality (e.g. book, human being, sport): see the definitions at 51b8–11, where Aristotle argues that POETRY tends to REPRESENT universals, history particulars.

particular to, proper to, *idios*, particular to, *oikeios*   These are used interchangeably to denote that which relates especially closely to something else; thus there is a pleasure "particular to" tragedy, which differs from the pleasure "particular to" comedy (53a35).

pathēma, pathos   EMOTION, SUFFERING

pepoiēmenos   MADE-UP

peplegmenos   COMPLEX

perception, *aisthēsis*   At 50b38 and 51a6 this has its basic sense of noticing something with one of the five senses, here sight (it is connected with OBSERVATION). Elsewhere it has the extended sense of "reacting" to or "noticing" the dramatic performance, and is translated "react": see on 54b15–18.

perform   See COMPETE.

peripeteia   REVERSAL

phainesthai, phaneros   See APPEAR.

phaulos   INFERIOR

philanthrōpia   MORAL SATISFACTION

philos   FRIEND

phobos   TERROR

phōnē   SOUND

phortikos   VULGAR

phusis   NATURE

phōnēen   VOWEL

pistis   PROOF

pithanos   BELIEVABLE

pity, pitiable, *eleos, eleeinos,* **compassion, arousing compassion,** *oiktos, oiktros*   A painful EMOTION, which (like TERROR) is aroused by tragedy and epic, and is subject to CATHARSIS. See on 53a4, and CATHARSIS. "Compassion" is an exact synonym (see on 53b15).

Plato   An Athenian philosopher, the teacher of Aristotle: see Introduction, Section 2.

pleasure, *hēdonē*   This noun corresponds to the verbs *chairein* "delight" and *euphrainein* "give enjoyment"; its opposite is "pain" (*lupē, odunē*). It is natural to desire pleasure, and we aim at pleasure when we obey our EMOTIONS; these are divided into those that are pleasant (e.g. confidence, joy or LAUGHTER), and those that are painful (e.g. ANGER, PITY or TERROR). So to attain to VIRTUE we must become habituated to feel pleasure and pain correctly, i.e. at the right time, toward the proper object, to the right degree etc.; both EDUCATION and CATHARSIS can contribute to this process of habituation. There are different kinds of pleasure, and they are not all equally good. Tragedy and comedy have different emotional effects, and therefore produce different pleasures: see on 53a35, 53b1–11. It is a paradox about tragedy that the pleasure it produces arises from painful emotions like pity and terror; this is possible because tragedy is REPRESENTATION (see further CATHARSIS).

plekein, plokē, **develop, development**   See COMPLICATION.

plot, story, *muthos*   The best translation for *muthos* would perhaps be "story", since Aristotle applies it to both a pre-existing story, such as the Trojan War, and the CONSTRUCTION of the INCIDENTS put into the poem by the poet (50a4). "Plot" has connotations of intrigue lacked by the Greek term, but it is the traditional rendering, and at 50a4 Aristotle indicates that he is using it in a technical sense. Thus I translate *muthos* in its first sense as "story" (see on 51a22; *logos* sometimes has to be translated "story" also, see SPEECH), and in its second sense as "plot" (a synonym for this is *mutheuma,* translated "plot-structure": see 60a28). As the construction of the incidents, plot amounts to the END of tragedy, that by means of which it performs its FUNCTION; hence Aristotle sometimes equates plot with "structure" (see CONSTRUCT) and even with the poem itself (see on 60a28). It is the main QUALITATIVE PART of tragedy (50a15–b4), and should represent a SINGLE, COMPLETE ACTION containing a CHANGE of FORTUNE constructed in accord with NECESSITY or PROBABILITY (50b21–51a35). Its KINDS are SIMPLE and COMPLEX (51b33–52a21), its PARTS are RECOGNITION, REVERSAL and SUFFERING (52a22–b13; see also on 59b10). See also CHARACTER, EPISODE, ERROR; for plot in comedy, see on *T.C.* 6(i)–(v), 11.

poem See COMPOSITION.

poet See COMPOSER, POETRY.

poetry, *poiēsis* This means literally "making", from *poiein* "make": see ART, COMPOSE, MAKE. It has two senses. In its popular sense poetry is composition in VERSE, whatever its content; thus Aristotle sometimes refers loosely to writers of versified scientific treatises or the like as "poets" (see on *T.C.* 1). But at 47a28–b24 he argues that a better criterion for what is poetry is whether it is REPRESENTATION, regardless of whether it is in prose or verse; and at 51a36–b32 he adds that poetry tends to represent UNIVERSALS rather than PARTICULARS; the representation of particulars is more appropriate to history. See Introduction, Section 4.

poiein   COMPOSE, MAKE
poiēma   COMPOSITION
poiēsis   COMPOSITION, POETRY
poiētēs   COMPOSER
poiētikē   ART, POETRY
politikē   CIVIC LIFE

possible, *dunatos* See IMPOSSIBLE.

potential, *dunamis* This originally meant "power", and is related to *dunatos* "able, possible"; Aristotle uses it as a technical term for the capacity or potentiality of something, which is not actualised until it is put into ACTIVITY: see on 47a9.

pragma   INCIDENT
praktikos, prattein, praxis   See ACTION.
premiss   See INFERENCE.
prepon, **suitable**   See APPROPRIATE.
pro ommatōn   See VIVID.

probable, probability, *eikos* *Eikos* is related to *eoikenai* "seem", and means that which seems reasonable; its opposite is that which seems contrary to reason (*logos*), the IMPROBABLE (*alogon*). What is probable can be approved and is BELIEVABLE. It is broadly equivalent to what is probable in a statistical sense, although quantified statistics are a modern discovery (see on 50b30). For further details see IMPOSSIBLE, PLOT.

produce   See MAKE.

prohairesis   DECISION

proof, *pistis* A proof is something which makes us believe (*pisteuein*), and so is important in proving someone's identity (see RECOGNITION). For the different kinds of proof see on *T.C.* 13.

proper to, *idios* See PARTICULAR TO.

proportion See DUE PROPORTION.

psogos See LAMPOON.

pseudos UNTRUTH

psuchagōgia ENTHRALMENT

psuchē SOUL

purify See CATHARSIS.

qualitative parts Since both tragedy and comedy use different MEDIA in different parts of the play (i.e. SONG in some parts and DICTION in others), they have parts like prologues, choral songs and EPISODES (acts) into which they can be divided (see 52b14–27, T.C. 17); Aristotle calls these their "parts according to quantity" (52b15). But they also have parts like PLOT, CHARACTER and SPECTACLE, which can give the play a certain quality, as Aristotle puts it at 50a8 (see also on 55b32–56a3, 59b7, b10); so it seems reasonable to call these the "qualitative parts", although Aristotle usually calls them "ELEMENTS" to distinguish them from the quantitative "PARTS". For the deduction of these parts see 49b31–50a14, T.C. 5–6, and see further PLOT, CHARACTER, REASONING, DICTION, SONG and SPECTACLE; epic has all except the last two (see on 49b16). Not every tragedy or comedy need contain them all, since, for example, an ACTION can be represented without explaining the CHARACTERS of those in action (see on 50a12, a25, T.C. 16), just as not every plot need contain a reversal. This may help to explain how these parts relate to the four "kinds" of tragedy and epic (see ELEMENT).

quantitative parts See QUALITATIVE PARTS.

random, at random This renders either the noun *tuchē* "chance" (connected with *eutuchia* "good fortune") or the participle of the related verb *tunchanein*. *Tuchē* is translated "chance" at 54a11. Random events are the opposite of those that happen in accord with NECESSITY or PROBABILITY.

react See PERCEPTION.

reason "For this reason" translates *dio* and similar expressions. See also CAUSE.

reasoning, *dianoia* This means rational thought generally, but, since poetry is a REPRESENTATION which uses words, it is used in the *Poetics* to mean especially such thought expressed in words; this is why Aristotle refers to the *Rhetoric* for a full account of it (see on 50a6, 56a34–b8). It is one of the QUALITATIVE PARTS or ELEMENTS of tragedy, epic and comedy. For its relation to PLOT and CHARACTER see on 49b36–50a7; see also CHARACTER, DECISION.

recitation, *rhapsōidia* Epic poems were performed by "rhapsodes", i.e. reciters, in public competitions: see on 47b21.

recognise, recognition, *anagnōrizein, anagnōrisis, anagnōrismos* One of the parts of PLOT, a change from IGNORANCE to knowledge (52a29–32);

for a classification of its kinds, see 52a33–b8, 54b19–55a21. Recognition and REVERSAL are particular to COMPLEX plots, and are found in epic too (59b15).

relaxation, *anapausis* See on *On Poets* Testimonium A(ii) 1341b32–1342a18.

represent, *mimeisthai*, representation, *mimēsis* In Greek in general *mimēsis* covered the whole range of what we call copying, imitation, impersonation and representation, particularly in the arts. Plato tended to stress the idea that art is imitation (see Introduction, Section 2). Aristotle, in reaction to this, developed the concept of art as representation, when one thing is LIKE another (see 48b4–19, and Introduction, Section 4). For its different KINDS, distinguished by their different MEDIA, OBJECTS and MANNER, see on 47a13–b28 and PAINTING, POETRY (which Aristotle regards as essentially representation, not versification). Its emotional effect depends on our recognition that the representation *is* a representation (see on 53b11, and CATHARSIS). PLOT is the representation of ACTION; similarly words themselves are representations of things, and METAPHOR is a word which represents another (see on 59a6). Greek has different words for the process of representation (*mimēsis*) and its product (*mimēma*); see on 48b9. "Representational artist" translates *mimētēs*, literally "representer" (48a26, 60a8, b8); in the second passage Aristotle plays on the Platonic sense "impersonator". The verb *mimeisthai* is used in a non-technical sense at 54b9, where it is translated "emulate".

result "As a result of" and similar expressions render the preposition *ek*.

reversal, *peripeteia* One of the parts of PLOT, the reversal of the actions to their opposite, so that the result is the reverse of what the characters (and often the audience) expect: see 52a22–9. It is closely related to RECOGNITION as an essential feature of a COMPLEX plot. See also 50a33–5, 54b26, 56a19.

rhapsōdia RECITATION

rhēma VERB

rhēsis SPEECH

rhetoric, *rhētorikē* Rhetoric is the art of finding and expressing what is persuasive or believable; Aristotle treats it fully in his *Rhetoric*. Thus REASONING in poetry falls within this art (see 56a34–b8), as do DELIVERY and, to some extent, DICTION (these are dealt with in *Rhetoric* III).

rhythm, *rhuthmos* This is the concept of metre itself; a measured unit of it is a VERSE (see on 47a29). Rhythm, SPEECH and MELODY are the MEDIA of poetry.

satyric, *saturikos* For the "satyric" nature of early tragedy, and its relation to satyr-play, see on 49a20.

saphēs CLEAR

schēma FORM

seem See APPEAR.

semnos GRAND

sēmainein SIGNIFY

sēmeion INDICATION

semi-vowel, hēmiphōnon See on 56b25–31.

serious, spoudaios See GOOD.

shocking, miaros See on 52b36, and CATHARSIS.

shortened, aphēirēmenon, shortening, apokopē, aphairesis A kind of NAME: see 57b35. *Aphairesis* (*T.C.* 5(iv)) is literally "subtraction" (see LENGTHENING). This is also called a "reduced" NAME at 57b3 (*huphēirēmenos*).

sign, sēmeion See INDICATION.

signify, significant, sēmainein, sēmantikos Something is "significant" when it "stands for" something else: see on 56b38 (the verb is translated "indicates" at 52a30). These terms are related to *sēmeion* "sign": see INDICATION.

simple, single, haplous *Haplous* means single and uniform, as opposed to multiple and complex; I have translated it "simple" or "single" according to context. Thus the VERSE-FORM of epic is "single", whereas tragedy has many different verse-forms (49b11); and NAMES are either "single" or "double", i.e. either not compounded of other NAMES or so compounded (57a32). Similarly PLOT can be "single" as opposed to "double" (when it ends well for the good and badly for the bad): see 53a13. But it can also be "single" as opposed to "COMPLEX": complex plots have REVERSAL and REC-OGNITION, simple plots do not (see on 52a1–11). In other contexts "single" translates *heis*, literally "one": see UNIFIED.

Socrates An Athenian philosopher, the teacher of Plato: see Introduction, Section 2.

solve, luein, solution, lusis This originally meant "undo" (as at 53b22), and is used in two main contexts. (1) It is that part of tragedy or indeed of plot opposed to the "complication": see COMPLICATION, and notes on 54a37, 55b24–56a10. (2) It refers to solving or refuting the problems and criticisms which critics raise (60b6, cf. "refutation" at 56a38); "resolve" at 61a10 renders *dialuein*.

song, melopoiia, melos Although *melopoiia* means literally "the composition of songs", Aristotle uses these terms synonymously, as at 50a10. He broadly equates song and MUSIC (see 62a16); it means specifically the combination of RHYTHM, SPEECH and MELODY, as opposed to VERSE which means speech and rhythm without melody (see 47b25, 49b34). Thus "song" includes the words that are sung, and DICTION excludes them. The use made of song is one of the points of difference between the kinds of REPRESENTATION (47a21–8, b24–8). Among the kinds of poetry that are sung throughout are the DITHYRAMB and NOME, whereas tragedy and comedy use song in some parts and DICTION in others. Hence "song" is both a qualitative part of these genres, like DICTION, SPECTACLE etc. (see QUALITATIVE PART), and a quantitative one like the prologue (see CHORAL PART). Aristotle has rather little to say about it (see on 49b34), and presumably regards it as falling under music (cf. T.C. 15), although it is still a part of tragedy (see *On Poets* frag. *3.11–18), just as he regards REASONING as a part of RHETORIC. Epic lacks it (see on 49b16).

sophist Sophists like Protagoras (56b15) and Polyidus (55a6) were itinerant professional lecturers who offered courses on how to succeed in public life by means of rhetorical and political skill; they charged high fees. Plato and Aristotle were hostile to their lack of theoretical underpinnings and tendency to use verbal trickery to win arguments.

Sophocles An Athenian tragic poet: see on 48a26.

sort See ELEMENT.

soul, *psuchē* Aristotle defines the soul as the ORIGIN of living beings; thus it is both their FUNCTION and their END (see on 50a38). The soul has rational and non-rational parts (see on *On Poets* *4.6), both of which contribute to VIRTUE. The first, which we call the intellect, is concerned with REASONING; this is why Aristotle says "soul" in contexts where we might say "mind" (60a25, T.C. 8). The second part is concerned with EMOTION. It seems that catharsis applies to both parts of the soul (see CATHARSIS).

sound, *phōnē* This means literally "voice" (see 47a20), but Aristotle defines it as the sound made by animals with their throats, as opposed to mere noise (*psophos*) produced by inanimate objects, and to articulate SPEECH (*dialektos*): see on 56b21 and *On Poets* frag.*3.12.

species, *eidos* See ELEMENT.

spectacle, *opsis* This means literally "sight" (58a5), and so "the visual element" in tragedy (49b31) and comedy (T.C. 15); since drama is enacted by people visibly acting and is not narration, spectacle corresponds to the MANNER of dramatic REPRESENTATION (50a11). It is thus one of the QUALITATIVE PARTS of drama, but, like SONG, it is absent from epic (see on 49b16). It also has the extended sense of "spectacular effects" like elaborate staging, costumes and so forth; Aristotle is aware that this is ENTHRALLING, but regards it as lying outside the ART of POETRY as such (see 50b16– 20, 53b1–11). "Spectacle" in this sense forms the basis of one of the four kinds of tragedy (see on 56a2).

speech, utterance, story, *logos*, [everyday] speech, *dialektos*, speech, *rhēsis* *Logos* is related to *legein* "say, tell" (translated "use speech" at 50a6), and refers to both what is said and how it is said. In the *Poetics* it has three main uses.

(1) "Speech" in general, i.e. language: this is synonymous with the wider sense of *lexis* "DICTION", and also with *dialektos*, translated "[every-

day] speech" (49a26, 58b32). Compare the adjective *lektikos*, "suited to [everyday] speech" (49a24, 27). *Logos* can also be equivalent to DICTION in its narrower sense, i.e. it excludes the words of songs (49a17); thus the MEDIA of POETRY as a whole are RHYTHM, speech and MELODY (47a22, cf. 49b10, b25). Speech is also opposed to ACTION (54a18), and is the means by which REASONING is expressed (56a37, b6–8). In the analysis of DICTION at 56b20–57a30, *logos* is used in the technical sense of "utterance" (see UTTERANCE).

(2) The plural *logoi* is translated either "words" (47a29, *On Poets* frag. *3.12), or "speeches", referring to more organised speaking whether in verse or prose (Aristotle had no word for "prose"); when prose speeches are clearly meant, I have supplied "prose" (50b15, 54a13, *On Poets* frag. 1). A synonym for a formal speech is *rhēsis*, also translated "speech" (50a29, 54a31, 56a31); this is cognate with "rhetoric". *Logoi* can also mean "dialogue" (47b11, and perhaps at 54b18, where I translate it as "work"): *dialogos* is a synonym for this (*On Poets* frag. 1).

(3) *Logos* also means "reason" in general, e.g. a philosophical "argument" (61b16) or "topic" (49a9); hence it is related to the IMPROBABLE (*alogon*), that which is contrary to reasonable expectation. Based on this sense, Aristotle also uses *logos* for the argument or "story" that is used in a poem (55a34, b17, 60a27); he uses *muthos* in the same sense (see PLOT).

spoudaios, good, serious See GOOD.

standard, *kurios* This is one of the kinds of NAME, i.e. the normal word for something: see 57b1–6. For its contribution to the VIRTUE of DICTION, see on 58a18, 59a14.

stoicheion ELEMENT

story, *muthos, logos* See PLOT, SPEECH.

structure See CONSTRUCT.

suffering, *pathos* For the basic meaning of *pathos* see under EMOTION. In tragedy and epic it is a part of PLOT, and means the deed of violence that one does or suffers (hence "suffering"): see on 52b10. Suffering forms the basis of one of the kinds of tragedy (see 55b32–56a3) and of epic (59b10).

suitable, *to prepon* See APPROPRIATE.

sullogismos INFERENCE

sumpathēs, sharing in emotion See EMOTION.

sumbainein, sumpiptein See ARISE.

sunthesis CONSTRUCTION

sustasis, sustēma, structure See CONSTRUCTION.

syllable, *sullabē* See on 56b36–7.

synonymy, *sunōnumia* See on *T.C.* 5(i)–(ii).

tapeinos COMMONPLACE

technē ART

teleios COMPLETE

teleutē conclusion   See WHOLE.

telos END

temperance, *sōphrosynē*   This is the VIRTUE connected with moderation in satisfying bodily appetites: see on *On Poets* *4.6.

terror, terrible, *phobos, phoberos,* **dread, dreadful,** *deos, deinos*   A painful EMOTION (like PITY) which is aroused by tragedy and epic, and is subject to CATHARSIS: see on 53a4. It may also be translated "fear"; I have used "terror" because it is the stronger word. "Shudder" is used as a synonym for "feel terror" at 53b5; "dread", *deos*, and "dreadful", *deinos*, are also synonyms (53a22, b15, b30, 56b3, *T.C.* 3: see on 53b15).

tetrameter   See TROCHAIC VERSE.

thaumastos AMAZING

theōria, theōrēma OBSERVATION

time, *chronos*   Aristotle's theory of time is scarcely reflected in the *Poetics* (see on 50b38). A verb is a NAME that contains an indication of time (see VERB). For the relation between the duration of a poem's performance, and the duration of the events represented in it, see LENGTH.

tragedy, *tragōidia*   This means SERIOUS DRAMATIC poetry (composed in a mixture of SONG and spoken VERSE). For its etymology and origins see on 48b1, 49a10, a20, *On Poets* *13–15. For its development, in relation to epic and in itself, see 48b34–49a31; for its similarities to and differences from epic see 49b9–20, 61b26–62b15, *On Poets* *3.8–10. Its definition and analysis into PARTS occupy 49b21–59a16. Like comedy (51b11), it represents UNIVERSALS, but the PLEASURE derived from it is quite different (53a37), since its FUNCTION, like that of epic, is to arouse PITY and TERROR by means of REPRESENTATION, and thereby to accomplish the CATHARSIS of such PAINFUL EMOTIONS. Thus "tragic", *tragikos*, means "arousing pity and terror" at 53a27 and b37 (compare 53b39).

trimeter   See IAMBIC VERSE.

trochaic verse   This means literally a "running" metre, and Aristotle associates it with dancing (49a21, 59b37). It was the main metre of early tragedy, but was replaced by the IAMBIC trimeter (see on 49a19–24, 59a12, *On Poets* *3.9); trochaic metres continued to be used in choruses (see on 52b22). Its usual form, the tetrameter, contains four "measures" (*metra*), each consisting of a heavy syllable, a light syllable and a heavy syllable, with an extra syllable at the end of each *metron* except the last.

tuchē   See RANDOM.

type   See PART.

ugly, ugliness, *aischros, aischos*   See on 49a34, *On Poets* *3.3, and FINE, LAUGHTER.

unfamiliar, *xenikos*   All those kinds of NAME that are not STANDARD: see on 58a21, where its opposite is the "everyday" (*idiōtikos*).

unified, unity, *heis* This means literally "one" or "SINGLE", and is used to describe a PLOT that is a single WHOLE (51a1, a16–7, 62b4). It is otherwise translated "single".

universal, *katholou* This means literally something considered "as a whole" (*holon*). Whereas a PARTICULAR is an individual person, object or situation (e.g. this book, Socrates, today's match), a universal is on a higher level of generality (e.g. book, human being, sport). Poetry tends to represent universals, not particulars: see on 51a36–b32, 51b5, 51b7–11. At 49b8 it is translated "generalised".

utterance, *logos* This is the most complex of the parts of DICTION: see 57a23–30 with notes. In two other passages it translates *lexis*: see DICTION.

verb, *rhēma* One of the parts of DICTION: see on 57a14, 57a31–58a17.

verse, verse-form, *metron* This means literally a "measure" (thus it is translated "due measure" at 58b12). Thus verses are measured portions of SPEECH with RHYTHM (compare 48b20). Poetry was popularly considered to be composition in verse, but Aristotle regards as a more important criterion whether the composition is a representation or not (see POETRY, REPRESENTATION). Since sung verse generally varied its verse-form, but recited or spoken verse often used long stretches of the same metre (especially hexameters and iambic trimeters), "verse" came to mean spoken verse, including its words, whereas the words of sung verse were included in SONG; see on 47a29. See also HEXAMETER, IAMBIC VERSE, TROCHAIC VERSE.

vice, *kakia* See VIRTUE.

virtue, *aretē* The virtue of X is to be a good X, e.g. the virtue of a poet is to be a good poet (compare *On Poets* *4.4); something possesses virtue when it performs its FUNCTION well. Thus DICTION will perform its function well by being clear and appropriate (see on 58a18). Human virtue, and its opposite vice (*kakia*, literally "badness") are basic to CHARACTER (48a3, 53a8). The virtue of character depends on habituation to feeling the right emotional responses, a process for which poetry can be beneficial (see *On Poets* Testimonium A(i) 1340a14–28, A(ii) 1341b32– 1342a18, *On Poets* *4.6–7); there are virtues of intellect, like intelligence, and of character, like bravery, and it seems that the catharsis which poetry can accomplish contributes to both kinds of virtue (see *On Poets* *4.6–7, Introduction, Section 5, and CATHARSIS).

vivid, *enargēs* See on 55a23.

voice See SOUND.

vowel, *phōnēen* See 56b25–31.

vulgar, *phortikos* See on 61b27, *T.C.* 6(vii).

whole, *holos* A whole is that which has a BEGINNING, a middle or middles, and a conclusion: see 50b25–33. PLOT should be a whole; see also SINGLE, UNIFIED.

wicked, wickedness, *mochthēros, mochthēria*, villainous, villainy, *ponēros, ponēria* These are used interchangeably (e.g. 52b36, 53a1; 61b19, 22). At 52b36 "wicked" is opposed to DECENT, and at 53a9 "wickedness" is equated with VICE, and opposed to ERROR as a cause of a fall into misfortune. Unnecessary wickedness is a fault in serious poetry (see 54a29, 61b21: see HARMFUL), but amusing in comedy: see *T.C.* 6(vi).

word   See SPEECH.

xenikos   UNFAMILIAR

zōon   ANIMAL

Bibliography

This list contains only a small selection from the mass of writing on the *Poetics*. A fuller selection may be found in *Articles on Aristotle. 4: psychology and aesthetics*, ed. J. Barnes, M. Schofield and R. Sorabji (London, 1979), cited as *Articles* below; and in S. Halliwell, *Aristotle's Poetics* (Chapel Hill, 1986). A number of the older books are available in modern reprintings: I give the original date of publication, since this will often affect how up-to-date the book's contents are.

Ancient Literary Criticism

For a collection of essential texts see:

D.A. Russell and M. Winterbottom (eds.), *Ancient Literary Criticism: the principal texts in new translations* (Oxford, 1972).

General surveys:

G.M.A. Grube, *The Greek and Roman Critics* (London, 1965).

D.A. Russell, *Criticism in Antiquity* (Berkeley, 1981).

W.J. Verdenius, 'The principles of Greek Literary Criticism', *Mnemosyne* 36 (1983) 14–59.

It is especially useful to read Plato's *Ion* and *Republic* Books II–III and X, and also (amongst his later dialogues) the *Phaedrus* and *Philebus*.

See also:

W.J. Verdenius, *Mimesis: Plato's doctrine of artistic Imitation and its meaning to us* (Leiden, 1949).

P. Vicaire, *Platon: Critique Littéraire* (Paris, 1960).

I. Murdoch, *The Fire and the Sun* (Oxford, 1977).

J. Moravcsik and P. Temko (eds.), *Plato on Beauty, Wisdom and the Arts* (New Jersey, 1982).

E. Belfiore, 'A theory of imitation in Plato's *Republic*', *Transactions of the American Philological Association* 114 (1984) 121–46.

Aristotle in general

Short accounts of his essential views:

J.L. Ackrill, *Aristotle the Philosopher* (Oxford, 1981).

J. Barnes, *Aristotle* (Oxford, 1982).

More detailed introductions:

227

W.D. Ross, *Aristotle* (London, 1923).

W.K.C. Guthrie, *A History of Greek Philosophy. 6. Aristotle: an encounter* (Cambridge, 1981).

The standard English translation of Aristotle's complete works has been revised and reissued by J. Barnes (Princeton, 1984). In connection with the *Poetics* it is especially useful to read the *Ethics* and the *Rhetoric*. See also:

W.F.R. Hardie, *Aristotle's Ethical Theory* (Oxford, 1980).

T.H. Irwin, *Aristotle: Nicomachean Ethics* (Indianapolis, 1985).

M.C. Nussbaum, *The Fragility of Goodness: Luck and Ethics in Greek tragedy and philosophy* (Cambridge, 1986).

A.O. Rorty (ed.), *Essays on Aristotle's Ethics* (Berkeley, 1980).

R. Sorabji, *Necessity, Cause and Blame* (London, 1980).

The *Poetics*: general

Commentaries:

S.H. Butcher, *Aristotle's Theory of Poetry and Fine Art* (London, 1907).

I. Bywater, *Aristotle on the Art of Poetry* (Oxford, 1909).

A. Rostagni, *Aristotele: Poetica* (Turin, 1945).

G.F. Else, *Aristotle's Poetics: the Argument* (Harvard, 1957).

G.M.A. Grube, *Aristotle on Poetry and Style* (Indianapolis, 1989).

D.W. Lucas, *Aristotle: Poetics* (Oxford, 1968).

R. Dupont-Roc & J. Lallot, *Aristote: La Poétique* (Paris, 1980).

Short accounts of the whole work:

H. House, *Aristotle's Poetics: a course of eight lectures* (London, 1956).

F.L. Lucas, *Tragedy: serious drama in relation to Aristotle's Poetics* (London, 1957).

More exhaustive studies:

J. Vahlen, *Beiträge zu Aristoteles' Poetik* (Leipzig, 1914).

S. Halliwell, *Aristotle's Poetics* (Chapel Hill, 1986).

Representation and catharsis

J. Bernays, *Grundzüge der verlorenen Abhandlung des Aristoteles über Wirkung der Tragödie* (Breslau, 1857). Translated in *Articles* 154–65.

L. Golden, 'Catharsis', *Transactions of the American Philological Association* 93 (1962) 51–60.

L. Golden, 'Mimesis and catharsis', *Classical Philology* 64 (1969) 145–53.

A. Nicev, *L'énigme de la catharsis tragique dans Aristote* (Sofia, 1970).

J.M. Redfield, *Nature and Culture in the Iliad* (Chicago, 1975), Ch. 1–2.

W.W. Fortenbaugh, *Aristotle on Emotion* (London, 1975).

W.W. Fortenbaugh, 'Aristotle's *Rhetoric* on emotions', in *Articles* 133–53.

N. Gulley, 'Aristotle on the purposes of literature', in *Articles* 166–76.

D. Keesey, 'On some recent interpretations of catharsis', *Classical World* 72 (1979) 193–205.

B.R. Rees, 'Aristotle's approach to poetry', *Greece and Rome* 28 (1981) 23–39.

K. Eden, 'Poetry and equity: Aristotle's defense of fiction', *Traditio* 38 (1982) 17–43.

Carnes Lord, *Education and Culture in the Political Thought of Aristotle* (Cornell, 1982).

A. Nicev, *La catharsis tragique d'Aristote* (Sofia, 1982).

E. Belfiore, 'Pleasure, tragedy and Aristotelian psychology', *Classical Quarterly* 35 (1985) 349–61.

The origins and performance of tragedy

A.W. Pickard-Cambridge, *Dithyramb, Tragedy and Comedy* (Cambridge, 1927).

A.W. Pickard-Cambridge, *The Theatre of Dionysus in Athens* (Oxford, 1946).

A.W. Pickard-Cambridge, *The Dramatic Festivals of Athens* (Oxford, 1953).

G.F. Else, *The Origins and early form of Greek Tragedy* (Cambridge, Mass., 1965).

Carnes Lord, 'Aristotle's history of poetry', *Transactions of the American Philological Association* 104 (1974) 195–229.

A. Lesky, *Greek Tragic Poetry*, translated by M. Dillon (Yale, 1983), Chs. 1–3.

C.J. Herington, *Poetry into Drama* (Berkeley, 1985).

Tragedy and its structure

John Jones, *Aristotle and Greek Tragedy* (London, 1962).

J.M. Bremer, *Hamartia* (Amsterdam, 1969).

B.R. Rees, '*Pathos* in the *Poetics* of Aristotle', *Greece and Rome* 19 (1972) 1–11.

T.C.W. Stinton, '*Hamartia* in Aristotle and Greek Tragedy', *Classical Quarterly* 25 (1975) 221–54.

J. Moles, 'Notes on Aristotle, *Poetics* 13 and 14', *Classical Quarterly* 29 (1979) 77–94.

O.J. Schrier, 'A Simple View of Peripeteia', *Mnemosyne* 33 (1980) 96–118.

G. Xanthakis-Karamanos, *Studies in Fourth-Century Tragedy* (Athens, 1980).

R.D. Lamberton, '*Philanthropia* and the evolution of dramatic taste', *Phoenix* 37 (1983) 95–103.

E. Belfiore, 'Aristotle's concept of *praxis* in the *Poetics*', *Classical Journal* 79 (1983–4) 110–24.

J. Moles, '*Philanthropia* in the *Poetics*', *Phoenix* 38 (1984) 325–35.

S. Halliwell, 'Plato and Aristotle on the denial of tragedy', *Proceedings of the Cambridge Philological Society* 30 (1984) 49–71.

Epic and comedy

Lane Cooper, *An Aristotelian Theory of Comedy* (New York, 1922).

J.C. Hogan, 'Aristotle's criticism of Homer in the *Poetics*', *Classical Philology* 68 (1973) 95–108.

T.G. Rosenmeyer, 'Design and Execution in Aristotle, *Poetics* ch. XXV', *California Studies in Classical Antiquity* 6 (1973) 231–52.

R. Friedrich, '*Epeisodion* in Drama and Epic', *Hermes* 111 (1983) 34–52.

G.F. Held, '*Spoudaios* and teleology in the *Poetics*', *Transactions of the American Philological Society* 114 (1984) 159–76.

R. Janko, *Aristotle on Comedy* (Berkeley, 1985).

The influence of the *Poetics*

Lane Cooper, *The Poetics of Aristotle: its meaning and influence* (London, 1923).

M.T. Herrick, *The Poetics of Aristotle in England* (New Haven, 1930).

M. Kommerell, *Lessing und Aristoteles* (Frankfurt, 1940).

B. Weinberg, *A History of Literary Criticism in the Italian Renaissance* (Chicago, 1961), I 349–423.

J. Hutton, *Aristotle's Poetics* (New York, 1982), 24–34.

K. Eden, *Poetic and Legal Fiction in the Aristotelian Tradition* (Princeton, 1986).

Index of Names and Titles

This index lists all proper names and titles of literary works mentioned in the texts translated here. References to the *Poetics* are given by Bekker numeration only, e.g. 54b14. References to the *Tractatus Coislinianus* are abbreviated *T.C.* A reference in parentheses, e.g. (55a4), means that the poet or work is mentioned or quoted without the name or title appearing in the text. In all cases, further details should be sought in the relevant Notes. Other names and references found in the Introduction and Notes are listed according to the page-numbers where they appear. Aristotelian references are indexed by book and chapter number only, e.g. *Rhetoric* III 6.